NORTHSIDE
APR 1 4 1997

D0326880

NS

LOVEJOY

L O V E J O Y

A Year in the Life of
an Abortion Clinic

P e t e r   K o r n

KENOSHA PUBLIC LIBRARY
KENOSHA, WI

The Atlantic Monthly Press
New York

3 0645 5361593

363.46
K843

Copyright © 1996 by Peter Korn

All rights reserved. No part of this book may be reproduced in any form or by any
electronic or mechanical means, including information storage and retrieval systems,
without permission in writing from the publisher, except by a reviewer, who may quote
brief passages in a review.

Published simultaneously in Canada
Printed in the United States of America

FIRST EDITION
Library of Congress Cataloging-in-Publication Data

Korn, Peter, 1954–
    Lovejoy : a year in the life of an abortion clinic/Peter Korn.—1st ed.
        p.   cm.
    ISBN 0-87113-659-7
    1. Lovejoy Surgicenter.   2. Abortion services—Oregon—Portland.
I. Title
RG734.K67   1996
362.1'9888'0979549—dc20   96–9527

Design by Laura Hammond Hough

The Atlantic Monthly Press
841 Broadway
New York, NY 10003

10 9 8 7 6 5 4 3 2 1

To Betty

Prologue

The first thing Allene Klass noticed was the sound of hoofbeats on cement, pounding, clattering, relentless. Horses on Lovejoy Street. No, not horses, she thought, beasts, big black beasts, not a gray or white one in the bunch. She'd been warned but not prepared for a sight so incongruous: a formation of six horses and riders in two per-fect lines with twenty uniformed police officers following them up the tree-lined city street—all coming to her rescue.

When Allene had arrived at the Lovejoy Surgicenter a few hours earlier she had sensed the electric feeling in the air. Lovejoy had been the target of a protest of one kind or another nearly every day for fourteen years. Lately the crowds had been growing, the protestors increasingly emboldened. Allene had resisted reacting. Partly her restraint had been philosophical: She supported First Amendment rights, even when those rights were exercised by her adversaries. It was also tactical: She had not wanted to give the protestors any cause to increase their fervor. But like a good and patient general, Allene knew when the time had come to respond.

The protestors had never succeeded in their primary objective— to shut down Lovejoy, one of the country's busiest abortion facili-ties. Not even for a day. They'd come close. It had become standard procedure to instruct patients not to drive directly to the Surgicenter when major protests were anticipated. Instead Allene arranged to have all the day's patients meet in the morning a few blocks away, where a van would be waiting with a police escort. The van would then drive right up to the clinic's side door and the police would force open a path between protestors so that the women could enter.

On other mornings, before the protestors arrived, Tim Shuck, Lovejoy's director of counseling, would park his car as close to Lovejoy's back entrance as he could, practically beside the building. When patients arrived he would shove them through a door of the car, using the vehicle as a tunnel through the blockaders. The patients would exit out the door on the car's other side, next to the building entrance. On more than one morning the parking lot behind Lovejoy had become the setting for shoving matches, which deteriorated into small-scale riots as protestors and escorts fought for control of the facility's entrances.

Allene was proud that each time she and her staff had found some way to get the day's patients inside the building and through their procedures. But even a succession of victories had taken its toll. The blocked doorways and the malevolent stares of protestors who were continuously peering through windows and doors had contributed to a sense, among the people who worked at Lovejoy, of being trapped inside their own building. The staff had become battle weary, Allene knew. Every day they had to walk in the building to shouts of "baby killer" and "murderer." Every day they had to begin work feeling unconditional hatred directed at them. Allene recognized the psychic cost better than any of her employees; she had been primary target for the venom. Arriving today she heard "Jewish bitch" directed at her. It was beginning to look like this morning might bring a wonderful morale builder.

The horses were almost on top of the protestors. Allene looked for Andrew Burnett, the man who had organized the blockade. Burnett was the leader of Advocates for Life, the most radical and daring of the anti-abortion organizations. He was walking from group to group, talking to individuals among the fifty to sixty protestors. Most of them were lying or sitting in front of the entrances to Lovejoy. Half an hour earlier they had been milling about. Then somebody had blown a whistle and everyone had scurried to an assigned place, blocking each of the building's six doors. For much of the last thirty minutes they had chanted songs, yelled epithets, generally made as much noise as they could. Now Allene noticed an eerie quiet descending over the crowd as they became aware of the approaching horses, their confidence gradually replaced by fear.

Until now fear had been felt only inside the building, Allene knew. She was also aware that even today the tumult would harm her patients considerably more than the protestors. She had attended at least a half dozen meetings with city officials trying to devise a plan that would allow women to pass safely inside the building without confronting protestors. The police were getting as frustrated as Allene. They could not act as permanent escorts, and nobody knew when a blockade would take place.

But the protestors finally might have become too daring. Last week they had called a press conference to announce their intentions: to perform a rescue at Lovejoy on Saturday with the purpose of shutting down the abortion facility by blockading entrances and disrupting the work inside. Allene had called the district attorney and the local police precinct captain. She wanted a show of force that might discourage future protestors. The police told her they already had a plan, but it would involve both night shift and day shift officers, and implementation would result in a serious shortage of police throughout the rest of the city. Allene would have to keep it a secret—a condition to which she agreed.

Previously the police had dealt with protestors by hauling them away, two police officers to a body. The blockaders had been instructed by their leaders to go limp, which made them almost impossible to hoist. A few of the officers had complained to Allene that the lifting was beginning to hurt their backs. Two had actually become disabled with back injuries.

The police were tiring of these tactics, the precinct commander told Allene. It was not practical to continually commit officers as escorts. But by announcing their intentions the protestors had finally given the police an opportunity to take the offensive. The commander suggested a major counterattack in the hope it would deter future blockades, but he did not tell Allene about the horses.

The horses snorted and bayed as their riders struggled to control them. The mounted police moved in among the protestors, who were now rising from their positions in front of the building's side entrance and scattering. Most were grabbed by police officers, who herded them into waiting vans. But some refused to budge, especially those at the top of the stairs that led to the front doors. Undeterred, the police riders drove their horses right up the stairs. Then the horses themselves became a tunnel, nose to tail in two parallel lines as the day's patients rushed through and into the building.

Allene retreated inside and viewed the riot from behind two glass doors in the building's entryway, doors she knew to be shatter resistant, specially ordered six months ago. Most of Lovejoy's staff had gathered around her—nurses, counselors, even a few doctors. As patients entered the building the staff began cheering, exactly the sound Allene wanted to hear.

She found herself overcome with emotion. There was concern for her patients and staff. She knew that after these incidents the pregnant women who made it into the lobby were often distraught. The protestors seemed to have a sense of which women were most vulnerable, and they would aim their taunts and pleas at them. All the women who came in today would need an extra measure of soothing. Allene would remind each one that an abortion was her right, and that the protestors outside were trying to take away that right. She knew that a few of the women might change their minds and walk back out the door. But usually those women returned later, certain they wanted an abortion after all.

But what dominated Allene's thoughts as she watched the police rout the protestors was the magnificence of the spectacle. How many people can say that the cavalry once came to their rescue? She loved it. She was thinking about the American flag and apple pie, of all things, and in her excitement actually thought she heard a marching band in the background. She was proud of the police and sure that such a scene could happen only in America. In her mind, the entire city of Portland, her city, was saying, "Women, you have a right to be here."

Chapter One

1995

On an early spring morning that hints of an early summer, Allene Klass directs her jet black Jaguar past the solid, two-story cinder-block structure on the corner of Lovejoy and Twenty-fifth Streets. She does not hesitate as she pulls into the small lot behind the building, hardly slows as she glides into a diagonal space and cuts the engine. The transition from movement to stillness has been nearly seamless.

The Jaguar is a low car and Allene, fifty-six, is a tall, leggy woman. She is aware of her legs as she bends knees together and pivots at the hips. Across the street and three floors up there is a doctor who recently told a friend of Allene's, "Watching those legs come out of that Jag is the highlight of my day." Allene has always preferred short, tight skirts and she's happy to oblige her admirer.

Allene's dress defies easy classification. She clearly has paid great attention to her appearance, but the black skirt is a little shorter than expected and the black silk blouse is cut just a little bit too low at the neck to complete the classic look of a professional woman. She favors rich colors and contrasts. Her long sculpted nails are bright red, as are her lips; her wavy black hair frames a face that appears tanned even now, with summer months away. Outsized jewelry completes the ensemble—a large diamond ring, a shiny silver bracelet, dangling earrings. The effect—the clothes, hair, nails, makeup, even the car—is of someone who wants to be noticed. Her enemies simply consider her appearance further evidence. They call her witch and devil woman.

Quickly she enters the building through a rear glass door, her spike heels clicking against the pavement, then muffled by carpet. She appears to be moving effortlessly, without need to consider a single decision or alternative, a Lear jet on automatic pilot.

You would not know that as Allene has driven here she has surveyed the side streets with the attention of a mother owl searching for predators near the nest of her brood. You might not realize she noted each car parked on the block, or that she accounted for the two men standing near the side of the building.

Once inside the building's rear door Allene moves through a short hallway toward the front reception area, to a waiting room that could serve as a patients' lounge in any doctor's office in any city or town in the country. The walls are covered with textured plaster. The chairs arranged around the room have rounded wooden backs and plush purple cushions. An oil painting of a landscape with mountains and a river dominates a wall facing the front entrance. The carpet is an unobtrusive brown weave, the lighting fluorescent. A six-foot metal sculpture of a sunflower and a vase with fresh flowers are the only distinctive decorations. The flowers are exactly what you would expect this woman to have in her waiting room: gladiola, showy and grand, pink trumpets rising up each stem.

As in many medical offices a glass panel separates a seated receptionist from the lounge. But here there is a difference: The glass panel is bulletproof, Mylar-coated Plexiglas, the same as used in the storefronts of ghetto convenience stores. Allene had it installed when the shootings began.

Allene wheels past a corner, smiling and greeting the woman behind the glass. In most business settings, hierarchy is easily discerned by the placement of offices. Not here. Allene's office sits at the rear of the building, across the hall and a few steps away from the receptionist's station. It would look out on the parking lot if the shades were not always drawn. There is no view to speak of and no natural light. It is a bit like a cave, the only lighting coming from spot lamps on the ceiling. A visitor's attention is never divided in this room. The only possible focus is where the spotlight falls—on Allene.

But Allene is alone now. She surveys her orderly desk where three neat piles of papers await her attention, along with a copy of the *Wall Street Journal*. If only the organization in her office were a metaphor for Lovejoy. Anyone who has ever run a hospital or medical center would laugh at that wishful thinking, she knows.

For all the talk of women's rights, of providing a necessary service to women, of moral choices and political battles, when you get past all the rationale, you find Allene Klass, a woman behind a desk with a business to run in an increasingly competitive market. When they write Allene's epitaph, whoever is doing the writing might paint her as hero or villain. The one thing she is sure the epitaph will say, no matter who the author, is that she was one tough businesswoman. Lovejoy would not still be around if she were anything less.

In the year 1995 abortion facilities around the country are closing. Obstetricians are getting out of the business. The federal government is forcing medical schools to teach abortion procedures; the schools prefer to avoid the controversy. In the last three years the number of American hospitals willing to provide abortions has fallen 48 percent.

The terrorism is working. Some administrators and doctors are afraid of Andrew Burnett and his compatriots. And some are simply unwilling to put up with the pickets and threats; they do not want to expose their patients to the inconvenience and emotional trauma. One of Lovejoy's doctors, fearing for the safety of his family, has ceased performing abortions, retreating back to the privacy of his obstetrics practice.

You run a hospital. Hundreds of procedures are performed there every day—nose jobs, arthroscopic knee surgery, heart surgery. Babies are delivered in the obstetrics ward. If you choose to add abortion to that list, all your patients will be subjected to the taunts of the anti-abortion pickets. Is it fair to them? Is it good for business? Most hospitals have decided it is not.

Five years ago Allene Klass reached an agreement with Kaiser Permanente, the large health care provider. Kaiser's Portland-area patients need access to abortion, but Kaiser, which runs its own hospitals, doesn't want to provide them. Now when a woman on a Kaiser health plan needs an abortion, Kaiser pays for her to go to Lovejoy. Good business for Lovejoy. Allene would like to increase business by convincing more local obstetricians to perform their abortions at Lovejoy, but it will be a hard sell.

Oregon is not and never has been like the rest of the country. A state of political dichotomy, it can lay claim to some of the most progressive and farsighted environmental legislation and at the same time be home to some of the most reactionary Aryan Nation and antigovernment militia groups the Far Right has to offer.

This dichotomy extends into the area of abortion rights. On one hand, Oregon's abortion landscape is among the most open in the country. Most states have enacted some limits on abortion, Oregon practically none. There is no mandatory twenty-four-hour delay before an abortion can be performed, no bias counseling in which a woman must be shown material that might make her rethink her decision to have an abortion, no law that says parents of all minors must be notified before an abortion can be performed on a teenager.

In addition, Oregon continues to provide public funds for abortions for the poor, even though by 1995 most other states have discontinued the practice. In fact, Oregon was chosen as one of the U.S. test sites for the National Institutes of Health study of RU-486, the controversial French abortion pill.

And yet Oregon also is home to Advocates for Life Ministries and, for the last twenty years, one of the most active and radical anti-abortion campaigns in the country. Oregon Right to Life is the second largest political action committee in the state. There probably is no abortion facility in Oregon that has not been hit by major protests and violence.

Through all this, access to abortion has defied the national trend and thrived in Oregon. Depending on how the counting is done, there are as many as eight abortion providers in Portland. Some think the courage displayed by Allene Klass over the last twenty years is one of the reasons. For her part Allene is proud of her contribution, but she's not totally happy with the results. Nobody who runs a business welcomes competition.

Some of her competitors think Allene too much a businesswoman. Certainly Lovejoy is run differently from the two other high-profile Portland abortion clinics. One, the Feminist Women's Health Center, is nonprofit, the other, the Downtown Women's Center, is run as a cooperative, which means neither has to be particularly concerned with making a profit. At Lovejoy, economy is a watchword. Operating room gowns and towels are laundered on-site, surgical instruments are sterilized and recycled rather than discarded in favor of plastic tools as at other medical facilities. The staff is kept to a minimum. One consequence is that abortion prices at Lovejoy are among the lowest in the country, an important consideration for the legions of low-income women who make their way there. "We do a volume business," Allene says.

As she takes her seat Allene feels energized. Early this morning she accepted delivery of a three-thousand-pound Japanese garden stone she has coveted for days. The stone has a natural indentation at the top that will serve as a birdbath. Allene first spied the stone at a garden shop, and she has been anxious to see what it would look like in the garden in back of her house, her sanctuary surrounded by ancient cedar and fir trees.

When the stone arrived this morning it appeared a perfect fit. Outstanding but not obtrusive, it draws the eye but does not dominate its surroundings. The rock, in Allene's view, possesses a pure integrity, as if it had thought out its own design in the course of

millions of years of shaping itself. Its strength, the sense of perma-
nence it projects, reminds Allene of her family. Seeing the rock in
her garden this morning has given Allene the little lift that will carry
her through the day at Lovejoy, no matter what happens there. Allene
feeds on this feeling, the sense that she can handle whatever comes
her way; it is one of the things she most likes about coming
to work and one of the things others most like about her—pure
confidence.

The last few weeks have presented Allene with a number of
administrative decisions, the types of decisions that she faces routinely and have little long-term impact. But there are weightier
choices at hand as well.

On the administrative side Allene considers the issue of staff
turnover. This week Kimo, the head nurse, informed Allene she
would be leaving in a month to begin a nurse practitioner's master's
program at the local medical school. A calm, competent woman,
Kimo has been running the second floor, where surgeries are performed, since she started working at Lovejoy six months ago. Her
loss will cause problems, Allene knows.

Lovejoy has gone through five head nurses in four years. The
job is a difficult one, at least partly because of the nature of the
second-floor operation. On certain days as many as twenty-five first-
trimester abortions might be scheduled in one operating room.
Women coming in for abortions are often suffering great emotional
stress; of those that appear, it is not unusual for half to be late for
their appointments, some by as much as two or three hours. The head
nurse must keep the surgical area running efficiently in the face of
such unpredictability. At one moment pre-op, the operating room,
and post-op can be functioning smoothly and on time. Then six,
seven, or eight women will arrive simultaneously for their abortions.

That is when the upstairs stress levels skyrocket, and it helps
explain why in spring of 1995 practically all the support personnel
upstairs have worked at Lovejoy less than a year. On hectic days
nurses complain that the Surgicenter is trying to squeeze in too many

patients. But at other times the upstairs waiting room is empty for hours. Allene hasn't yet found a solution to this problem. But Kimo's departure will force her to consider the situation again.

Allene thinks Lovejoy will inevitably suffer a transient staff. Much of the work upstairs is handled by certified medical assistants (CMAs), and over the years she has observed a pattern of behavior among these women that she calls a syndrome. It starts as a reaction to the patients. The stream of scared and needy women can seem endless, and after a while, the patients themselves become faceless. The medical assistants, Allene has observed, become complacent, sometimes flippant. The patients wear them down. And when that happens they lose sight of the one rule that Allene says must always govern their work: that each woman be treated with respect. Many of the assistants quit once they reach that level of exhaustion. Sometimes Allene dismisses them. For their part, some of the upstairs CMAs think their stress would be alleviated if there were more of them.

On Wednesday Leanne, a receptionist, told Allene she too was leaving. Dr. Jessel also gave notice this week that he is moving back east. So Allene will be looking for an obstetrician to take over the abortions Jessel performed one afternoon a week. For a long time Allene has wanted to find a woman to take on some of the procedures at her hospital. Allene thinks Jessel's departure might provide the opportunity. The abortion procedure is an intensely personal one for most women, and Lovejoy is very much a women's place; days go by when men simply aren't seen outside the operating rooms.

But there is another stress point in the Lovejoy infrastructure with even more serious ramifications. For some time it has been clear to Allene that Harold Suchak, the center's medical director and chief surgeon, and Carye Ortman, director of counseling, are involved in a deep-seated conflict. Suchak accuses Carye of dishonesty. Carye complains Suchak is shirking the responsibilities of medical director, doing no work at Lovejoy other than his surgeries. Allene has thought extensively about the battle and has not been able to puzzle

out where it began, what its root cause might be. The two certainly
are different types of people but their current behavior reflects more
than just contrasting personalities, and it threatens to develop into
a major rift that could become divisive within Lovejoy.

Monday morning Suchak and Carye confronted each other in
Carye's office. There had been miscommunication about who was
looking after security on Saturday. Carye, who was not going to be
there, had left someone in charge but had not informed Suchak.
When a protestor who was not recognized as a regular began shouting from just outside the front doors Suchak called the police. Carye
thought he overreacted, Suchak disagreed. The event itself is incon-
sequential, Allene thinks, but not Monday's confrontation. Allene
has never seen Carye as upset as she was after the blowup. And Suchak
came into Allene's office and offered to resign on the spot, something Allene thought she would never hear.

Allene believes she has maintained a loyalty to Suchak far beyond what he deserves. For some time she has been aware that he is
moonlighting at other abortion facilities behind her back, though
for the life of her Allene can't figure out why: Suchak earns over three
hundred thousand dollars a year at Lovejoy, paid not as a salary but
as a set amount for each abortion he performs. What's more, Allene
was recently called by a woman who runs an abortion clinic in a
neighboring state. The woman told Allene that Suchak had made
inquiries about a job there. But Allene knows well how difficult it
would be to replace Suchak. There are few obstetrical surgeons as
technically proficient, fewer willing to devote their entire practices
to abortion.

Suchak is nearly irreplaceable, but Carye is practically Allene's
right hand. A large woman with a quick wit and versatile intellect,
Carye has as her primary job helping women decide whether they
want an abortion, and if so, preparing them for it before they meet
with a surgeon. For the most part she is in charge of running the first
floor of Lovejoy, where patients spend their time before heading
upstairs for their operations.

Carye adores Allene, is amazed by her strength and competence. Both women have battled through difficult lives—Carye's mother suffered from recurring emotional problems and deserted the family for a period when Carye was a young child; Allene lost a three-year-old son to a congenital disease years ago. Carye likes to tell stories about her boss: Allene goes off to an afternoon appointment with a hairdresser nobody can stand because the woman talks incessantly, and the hairdresser and her husband end up at Allene's house that evening for marriage counseling. "This is a woman who walks into a restaurant and the waiters are thinking, 'Oh no, it's her.' And by the end of the meal they love her," Carye says with a laugh.

Both women present first impressions that reveal little of their true selves. Allene's flashy appearance belies the fierce mothering instinct that has allowed her to raise four children in a tight family while running Lovejoy. The first thing you notice about Carye is her size—she is five feet eleven inches and weighs well over two hundred pounds—but people who get to know her soon discover that size is not a defining aspect of Carye. Allene once said Carye's weight had always been a puzzle to her because Carye did not possess the personality of an obese person. Carye's husband once described her as someone ready to laugh at any moment. And Carye displays no sensitivity about her size. Another seeming anomaly is Carye's short hair, which is completely gray. Carye is just thirty-seven and her face is a pretty, delicate one. Sixteen years ago she developed leukemia. During chemotherapy her hair fell out, and when it grew back its color had permanently disappeared.

The Lovejoy staff is not working as a team, Allene thinks as she arranges papers on her desk. But running Lovejoy has always been about putting out one fire or another. At least these are symbolic fires, she notes. In recent years the Surgicenter has been the victim of two arsons.

For a moment Allene allows herself a thought of the one person who has come closest to being her partner through twenty years of running Lovejoy—Tim Shuck. Tim, a gentle, funny gay man who preceded Carye as Lovejoy's director of counseling, became Allene's best friend. He left Lovejoy when AIDS made work impossible. At moments like this Allene most wishes Tim were still here.

Brushing aside the thought, Allene considers the good news— the pressure from outside has abated. Lovejoy and its proprietor have been the target of anti-abortion protests of one sort or another since the facility opened in 1974. For the most part Allene ignored the commotion. By the late 1980s, however, local activists led by Andrew Burnett had begun raising the stakes. Sit-ins turned into blockading rescues. Burnett's influence grew; a word from him could bring three hundred protestors to Lovejoy on a Saturday morning.

Eventually Allene found it impossible to continue business as usual. Sidewalk escorts for women arriving at Lovejoy weren't enough, not with the entrances blocked by waves of shouting protestors. Even when women did make it through, some were so traumatized that the Lovejoy staff had to spend as much time comforting and reassuring them as preparing them for surgery. There were mornings when Lovejoy's ability to stay open had been in doubt. Even the legendary cavalry charge had accomplished little of a permanent nature. Know this about Allene Klass: She can be a very understanding woman, but don't try to shut down her business.

Allene took to the courts, filing a civil lawsuit against Advocates, Burnett, and twenty-seven other protestors. At the least Allene hoped for an injunction that would keep the protestors away from Lovejoy. Never in their wildest dreams did Allene and her attorney, Art Tarlow, anticipate that in addition Allene would end up with a landmark $8.2 million judgment for punitive damages against Advocates and individual protestors, $500,000 of it against Burnett himself.

The injunction, combined with new federal legislation protecting abortion clinics, has worked to some degree. Protests the last couple of years have become smaller in size and less violent in nature.

Burnett is not allowed to yell or scream outside Lovejoy, nor can he step inside a buffer zone around each of the building's entrances. Collecting the judgment has not been as rewarding, though. While he was in jail Burnett sold his roofing business. He transferred the title to his house to his brother-in-law. Knowing any money he made was subject to garnishment as part of the judgment, he went to work full-time at Advocates for Life, at minimum wage. He claims he has no money, so he and Advocates cannot pay Allene what the court says she is owed. He does not even have a checking account.

Despite his avowed poverty, every few months Burnett flies around the country organizing protests. He continues to publish his magazine. Allene is sure he has secret sources of funding from the anti-abortion movement, and she would love to use the $8.2 million award to get at it. Actually, it isn't Burnett's money she wants. It's his magazine.

Burnett is one of about six national leaders of the arm of the anti-abortion movement that advocates the use of force against doctors, even to the point of shooting them. But *Life Advocate* is the only established means the movement has of getting the word out to its members and prospective members. In 1993 the magazine "outed" Dr. George Tiller of Wichita, Kansas, publishing his picture, his address, his phone number, and the fact that he performed second-trimester abortions. A month later Tiller was shot by Shelley Shannon, who three weeks earlier had been protesting at Lovejoy.

Allene would like to return to court to collect her judgment, and she would be satisfied if the collection started and stopped with the revenue that supports *Life Advocate*. She recognizes this would deal a severe blow to the radical anti-abortion movement nationwide, and possibly a fatal one to Andrew Burnett as one of the movement's leaders.

But Allene has not pursued collecting her judgment in court. There are two reasons. First is the cost. Allene spent over $150,000 in legal fees pursuing her civil case. She has recouped maybe $20,000 of that through the judgment. Tarlow, her attorney, says a court action to collect on the judgment might run her another $50,000 and would net little financial return.

The other reason Allene has hesitated in going back to court is Burnett. She has watched him change his tactics over the last ten years, becoming increasingly violent, and, she thinks, increasingly power hungry.

"The man frightens me," she says. "He's been getting sicker and sicker. I sat in a courtroom twenty-two days and I felt the hate. He's like a Hitler."

Often Allene finds herself considering a question to which she rarely gives voice. Would Burnett, if pushed far enough into despair by his own diminishing power base, pick up a gun and go after Suchak or Allene? Allene does not think so. But she's not positive. And she does think he might encourage someone else to do the deed. Shelley Shannon, the Oregon woman who shot Dr. Tiller, was with Burnett in Portland shortly before she drove to Kansas City with a .25 caliber handgun, a Bible, and a doll that resembled a fetus in her car. Nobody has proven that a conspiracy exists among the radical fringe of the anti-abortionist movement or that Burnett had anything to do with Shannon's act. But Allene is concerned that by going after Burnett one more time in court, possibly bankrupting the man and taking away his pulpit in the form of *Life Advocate*, she might just be setting herself up as a target.

The solution, which Tarlow mentioned to Allene months ago, would be to get someone else to pursue the judgment—perhaps a national organization without any recognizable personality at the helm. Sell the $8.2 million judgment to them for a dollar, Tarlow suggested, let them keep whatever they can collect, and the final responsibility will not be Allene's.

For months Tarlow and Allene have been calling leaders of prospective partners such as the National Organization for Women and the Southern Poverty Law Center (which success-

fully pursued similar cases against the Ku Klux Klan and a neo-
Nazi leader). All have said the idea is a great one, that they would
love to see Burnett out of action. None have been willing to get
involved.

But yesterday a call came from an attorney with the Feminist
Majority Foundation's National Clinic Defense Project in Washington, D.C. They're interested. They are running an analysis to project
how much money they might be able to collect from the defendants.
They will get back to Allene in a few weeks.

Allene smiles at the possibility, but it is not her full grin. Her
enthusiasm is tempered by an understanding of what could go
wrong here.

Allene wishes whoever takes on the suit would hire Tarlow to
handle the case. She has confidence in his ability and she knows he
is most familiar with all the nuances of the situation. And he possesses the finesse she thinks is needed. That is the word Allene keeps
coming back to when discussing the matter.

When Lovejoy went after its protestors Allene decided she did
not want to expose the Surgicenter's patients in court. That meant
she could not pursue harassment charges against the protestors. The
civil suit, instead, was based solely on trespassing charges. No patients
were named in court or required to testify, and Allene still ended up
with an $8.2 million judgment. That, Allene thinks, is an example
of legal finesse. But she feels certain another group will try to find
less expensive counsel that might also be less experienced. And that
worries her.

If the Clinic Defense Project pursues the case and does a poor
job, Lovejoy and Allene will become even more vulnerable, just as
Lovejoy's patients might have been in the initial case. That is exactly what Allene is trying to prevent. This action cannot be allowed
to appear as if Allene is out to get Andrew Burnett. A long court
case, the wrong testimony, no significant diminution of Burnett's
power, and Lovejoy could find itself under siege once again.

*

Peter Korn

Harold Suchak does not need an alarm clock. He rises at 6:15 A.M., a man of habits and routines, a man who has been starting rounds at 7 A.M. for nearly thirty years. The rest of his family still slumbers.

Quietly he heads to the bathroom. He shaves as he showers, then dresses in a room off the bathroom. First his underwear, then socks, shirt, pants, shoes, and tie. He returns to the bedroom to kiss his just-awakening wife, Greta, good-bye. Downstairs, before heading out the door, he reaches for one final garment—a sport jacket with a Kevlar bulletproof vest hidden inside.

Some mornings Suchak stands before the downstairs closet and decides not to wear the vest. But lately the protests have been escalating. Twice recently the police had to be called because protestors grabbed women coming into Lovejoy. One afternoon a warning came from the police that a protestor outside held a permit to carry a concealed weapon and was believed to be armed.

There is no science to Suchak's decision. He is a practical man but there is no chain of logic in which to take comfort here. Somedays it seems as if logic has completely abandoned him to a world gone haywire.

The reliance on intuition continues as Suchak approaches work. He must decide whether to drive straight in or continue around the block two or three times. Should he park in the staff parking lot or on a side street several blocks away?

At least there have been no demonstrations at his house in over a month. The last one was fairly mild in comparison to some. Advocates for Life called it a "Nowhere To Hide" rally. About twenty protestors marched up and down the street on a Saturday morning, carrying signs, passing out leaflets featuring his name and picture and the slogan WANTED FOR CRIMES AGAINST HUMANITY, along with a picture of—they claimed—a twenty-week-old aborted fetus. "IF IT BOTHERS YOU . . . that a man in your neighborhood cuts off the heads of children and grinds them up in a garbage disposal . . . DO SOMETHING ABOUT IT!!" The flyers ended up on parked cars, doorsteps, stapled to neighborhood telephone poles. That afternoon, after the protest-

19

ors left, Suchak and his family scoured the neighborhood and collected about two hundred of them.

Suchak long ago gave up trying to be popular. He possesses none of Allene Klass's charm or flamboyance, and if given a choice, he would not wish to. Most of his life he has tried to do the right thing, as defined by the integration of his mother's Catholic faith and his father's blue-collar code. This is not a man who is supposed to find himself a target, at least not in peacetime. But Harold Suchak is Lovejoy's medical director, a doctor who performs over three thousand abortions a year. As far as the violent arm of the anti-abortion movement is concerned, he is one of the nation's twelve "most wanted" doctors.

Speak to a number of doctors who regularly perform abortions, and you will find some of the same ambivalence that exists in much of the general public. With any other procedure, surgeons exiting the operating room generally feel a sense of exhilaration, possibly even power, resulting from the work they have done. In some cases it's a feeling that they have beaten the devil, taken back a life. But after an abortion, there is usually little sense of great accomplishment. For starters, the vast majority of abortions are unchallenging surgery, easy work for an experienced surgeon. The deeper reason is the emotional and psychological impact that abortions can have on a surgeon. Except in a very few cases, performing an abortion does not feel like saving or healing a life. It might feel necessary and it may well feel like the right thing to do, but it rarely feels good.

Suchak insists he gets good feelings from his work. Sometimes this develops out of knowing the life situation of a patient, and being able to recognize that he has helped change the course of that life for the better. Still, Carye has heard him refuse a surgery saying, "I can't do this one. This one is a baby to me."

Chapter Two

"I want to do this really bad," says Anneke. She enters Carye's office. A wonderful, inviting smile plays across her face, but her eyes fail to keep up. They're searching eyes, looking for help. "Where should I sit?" she asks. There are four chairs in the room but no one to answer her question. Her eyes settle on the seat behind Carye's desk. "Here?"

Strawberry blond and very pretty, Anneke at twenty-three is about the same age as the equally nervous woman following her into the room. But the difference in their lives shows clearly on their faces. Anneke's smile is an easy one and it is her natural expression when beginning a conversation. It appears to be there even when it isn't.

Anneke grew up in the suburbs of Portland and entered college on a swimming scholarship. Last year she earned her psychology degree from Willamette University, a small college in nearby Salem. After working a one-year internship at a women's crisis center, answering the telephone emergency line and driving the center's car to pick up women who had to leave abusive and dangerous situations quickly, she answered a newspaper advertisement Carye had placed for a receptionist/counselor. Anneke has worked at Lovejoy two months.

Until now Anneke has been stationed behind the sliding glass window near Lovejoy's front entrance, mostly answering phones, greeting and instructing patients and scheduling appointments. Earlier in the week Carye told Anneke she would soon get her first opportunity to do some abortion counseling. Five minutes ago Carye wandered over to the front desk and told Anneke the next appointment of the morning would be hers.

If Anneke's face betrays her nervousness, the look on the woman following her into Carye's office conveys something a level beyond—outright fear, perhaps. Peggy is a heavyset blonde, a woman with a face that begs to be liked. But something is off; if she were a doll, you would think someone had not been careful enough in assembling her. The studious, Malcolm X–style glasses don't quite fit with the girlish barrette in her hair. Throughout this session she will constantly chew on the inside of her mouth. The effect is of someone balancing on a tightrope between adulthood and adolescence, uncertain which way she should jump.

Last month Peggy, who dropped out of high school after her junior year, completed a two-year certified nurse's assistant degree at a community college. She has a fifteen-month-old son, and she has been sick throughout her current pregnancy. She says she was engaged to marry the man responsible for the pregnancy but they recently broke up. Now she has another boyfriend, "but this is kind of in the way." She never says what "this" is.

Peggy takes the seat beside Carye's desk. Carye follows her in and forms a triangle with Peggy and Anneke by taking the chair in the room's near corner.

"My name is Anneke, and this is my first time doing this." The next line does not come so easy. Anneke begins looking down at the papers in her hands, and looks . . . and looks. Carye, after glancing at the sheets Anneke holds—Peggy's admitting forms—jumps in.

"Tell me about the surgery," Carye says. Peggy's first pregnancy and delivery were full of complications. She gained one hundred pounds over the nine months, suffered severe toxemia, which could have killed her, and experienced a heart problem during delivery. A few months after the delivery, about a year ago, she had her gallbladder removed, possibly a result of the toxemia.

Carye has asked precisely the right question. Peggy begins talking. "That's why I'm really freaked out," she says.

"Well, we're going to take really good care of you," Carye responds, her smile close to a laugh, ready to go either way depending on Peggy's interpretation. All three women laugh. Progress—the tension in the room recedes. But it hasn't disappeared. Now they're three women just sitting around chatting, gossiping a bit. Laughter comes quickly, maybe too quickly, but at this point any laughter is a welcome relief.

Anneke remains silent. She cannot take her eyes off the papers in her hand for more than a few seconds at a time.

"I've thought about it a lot," Peggy says. "I don't think I can love it at all. Things are going good now."

"It's one of those things, it's going to hurt," Carye says. She launches into an explanation of the situation as she sees it, as she has seen it through the eyes of hundreds of young women like Peggy. There are no easy choices here, no simple solutions, Carye emphasizes. Nothing fully ends when Peggy leaves Lovejoy, it is a question of which baggage she wants to carry with her when she does. Carye validates what appears to be Peggy's primary concern, her own health risk if the baby is carried full term and delivered. The combination of Peggy's weight, heart problem, and pregnancy history make her a prime candidate for a dangerous, possibly fatal delivery. Carye mentions the possibility of adoption, but Peggy closes off that discussion when she says she does not think she could give up a child if she gave birth to it.

In a confiding tone, Carye asks about the father. Peggy begins with the nervous laugh that accompanies most of her thoughts. "I used to think he had ambition, and then he kind of turned into a log," Peggy says. The three women laugh knowingly.

Anneke leans her elbows on Carye's desk, chin in hand, not yet a participant, waiting to be pushed into action.

Peggy says she is afraid of needles, and Carye says a compromise is possible. Instead of the standard two needles at the time of the abortion—one blood test and one local anesthetic—they can draw blood this morning for analysis. Then only the anesthetic injection will be necessary when Peggy returns for the operation.

"But it won't be today, right?" asks Peggy. Clearly she is not ready for the procedure.

Both counselors rush to assure Peggy that was never the plan. But because Peggy is close to twelve weeks pregnant, she is nearing the cutoff line for the simpler "tab local," shorthand for "therapeutic abortion under local anesthetic." There are only two more weeks in which this procedure can be performed. Carye leaves the room, and Anneke, now on steadier ground, conveys the necessary information she knows almost by rote at this point. This is the informed consent process.

Anneke explains what will occur on the day of Peggy's surgery, tells her where she will be admitted, asks if Peggy will have arranged a ride home and child care for her son. Women are usually asked not to bring small children into the waiting area out of consideration for other patients there. Counselors at Lovejoy know they must routinely ask these questions. Counseling here is seldom limited to the procedure; it extends to the fabric of the patients' lives because their pregnancies are both consequences and reflections of those lives. If Anneke doesn't ask about child care, she might get a call from Peggy on the morning of the procedure explaining she can't come in because nobody is available to take care of the baby. For many patients here, any excuse will do.

Peggy will be given Valium during the operation. "It will make you mellow, like you had three glasses of wine and haven't eaten all day," Anneke says, smiling. Next on her list is an explanation of risk to the patient. In reality a simple early abortion poses little medical danger to the patient. An infection making its way up the uterus is probably the worst scenario, and the risk of that is estimated at one in five hundred, but the full explanation is legally critical. Informed consent helps keep doctors and hospitals out of trouble.

"I have a question. Can I still change my mind at any time?"

"Absolutely."

Carye returns to the room, shutting the door behind her. "The only time you can't change your mind is once the instrument is in your body," Carye adds. "Then it's too late."

Anneke takes this as a cue and picks up scattered plastic rods called cannulas to show Peggy how the procedure is done, using a plastic model of the female reproductive system that permanently resides on Carye's desk.

"After the surgery you need to take really good care of yourself," Anneke says. She tells Peggy to monitor her blood flow; if it appears she is passing too much blood, she should call Lovejoy's twenty-four-hour-a-day emergency number. She should take her temperature three times a day and stay away from spas, saunas, hot baths, tampons, and intercourse for a week.

"Just basically listen to your body because you will know if something's not right."

"And call us day or night," Carye adds.

Peggy's mind is off on a different track. "Is it true that at six weeks it has a heartbeat?"

Carye says nobody is sure exactly when the heart begins beating, and tries to deflect that concern. "This pregnancy and you are the same thing," she adds, explaining to Peggy that prior to twenty-four weeks the fetus cannot survive outside her womb.

"This tells me you're wondering if this is an okay thing to do," Carye continues. "To look at something from a moral point of view, that's a good thing. It's really important to know that you're going to let yourself know the sadness and the grief. This is a loss. It's something inside of you."

Peggy confesses that in recent days she has been hoping she would miscarry. Actually, she admits, she has been jumping up and down on her bed hoping to induce a miscarriage. The image of 230-

pound Peggy launching herself from a mattress brings a hearty laugh to all three women, and allows Carye to steer the conversation back to Peggy's concern.

"You have to know that when you did something you were only going into it with the best of intentions," Carye says. "I think it's really important you know that afterward there will be times you're going to say, 'Shit, why did I do this?'"

Which seems, to Carye, an appropriate ending for this unfocused session. She is disturbed by Peggy's inability to pursue specific concerns, to stick to one line of inquiry at a time. Every time Carye thinks she had addressed one of Peggy's concerns, it comes back again later in conversation. Peggy is a puzzle.

The stand-up comic in Carye takes over as she explains why they need a sample of Peggy's blood. "There's something about your blood," she says in classic Bela Lugosi vampire voice.

Anneke completes her explanation of the risks and consent forms. But Peggy voices another fear.

"I heard sometimes they show you the tissue."

Carye says there is one doctor in town who does. "And I think it's sadistic," she adds.

"I don't know if I'm mentally prepared, but I know I have to do this," Peggy says.

Carye takes that as a statement that Peggy is ready to go ahead, though she suspects Peggy is capable of changing her mind two or three times before the morning is out. She moves the conversation to the doctors. There are four doctors who regularly perform abortions at Lovejoy in addition to Dr. Suchak, although, as medical director, Suchak performs most of the surgeries. In fact, one of Allene's goals for the coming year is to have more local physicians perform their abortions at Lovejoy. She knows Suchak will object to this, and balancing Suchak's satisfaction with her goal of increasing Lovejoy's business will be a delicate matter.

Carye is in the position of deciding which cases go to which doctors. She tries to match a difficult case—and Peggy is an emotionally difficult case—with the surgeon whose approach will be most suitable. Some of the surgeons appear to her more gentle or willing to take more time with younger patients. One is distinguished by his willingness to carefully explain each procedure he is about to perform to the patient. Some women are comforted by this. Other women prefer a doctor who is all business and who gets them through the operation as quickly as possible. Suchak is reputed to work that way. In her office, when no doctors are around, Carye occasionally will entertain the downstairs staff with her imitations of the different doctors, right down to the way they walk around the operating room and brandish their instruments. One surgeon, when completing a procedure, routinely waves his speculum like a pistol, blowing at invisible smoke coming out of the instrument's imaginary barrel.

Carye tells Peggy she wants to schedule the abortion with Dr. Chandler. "He's really kind and really gentle. He'll talk you through it." Chandler's next opening is three days away, so Peggy will have plenty of time to think about her decision.

Carye hands Peggy a supply of birth control pills to start the Sunday after the surgery. This is standard procedure at Lovejoy, where various types of birth control are dispensed, including morning-after pills. Carye rises and the two other women follow suit. Carye congratulates Peggy on her CNA degree and touches the woman's hand as they part in the hallway.

Minutes later Carye and Anneke, still in the hallway, review Peggy's situation. "I can almost guarantee that she will have an abortion," Carye says. She also ventures that Peggy probably will fail to come in for her appointment Friday. It is hard to believe anyone would try to predict the actions of a woman as conflicted and scattered as Peggy.

"She wants to have somebody to help her, to say, 'It's okay,'" Carye explains. "That's something I won't say. But I'll say, 'You can do this,' and that it will be a part of who you are."

Simple solutions are not in Carye's power and she refuses to pretend they are. She never offers what many of the women who visit

Lovejoy want most—a closed chapter, their old lives restored. Those old lives are gone, Carye tells them. Choose a new life. Abort, have your child, or deliver the child and adopt the child out. But be prepared to live as a changed woman.

Carye and Anneke discuss what they have observed about Peggy. Carye says she noticed every other button on Peggy's blouse was missing, with straight pins substituted for the missing buttons. Carye tends to pick up on details such as this. She sees the missing buttons as a signal that Peggy's life may be so out of control that she will never know what the best choice is for her, or she may be unable to follow through on any choice she makes.

"I think she'll probably reschedule once," Carye says. "I would probably make book on that." Peggy needs to make a decision fairly soon because her pregnancy is closing in on the end of the first trimester, beyond which she will need a more complicated surgery necessitating a general anesthetic.

Carye takes Anneke back to her office and instructs her on filling out the counseling notes that will be attached to Peggy's medical file. Peggy's surgeon will read these notes before the actual abortion. "Remember, this is subjective, so you write what you observed and what you felt," Carye says before leaving.

At the front desk Leanne is giving directions over the telephone. "What makes us stand out? There's a little old man on the corner with a sign in his hand, that's what makes us stand out," she says.

Allene has just arrived for the day. In the middle of her desk she finds a sheet of paper: a shooting target with concentric black and white circles. A dozen bullet holes are scattered throughout the target. She knows Carye had her weekly outing at the shooting range last night. With a playful smile Allene remarks, "She's ready."

FRIDAY, MARCH 31

Carye may have been mistaken. Shortly after lunch Peggy shows up in the waiting room, just in time for her appointment. Accompanied by a friend who calls herself Ike, she is sent straight to the first-floor laboratory.

Peggy was telling the truth when she said she was afraid of needles. She alternately laughs and then breathes out heavily, as if fighting off hyperventilation, as Joan, the lab technician, tries to prick her finger. "You have to relax your arm," Joan exhorts. "Come on, you've got to loosen it!"

Ike is holding the other arm, rubbing Peggy's back. Finally, the blood is drawn. "You did it," says Joan, adding, "That's the little part." Ike quickly adds, "That's the big part for you."

Within minutes Peggy and Ike are sent to the second floor. There they find another sliding glass window, another admitting ritual. Peggy gulps as if trying to clear something stuck in her throat, writes her name on the appropriate sheet of paper, and then breaks out in her characteristic nervous laughter.

Peggy is wearing sandals and blue stirrup pants today. She has not made the effort to affect a style. Ike has enough for both women—Doc Martens boots up past her calves, a short skirt over leggings, worn Levi's jacket, blond hair cropped short on the side but long on top. There was a time when her look would have been labeled punk, or butch, before styles became indefinable and cultural boundaries nearly indistinguishable. Now it is just a look.

Peggy and Ike take seats in the second-floor waiting room. There are two women sitting across from them.

Peggy directs a question across the room. "Did that guy outside bug you guys?" The two women have a streetwise air that sets them apart from Peggy, whose vulnerability drapes her like a Halloween costume.

"Oh I don't care," says one woman. "I told him, 'If you bother me I'm going to knock you out.'"

"Well, I'm kind of paranoid," Peggy says.

Peggy looks down at the form she was given at the admissions window. She nudges Ike, points to the word "abortion," and gulps again. She signs the form. She looks again at the two women opposite them.

"Did you already take your stuff? Did it make you loopy yet?"

But nobody has taken the Valium yet and nobody is ready for small talk, except Peggy. Ike is leafing through a *McCall's* and Peggy occasionally peeks at the magazine. She points to pictures of food that accompany recipes. Her nervous laughter is the room's dominant sound, the only competition the hum of a Pepsi machine a few feet away.

Peggy looks at Ike's magazine again and points to a story titled, "What Couples Fight About Most." "What, getting pregnant?" Peggy chortles. Ike shares her laughter.

Looking around the room, the blank peach walls, Peggy mutters, "It's a little morbid."

One of the other women tells her friend she is going outside to smoke. "Are you nervous?" the friend asks. Peggy leans over to Ike and whispers, "What's to be nervous about?"

Peggy did not sleep well last night, or much. Her son woke up at 5 A.M. "I haven't slept well since I found out I was pregnant," she confides. That was three weeks ago. Her stomach has been upset and she has been vomiting since then, but she thinks it may be more related to stress than the pregnancy itself.

This morning she called her ex-boyfriend and asked him to come to Lovejoy with her. He said he had a job interview. "He'd promised before," she says. "I wasn't thinking about an abortion until he mentioned it."

A medical assistant, Tamara, steps into the waiting area. She has dark hair and exudes competence, but at the same time there is warmth in her manner. "Peggy? Come on back." She watches Peggy produce one of her exaggerated breathing sounds then adds, "Or not."

Peggy begins to rise from her chair, then hesitates, finishing up by Tamara's side. Turning to Ike, Tamara says gently, "You wait here. She'll be back in an hour." Then, looking again at Peggy, "Or sooner."

Peggy's state could not be more obvious to Tamara if she had FEAR tattooed on her forehead.

"If you're not sure, do you need to see a counselor again? Because if you do, that's okay," Tamara says. She has tried to open a door of possibility that Peggy might have been afraid to open by herself, but Tamara does not want to influence events one way or the other. A sympathetic look on her face seems to bolster Peggy, who takes a deep breath as if she's about to blow up a balloon, sighs, and walks beside Tamara through the double doors leading to the surgical area.

Peggy's departure has not reduced the level of tension back in the lounge. It is clear that the three remaining women are affected by the inner struggle they have just witnessed. "It's against her ethics but she knows it's what she should do," says Ike quietly.

The other two women are silent until one says, "I just can't wait to fit into my pants again."

Ike wonders if Peggy would have benefited from more counseling downstairs. Peggy's uncertainty over the procedure has been clear from the start. But in view of Tuesday's session, more time with Carye probably would not help. Lovejoy is not a therapist's office. It's about surgery and about abortions, and the work the counselors do is much more in the line of crisis counseling than long-term therapy. Carye and Allene know they can't turn around the lives of these women. If this were an abortion in an obstetrician's office, Peggy most likely would have had no counseling at all—the price of privacy.

Still, a woman as ambivalent as Peggy is rare at Lovejoy. Most women who step through Lovejoy's front doors know what they want or they wouldn't have gone through the trouble of coming in.

For better or worse Peggy is now in the surgical area. She has remained behind the double doors for fifteen minutes, and the procedure should soon be over.

Tamara appears in the lobby, a crying, red-faced Peggy behind her. Peggy is looking down at her hands, which are working a crumpled piece of tissue this way and that, trying to make it smooth.

"We're going to send Peggy back downstairs," Tamara says to Ike. Her arm stretches around Peggy's bulky shoulders. Turning to Peggy she says, "You think about what I said." And to Ike, "I'm not comfortable going through with a procedure that two days from now she might regret because she was on narcotics."

Peggy and Ike head downstairs in the elevator. As soon as the door opens, Ike heads toward the business office off the front lobby. Peggy follows. Ike begins dialing the telephone. She is trying to reach the boyfriend or ex-boyfriend or friend—the father. His role has changed each time Peggy has told the story.

"This is to make her feel better," Ike says, nodding at Peggy. But nobody answers the phone. Outside Carye has been briefed on the morning's events, and she shuffles her afternoon schedule to fit in a session with Peggy.

Peggy and Ike wait in the empty business office. Ike keeps her arm around Peggy's shoulders and listens. Their relationship is remarkable in itself. The staff at Lovejoy assumes they are longtime friends but Peggy and Ike have known each other three months.

"It's really bad not having any support. I don't see why I have to do all this by myself," Peggy says. "Going up there, it's just like a big old tomb. I felt like I was playing God all of a sudden."

She describes her experience behind the double doors. In the hallway, being led to the pre-op room, she saw another patient through an open door. Just a moment's glance at the woman's frightened face opened a floodgate of emotions for Peggy. When she reached pre-op Peggy sobbed the entire fifteen minutes she was out of view, comforted by Tamara, who waited for the tears to stop before bringing her back out.

Peggy has resumed her shotgun approach to conversation. "The funny thing is, I would have been one of those people out on the street holding a sign until a year ago," she says. "I wish I were under heavy narcotics right now. I'm almost starting to feel a little brave, and once I do I think I'm going to go up there quick."

Twenty minutes later Carye ushers both women into her office. Ike takes the chair in the corner.

"When we talked the other day," Carye begins, but never finishes. Peggy does that for her: "I was brave."

Looking straight at Peggy but still managing a bit of nonchalance, Carye asks Peggy what it is she fears most. Is it the actual procedure, or the idea that having an abortion might be the wrong thing for her to do? It is an indication of Peggy's internal chaos that the normally insightful Carye still doesn't know the answer to this fundamental question.

Peggy giggles nervously.

"When this is over you're going to be sad," Carye says. "But it's not going to be something you won't be able to go through." Again she shows Peggy the plastic model of a woman's reproductive system, explaining that the doctor's work will take a minute at most.

"If your fear is the actual procedure, I know I can get you through that part. But I want to know on that other level—is this what you want to do?"

Peggy talks about her fear of doctors, her childhood heart surgery. She says that in recent years her memory of stifling tears through the ordeal has come rushing back to her. "I feel like I'm four right now," she says.

She is saying nothing new and nothing that will help Carye help her. Childhood trauma is a subject for long-term psychotherapy, not abortion counseling. Carye cannot follow leads that will take months to unravel. There are women waiting in the lobby.

"The other thing I'm really concerned about is you have a kind of manic personality," Carye says, trying a new approach.

Peggy ignores the comment. She says she's had pains on one side lately. She's shifted the conversation from the emotional to the more manageable physical. Carye mentions the possibility of an ultrasound, and Peggy says that's what she has wanted all along. Carye picks up Peggy's chart, reads awhile, asks about her gallbladder, bowel movements. She knows what Peggy is wishing for—that the decision be taken out of her hands—and she knows an ultrasound will not do that.

"It's unlikely you have an ectopic pregnancy if you haven't ruptured to this point," Carye says. An ectopic pregnancy, in which the fetus grows outside the uterus, would require a surgical procedure that would preempt the need for an abortion.

Carye brings up the possibility of having Peggy under general anesthetic during her abortion. Usually this is reserved for procedures after twelve weeks. Nevertheless, having Peggy unconscious might be the only way of getting her through an abortion. But the anesthetic itself involves an IV needle set into her arm, which probably would be harder for Peggy to bear than a local anesthetic by cervical injection, hidden from her view.

"I know if I go to option two, which is putting you to sleep, you're going to have to go through something that is worse, the needles. Right?" asks Carye. "But I keep coming back to, are you okay about having this abortion? Do you know it is the best thing, even though it may feel like the worst thing?"

"I just wish I had done it, and it was over with."

"Me too," says Carye. "I shouldn't be a counselor. I should be a fairy godmother."

The tension is broken with laughter. Through this session Peggy has continued her heavy breathing. Every few minutes she lets out a deep breath while making a sound, something like "Oooooh."

Peggy brings the conversation back to her own medical risk. Ike speaks up for the first time. "Would it be easier if the doctor said you can't deliver this baby?"

Carye puts a halt to that line of inquiry. "They'd put you in the category of high risk, but it doesn't mean that you couldn't carry this," she says.

"I'd like you to take some time," Carye continues. "We have some time here. Do you think it's the time that makes it harder?"

Turning to Ike she says, "Have you guys been talking a lot about this? What's your hit on Peggy being more scared of the procedure or more scared about having an abortion?"

"About equal," Ike answers.

"I'm just sorry I'm wasting so much of your time," Peggy says.

"You're not wasting my time because this is what I do," Carye says.

"I was, like, apologizing to it today."

"You know what, I talk to people about doing that, even writing letters," Carye says.

"I feel so guilty, that's what it is."

Carye is running out of ideas. She knows that no matter what Peggy might say here, tomorrow she may be of a completely different mind. Still, Carye tries to convince Peggy not to focus on guilt. Peggy isn't listening.

"I feel a big reality is hitting me in the face," Peggy says. "I'm just a basket case. I need a beer."

Carye relents. She proposes a general anesthetic next Thursday, a week away. Peggy appears to favor the idea. She apologizes for using up Carye's tissues and for filling up Carye's wastebasket with the used tissues.

"In the meantime, I want you to talk to the people at Boys and Girls Aid Society about some counseling, about your options," Carye says. The Boys and Girls Aid Society helps women arrange adoptions for their children, and will provide Peggy long-term counseling if she wants it.

"I don't feel like talking to a whole bunch of other people," Peggy says.

Exasperated, Carye turns to Ike. "I'm sorry, I don't know your name."

"Ike."

"I liked it when you and Tina were together," Carye says without missing a beat. The three women laugh, at ease again. The session is drawing to a close.

Ike says she starts a new job Wednesday and cannot accompany Peggy to a Thursday appointment. Apparently Peggy has no one else she can count on. She has not told anyone in her family about the abortion. Her mother is a churchgoing Catholic with strong feelings against abortion, and all of her family members are very judgmental, Peggy says.

"I think you've already made your decision," Ike says. "You made your decision a couple of weeks ago."

Peggy looks at Ike and says she might be ready for the abortion now. Carye takes out a new set of forms to prepare Peggy for the general anesthetic. She asks Peggy a series of questions regarding her overall health and fills out the paperwork. An appointment is set for an abortion under general anesthetic Saturday morning, tomorrow. Carye makes it the morning's first appointment in the hope that Peggy will arrive before the Saturday morning protestors; Peggy does not need any more roadblocks.

"Can I get a picture of the ultrasound?" Peggy asks. "I want to send it to Tommy. I just want him to think of it." These are the first words out of her mouth that hint at bitterness. "Part of the problem is it was Tommy's idea and he's not here. So maybe it's not such a good idea."

The three women walk to the ultrasound room. Peggy takes her position in the stirrups, Carye operates the machinery. The procedure takes about a minute. Carye points to the image of the fetus on the screen and says, "Absolutely perfect." The fetus is not out of position, as Peggy feared, or hoped. Peggy, still on her back, sticks her fist in the air and shouts, "I am woman!"

Returning to the front lobby Carye tells Peggy the hardest part of her procedure will likely be the hour or so she spends in the waiting room.

"If you're feeling scared while you're waiting, I want you to look beside you, because everyone around you is going to be feeling exactly the same thing." Then she adds, "If you're not going to show up in the morning, will you give us a call?"

Peggy utters one more of her patented "Oooooh" sounds, half-way between a sigh and the sound of a child blowing out candles on a birthday cake.

Back in the hallway outside her office after Peggy and Ike have left, Carye shakes her head and says Peggy is a woman whose emotional composition probably will never allow her to make a decision and live with it in peace. "We'll never really know if it's okay."

SATURDAY, APRIL 1

Just after Lovejoy opens for the day Peggy calls to say she will not be coming in. So Carye, though slightly off in sequence, was right with her original prediction that Peggy would cancel her appointment.

For the next three days Carye telephones Peggy but her messages are never returned. On Thursday Peggy calls and reschedules for Saturday morning. Saturday will mark Peggy's twelfth week, her final chance for a simple, one-day procedure. If she fails to make the appointment, the only remaining option will be a two-day tab gen—short for "therapeutic abortion with general anesthesia"—which entails an extra physician's examination.

APRIL 8

It is six-thirty on an overcast Saturday morning, the type of morning people who have lived in Portland awhile come to expect. Even the clouds are invisible. No streaks of sun or gentle coloring to the east can be seen through the front doors at Lovejoy. It is the type of day that makes desperate citizens think the sun will never appear, until, almost imperceptibly, there begins a faint tinting of objects around their edges. At Lovejoy the outlines of young maple trees lining the sidewalk are barely visible. Then a hint of color shows in a deep red rhododendron in front of the synagogue across the street. Portland mornings have a way of sneaking up like that. Sometimes you never notice the dawn.

At six-forty occasional cars roll past the clinic but no protestors are out. Inside, a light emanates from the receptionist's desk but
the business room is empty. The waiting room holds four people. A
relaxed young woman in Birkenstock sandals shares a joke with a
woman friend as she fills out her admissions forms. Both laugh naturally and easily. A black couple sit silently side by side, both wearing
baggy sweatshirts. The man is hunched over in his seat, forearms on
legs, lost in a book. The woman yawns. Apart from occasional comments from the two women, the room's only sound comes from a radio
in the business office tuned to a classic rock station.

Lovejoy sits close to downtown Portland, in an older neighborhood gentrified over the course of the last two decades. For
years northwest Portland featured cheap rents and an eclectic mix
of artists and longtime homeowners. Now most of the turn-of-the-
century homes are occupied by professional families; the artists
have been forced out by skyrocketing rents, and the old-timers
by skyrocketing property taxes brought on by increasing values
assessed to their homes. Today, many of the residents can be seen
running around the neighborhood and past Lovejoy in their Lycra
tights and hundred-dollar Nikes. A thirtyish woman jogs past now,
full of speed and balance, purpose and self-assurance, a startling
contrast to the women inside waiting their turn for another sort
of physical ordeal.

By 7 A.M. the protestors have begun to take their stations outside. They move slowly at first, as if they too are not quite ready
to begin. Two men and a woman gather at the corner just outside
Lovejoy's entrance. They have been meeting here every Saturday morning since 1978. Their protests have taken many forms,
but with court injunctions in place they tread much more carefully than they once did. One carries a sign that reads INNOCENT
CHILDREN KILLED HERE. Soon they begin to softly chant together
as they finger their beads, praying the rosary they call it, though
they are not all Catholic.

Peggy has found her resolve. Thursday she finally told her family she was pregnant and wanted to have an abortion. Her mother tried to talk her out of the operation, but Trudy, who is soon to be her sister-in-law, offered support, defending her choice. In fact, Trudy simply took charge. As a teenager she had an abortion performed. Today she is at Peggy's side as they enter Lovejoy. Amazingly, so is Tommy, quick to make clear he is not Peggy's boyfriend, just a friend. Trudy has somehow coerced him into coming along.

Today's is a slightly different version of Peggy, still afraid but steady enough to get through the operation. As Carye has planned, she is the first patient of the day. No waiting room tension this time. A medical assistant takes Peggy straight back to start the general anesthetic.

Waiting for Peggy to reappear, Trudy talks about the abortion she had nearly ten years ago. The operation was covered by her health insurance. What she doesn't understand is why her insurance won't pay for her birth control pills.

An hour later Trudy and Tommy walk alongside as a medical assistant guides Peggy's wheelchair out the back door to Trudy's waiting car. The operation went smoothly, says Dr. Suchak. For the first time since she arrived at Lovejoy over a week ago, Peggy is displaying little of her nervous giddiness.

Peggy never calls back to schedule the two-weeks-after-care appointment all women are asked to attend. Carye is sure she has seen her last of Peggy—unless there is another pregnancy. But two weeks later Carye receives an emergency telephone call late at night. Peggy, with Ike at her side, is clotting and bleeding heavily. She says she feels pain in her side, and she sounds panic-stricken. Ike gets on the phone and says Peggy is getting dizzy. Carye instructs Ike to take Peggy to a nearby hospital emergency room. The next morning Carye calls Ike and learns that Peggy never went to the hospital. The pain let up, the bleeding ceased. Carye urges Peggy to come into Lovejoy for a checkup, but she never sees her again.

*

Occasionally Portlanders will be treated to a day in early April that feels like August. Longtime residents know enough to enjoy the summerlike weather without getting fooled into thinking it is here to stay. The rain and the seemingly endless gray skies will return before the real summer breaks through.

Stepping from her car on this windless, sweltering afternoon Carye notices the enormity of the parking lot at the strip mall she is visiting. She looks about and finds another reminder that this is not her home territory: There are hardly any foreign cars in the lot. In fact, the few Toyotas and Subarus scattered about might be outnumbered by the Harley-Davidson motorcycles parked off to one side.

Approaching her destination Carye observes bars on all the windows. The sign above the store features three cartoon bears— Daddy Bear, Mommy Bear, and Baby Bear—each holding a gun. This is the place: Three Bears Guns.

She walks quickly, eager to finish the business at hand. But she cannot deny her curiosity. Basically an inquisitive woman, Carye is held in wonder by her circumstances, as one imagines many find themselves in wartime at a crucial moment of awakening— Ivy League English majors turned foxhole grunts, musicians made desk sergeants.

Inside the store Carye notices stacks and stacks of boxes to her left, each full of bullets. To her right are scopes and sights and various other shooting paraphernalia. Directly in front of her, handguns are displayed against the back wall. Carye approaches the counter and is pleased to find a familiar face in Chad, the man who sold Carye her handgun at a firearms show the month before.

Quickly Carye learns there are two choices here. Carye's gun is a .357 Magnum, a miniature version of the powerful weapon popularized by Clint Eastwood in his Dirty Harry movies. Carye can put two different kinds of ammunition in the gun: .357 bullets or smaller .38 caliber bullets, which will do less damage to a victim. Chad recommends the .357s, the bullet the gun was designed to shoot. He places boxes of both bullets on the glass countertop between them. Carye, acting as if she is late for an appointment, does not open the boxes. She buys two boxes of the .357s and six of the smaller .38s. She remembers to ask for earmuffs and targets to take to the shooting range. Gathering her change, she quickly leaves the store.

As Carye hurries back to the comfort of her car the plastic bag holding her purchases breaks, and all the boxes fall out on the parking lot pavement. Embarrassed, she hurriedly gathers up everything she has bought and rushes to her car, putting the bullets, targets, and earmuffs in the trunk. One box of bullets she keeps in her hand and takes into the car.

Carye locks the car doors. Now she is alone, back in a familiar space. Safe. Her breathing slows. She opens the box and immediately is struck by the sleek, compact design of each bullet. She compares the shiny brass casings to fine jewelry. They are beautiful, she recognizes. And now Carye begins to cry, not a little bit, but tears that seem endless because she is not even sure of their source. She continues for what seems minutes.

When Carye bought her gun the weapon did not scare her. It has never seemed beautiful or deadly in the way these bullets do. At most she has found herself marveling at the intricacy of its work, but it has always seemed a machine to her. It does not fuel her imagination beyond the moment at hand. In fact, Carye has laughed more than once at the thought of her gun, and how shocked most of her friends would be if they knew she carried such a weapon in a holster hidden behind her hip. Carye Ortman, who grew up in Forest Grove, a small town about thirty miles west of Portland, where the first weekend of deer season each year would bring a day off from high school because so few kids would be anywhere but in the woods. Carye Ortman, whose father was virulently antihunting despite his neighbors, and who repeatedly cautioned her to never take anything into the woods but a camera. Carye Ortman, who only once has so much as struck another human being in her life and then only in response to an attack on her; who, when she made the decision to buy a hand-gun, went through the same process as when she bought a dish-washer—checking out *Consumer Reports* for the best type of gun for her, then the various ratings of different models.

Carye is still in her car sobbing. The bullets have broken through her emotional defenses in a way the gun could not. These are the real killing machines, these are what rip through flesh and puncture organs and set blood to running out in rivers as life itself drains away. And still crying, Carye takes one of the bullets out of the box and begins to place it on different spots on her body, imagining the bullet going in at each place and doing its damage inside. And she begins to cry all the harder.

Later, driving home, Carye's mood lightens. Passing one more of the countless fast-food restaurants on this blue-collar avenue, she observes a giant balloon figure of a clown floating above a McDonald's and finds herself ruefully wondering how many bullets would be needed to deflate Ronald if she were to take out her gun, load it, and start firing.

At home Thom, her husband, will comfort her but he cannot resist an observation: "I can almost promise you you're the only woman on this planet who owns a Volvo and a revolver."

Two weeks later Carye drifts into Allene's office. Allene looks up and smiles; Carye is a surefire cure for the day's pressures, she knows.

Immediately the two women start discussing last weekend, when Carye and Allene were treated to four days at a South Carolina resort by pharmaceutical manufacturer Parke-Davis. Every year Parke-Davis invites the heads of the nation's largest abortion facilities to this conference. Allene enjoys the expensive accommodations, the fine food, the pampering, primarily because she feels the abortion providers are being acknowledged as an important group of people by an important member of the nation's business community. "It's the only time in my experience that we are singled out as good and valued businesspeople," she says.

Carye returned from the conference fired up about a renewed marketing effort. Business is slow at Lovejoy. The facility currently handles about three hundred abortions a month, down from last year's monthly average. This is right in line with a national trend toward fewer abortions. Baby boomers are aging and pregnancies are fewer. And Lovejoy has to face the added pressure of fierce competition from local providers.

But South Carolina has inspired Carye. She and Allene attended a workshop on marketing. Carye shows off a little black item that looks like a matchbook. On the bottom, instead of CLOSE COVER BEFORE STRIKING, it reads, OPEN FOR SAFETY. Inside, instead of matches, sits a condom encased in plastic, ready for use. And the name of the abortion facility is printed at the top. A facility on the East Coast increased their calls by 10 percent using these giveaways. Carye imagines distributing them in nightclubs and bars around Portland.

The thought of passing out condoms makes Carye think back to her first year on the Portland abortion scene. She was working at the local Feminist Women's Health Center when she became aware of the number of abortions resulting from Rose Festival trysts. The Rose Festival is a local institution—an annual month-long excuse for parades, concerts, and carnivals. Navy ships dock downtown, tourists and residents are given a chance to look the ships over during the day, and at night sailors prowl the city on leave. Inevitably, Carye learned, there would be an increased demand for abortions a month or two later.

That first year Carye was so upset, she recruited Thom to help her pass out free condoms at festival parades and at the fun center carnival downtown. She also pasted stickers proclaiming the benefits of safe sex inside the portable toilets lined up along the downtown park.

Later Carye figured out that Rose Festival was only one of many events contributing to the cyclical nature of abortions. December, for instance, is always a heavy month for the second-trimester abortions known as D & Es (for "dilation and evacuation"). Carye figures these are due to autumn's new school year: Girls who become pregnant at the close of summer return to school and are able to maintain their denial until about December. Then there is the first week of July, which usually yields a jump in abortions, the result of prom nights in May.

Allene, too, has been sparked by the marketing workshop. She thinks she has gotten lazy about pushing for business, or maybe just too consumed by other issues such as Andrew Burnett. She's been thinking about running radio ads for Lovejoy.

Allene and Carye share a laugh as they review their impressions of some of the other providers at the conference. One owner of an abortion clinic said he had spent one million dollars in security measures since last year; all people are now searched before entering or exiting his facility. Even the conference had a different look. "There were forty security people," Allene notes. "And the ones who were most scared were the Parke-Davis people."

But their favorite event came on the conference's last day. Parke-Davis paid for a cruise of the waters around the resort. The setting was idyllic—blue seas, dolphins mating, turtles nearby. On board a naturalist was describing the scenery as drinks flowed freely among the fifteen providers and the handful of Parke-Davis executives.

Then, offhandedly, one of the providers mentioned he had bought a gun during the year. Carye said that she had, too. The discussion went from one provider to the other—the most practical gun, which model is easiest to conceal in a purse, the advantages of four-inch barrels versus six-inch barrels, concealed-weapons laws in each of their communities, the atmosphere at their local firing ranges. It turned out ten of the fifteen abortion providers on the cruise were carrying weapons on a daily basis. Six of the ten were women. While the providers became drawn into the topic of guns, the tour guide kept trying to draw their attention to the dolphins off the side of the boat and the scenery in the distance. But basically, the providers were too engrossed in their own conversation. The gaping representatives of Parke-Davis simply listened, stunned.

Allene found her validation at the conference and Carye found hers. This, Carye says, was the support group she needed.

As Carye and Allene talk over business, a single-page flyer is being sent around the city. Across the top is bannered MEDICAL COMMU-NITY NEWS. Flashing across the bottom of the page are the words URGENT ALERT! URGENT ALERT! URGENT ALERT! Between these legends the flyer reads:

> Advocates for Life ministries has exposed one abortionist a month for the last six months through home picketing, leafleting and other activities protected under the First Amendment.
>
> We plan to continue these activities as a public service so that patients, colleagues, neighbors and friends of these abortionists will know that this person kills children for a living.
>
> Inside is a list of those already picketed and addresses and phone numbers where they might be contacted. Please use whatever influence you have to convince them to practice real medicine in keeping with their Oath.
>
> COMING SOON TO YOUR NEIGHBORHOOD!

There are days when Allene feels she is close to the end with Lovejoy. Her children, concerned for her safety, ask her to get out. At least wear a bulletproof vest, exhorts her daughter Leah, who works at Lovejoy as a counselor. The problems no longer appear as challenges but as hurdles she has leaped before, only to see them in front of her once again. These are the days it seems as though so little progress has been made, when the road ahead seems impossibly long.

Four years before *Roe v. Wade* irrevocably altered the national landscape, state legislation made abortion in Oregon marginally legal, but hardly bearable. Many of the state's abortions took place at Oregon Health Sciences University, the state's Portland-based public hospital and medical school. An obstetrician told Allene that women who came to OHSU for abortions often were placed in rooms with women who were delivering babies. Many of the medical center's nurses were unwilling to work on abortion patients. The need for a separate abortion facility clear. Allene, who had been trained as a nurse, decided to turn her mother's physical rehabilitation center into the state's first abortion clinic.

Even as a teenager Allene Klass felt she was destined for an extraordinary life of some kind. No obstacle seemed insurmountable. When she was twenty-five Allene lost her son, then three and a half. She came through the ordeal sure that her tragedy was not an isolated, horrible event, knowing there had to be a reason she had been forced to grow up so fast. She also learned a lesson fundamental to her later success: not to despair over matters beyond her control.

And on weary days such as this, Allene stands in the doorway of her office, or sometimes wanders out to the lobby, and looks at the women seated all about. Many appear no more emotionally engaged than if they were waiting for an optometrist. But usually Allene can spot the others, women with fear in their eyes, or anger, or a look of just plain giving up. And that, usually, is the antidote. Allene believes nobody could run Lovejoy as well as she has. Those women need her. But she also knows there will come a time when the needs of the women will fail to override her own needs. Allene is fifty-six, she has been taking care of the needs of others for twenty-five years, and she does not possess a martyr's sensibilities. When the job becomes more burden than joy, it will be time for a change.

A few years ago that might have meant looking for someone to buy Lovejoy, but no longer. Allene has a plan. Nobody at Lovejoy

knows. She's found a successor for that time when she wants out of
the daily decisions, the conflicts, the caution. Carye. She has not
even told Carye this, but sometime in the last year she began to
look at Carye as the woman who can take over and run Lovejoy.
Allene will still own the Surgicenter, she will need the income in
her retirement or semiretirement or whatever it becomes. But Carye
is smart enough, and, more important, she can be trusted. What
Carye doesn't see yet, Allene believes, is the overall picture of running a business, how to stick to a bottom line while making hundreds of little decisions each day.

And so Allene is teaching Carye, a little bit at a time. A comment here—"Politics, girl." An observation there—"I think she's
catching on." Carye senses she is a pupil on occasion, but she does
not know the job for which she is being groomed.

Chapter Three

You are Andrew Burnett and you are looking for something. You are thirty, moderately successful as a roofing contractor, a loyal husband, father to three children, and bored. You are living an unremarkable life.

Your father was anything but unremarkable, a respected Baptist minister who came to Oregon when you were nine and eventually left the congregation he led for eighteen years to set up shop as a family counselor.

You need to find some way to make a mark in the world, and one afternoon you're reading a story in the local newspaper about an abortion protest and you decide this cause is worthy of your efforts. Reticent, you call a friend and he agrees to join you at the protest. You go, and you keep on going, and then a small group forms around you and suddenly you no longer are the nearly friendless high school kid but a leader, a leader in the movement to end abortion. You believe abortion is equivalent to murder and you support and advocate nonviolent civil disobedience as a means of protest.

But one thing leads to another. Picketing leads to blockading. The rescue blockades become violent shoving matches with patients and escorts. Police intervene on the side of the escorts. Before long you find yourself organizing rescues with three hundred protestors, a

field commander in a war zone. And then the anti-abortion movement becomes radicalized further.

People start shooting doctors and you are one of the leaders
of the movement, so you begin a debate with your own conscience
and decide that if you truly believe abortion is murder you should
use your voice to justify the shooting of doctors who perform abortions. Not as execution, you insist, but as a defensive action—to
stop the murder of unborn children. Your voice is your magazine,
the one publication that keeps the radical anti-abortion movement together, and you defend the shooting of doctors not only
through stories justifying violence but by publicizing the work of
these doctors—printing their names, home and clinic addresses
and telephone numbers, along with their photographs. And some
of them get shot.

Your picture is in *Time* magazine, and not one of those tiny head-
and-shoulder shots used to break up a column of text. *Ms.* magazine
calls you one of fifteen "Enemies of Choice." Each month thousands
of people nationwide wait to hear what you have to say, and that
includes agents for the FBI and Alcohol, Tobacco and Firearms
(ATF), who read each word you print with the thoroughness of trea-
sure hunters scanning old maps—looking for clues to what you or
your followers might do next.

You advocate shooting the nation's abortion doctors but you
will not do it yourself. You don't want to go to jail for the rest of your
life. You are forty-one now and you don't want to say good-bye to
your wife and five children. You've finally climbed up high enough
to get others to listen and you are not ready to relinquish your plat-
form. So when asked, you call yourself a coward.

Andrew Burnett has been in jail fifty or sixty times since he
began protesting abortions. He's lost count. Most of the confronta-
tions that led to those jailings were with Allene Klass and the Lovejoy
Surgicenter.

The contrast between Allene and Burnett could not be more
vivid. One, Allene, Jewish, a strong woman, running the largest

abortion facility in the state. The other, Burnett, a fundamentalist Christian man unable to defeat what he perceives as evil in his own backyard, let alone the nation.

Even their appearances speak of different values. Burnett is tall, about six foot three, with small eyes set close together in a large face. His hairline is receding, his mustache well-trimmed. He gives little attention to his dress, which tends toward plaid shirts and brown slacks. Burnett usually keeps two pens in his front pocket, and his fingertips and nails often have a dirty blue look from running the printing press at the family business now registered in his wife's name. He's a big man with a slight paunch and he says that helps in jail; nobody has bothered him much there. That also may be due to the expressionless look he often displays, which falls just short of a glower. Allene calls it "brooding."

This look may be Burnett's greatest contradiction, considering his rhetoric. Whereas Allene speaks with passion and spontaneity, often changing her mind from one week to the next, Burnett offers a tone of rationality. His voice in conversation stays even, with little display of any emotion. Every question is carefully considered and every answer carefully thought out.

For years Allene and Burnett have been adversaries, natural enemies. Now they are like two wary prizefighters, heavyweights, slowly moving around a ring. They may hate each other but they respect what damage the other can wreak. Each claims to know how the other's mind works, but neither is quite sure of that. Neither will use the word "fear" when discussing the other. They do not get too close, and there is a reason. In their last encounter Allene threw what in boxing terms would be called a haymaker—the $8.2 million lawsuit.

In fact, the only emotion Burnett displayed in the course of many afternoons of conversation was a half smile at what he sees as the great irony of his eleven-year battle with Allene. The lawsuit, he says, turned him and the other leaders of Advocates for Life from part-time protestors with regular jobs into full-time anti-abortion activists. Now that each of them owes hundreds of thousands of dollars that could be garnished out of their wages, there's no point in trying to maintain a middle-class life. Burnett sold his roofing business. The house he lives in is legally owned by his brother-in-law. The key people at Advocates have become minimum-wage-earning activists with few possessions. Burnett owes Lovejoy five hundred thousand dollars but he scoffs at the figure, saying it might as well be five hundred *million*.

So Allene's civil award was not a knockout punch. But in the spring of 1995, despite the stories in *Time* and the FBI surveillance and the fear of violence that has succeeded in convincing many doctors and hospitals that they would rather not perform abortions, *Life Advocate* is reeling. Subscriptions are down. Finances are dwindling. Too many do not share Burnett's vision. If abortion is murder, Burnett says, then shooting a doctor before he can kill again is just, and any law that penalizes an abortionist with less than a murderer's sentence is wrong. When it comes to principles, Burnett will not budge.

"You're flushing your ministry down the toilet," another leader of the movement recently told Burnett. You are Andrew Burnett and you are now the radical fringe, an outcast even to the very anti-abortion movement you helped to foster.

FRIDAY, APRIL 21

The week's events have taken their toll. Nine P.M. and already Carye is ready for sleep. Her husband, Thom, settles in on his side of the bed they have shared for ten years. Carye takes her side. She reaches to turn off the light and mutters, "Oh shit, I haven't called, and they're going to change it tomorrow."

Carye rolls over on her side to the nightstand phone and dials a number too well committed to memory: 288-5493, the Advocates for Life Action Ministries hot line. The call is part of Carye's life every Monday, Wednesday, and Friday. The hot-line message, she has learned, is changed Tuesdays, Thursdays, and Saturdays. For Carye, calling the hot line is as much a part of her evening routine as making sure the dinner dishes are washed and brushing her teeth—finding out if she and her coworkers might be victims of an organized protest tomorrow.

She listens for about thirty seconds, hangs up the phone, turns off the light, and rolls over in bed. "Anything new?" Thom asks. Though Carye didn't say who she was calling, he knows the routine too. Carye isn't sure. Maybe. The message spoke of a protest tomorrow, Saturday. Participants are to meet at a parking lot in another section of town. At least now Carye can go to sleep.

SATURDAY MORNING, APRIL 22

His name is John and he is a man of conscience. He is tall with gold-rimmed glasses and a shock of pure white hair, and his manner is gentle. If this were any other corner in the city, you would bet the mortgage or the rent that here is a grandfather come to take his grandchildren for a walk. John has been protesting outside the doors of Lovejoy for twenty years.

John, unmarried, taught in a public elementary school for thirty years. When classes were over for the day he coached sports, and when school let out for the summer he worked as a camp counselor. "Kids have been my life," he says.

John abhors violence . . . and yet. And yet, when he thinks of Andrew Burnett his abhorrence softens. John's voice lowers just a bit, his eyebrows and mouth turn down, and he hesitates. He is not ready to condemn.

This is John's reaction when he reads in the newspaper that another abortion doctor has been shot: "It bothers me. Uh oh, it's going to make it more difficult for us." Prompted, he continues, "It is totally wrong." But there's that hesitancy in his voice again.

So many pictures show abortion protestors who claim to be motivated by love for children, with mean, twisted faces. This contradiction—the hypocrisy so evident in their features—makes them easy to dismiss. But consider John, a man with a sympathetic face.

Twenty years ago a friend of John's was arrested at Lovejoy during a protest. John, always against abortion, felt guilty that he had not been willing to take action on his principles. He began joining two or three friends for Saturday morning vigils at Lovejoy. Soon there were ten.

"This is the number one abortion clinic in the United States," John says. It's also convenient, he admits, since the front door right off the street makes Lovejoy an easy mark for effective demonstrating. There's less room for clinic employees and incoming patients to evade protestors' entreaties.

John comes about one Saturday a month now; when he was younger he was here every Saturday. He doesn't want to be associated with the more aggressive protestors. He thinks they begin shouting out of frustration. He grows worried when Leah or Anneke walks out the front door of Lovejoy and takes his picture. Was I standing somewhere I shouldn't have been? he wonders. Was I shouting? Blocking anybody's path? He's not even sure if he's allowed by law to stand in front of Lovejoy's side door.

Most women approaching Lovejoy have driven to this upper-middle-class neighborhood. John looks for their cars, often identifiable because the bulk of Lovejoy's patients are not upper middle class. If the women have parked further away, John tries to spot them heading toward Lovejoy on foot. It is important, he says, to approach people as far away from the clinic as possible. Distance is time. Time is what he needs.

Occasional pedestrians and joggers pass by, but most cross the street before reaching Lovejoy. After twenty years John has become adept at differentiating between "targets" and bystanders. Age is his first criteria: Women fifteen to thirty years old are the most likely Lovejoy patients. Beyond that, a certain look, possibly a hesitancy in their step. It might be something so simple as a quick twist of the head as they spot him. He knows almost all the women ignore him. He says he is here because he believes one in ten will at least listen or take his brochure.

A woman drives up in the passenger seat of a car. The man accompanying her is having trouble parallel parking in the one open spot beside Lovejoy. John is next to the car before it has come to a stop. Smiling, he motions with his hand, suggesting the driver instead move around the corner about fifty feet away to a larger parking spot. The man tries to park again. John again motions around the corner. More determined now than before, the driver works his way into the spot.

As the passenger side door opens, John is next to the woman with a rapidity that belies his age and appearance. "Good morning. Are you coming to the clinic?" he asks the woman as she exits the car. He looks and sounds like a valet. "It's not too late. Can I share some information?" he says, showing a pamphlet with a woman's face on the cover. In the picture the woman is lost in thought, composed. Beside her are the words "Pregnancy can be a hard thing to face." There is no hard sell here, no aggressiveness beyond the simple fact of John's presence and inquiry. Immediately an escort with an identifying orange band around her arm is at the woman's elbow and she is led inside Lovejoy.

Five minutes later the woman is out of the clinic, into her car, and away. And John is thinking maybe he planted a seed. He noticed she was smiling in his direction as she opened the door of her car. Maybe that was his one in ten, the one in ten who is receptive, the one in ten for whom he might be making a difference, the one baby in ten who otherwise would not have been.

Soon his morning's work is over. John prepares to walk back to his car. He nods in the direction of a group of protestors on the far corner. "They're the real heroes," he says. "I've been playing it pretty safe. I haven't been arrested. I haven't blocked any doors."

Every morning John looks at the Advocates for Life envelope that sits on his bedroom dresser and he feels guilty for not sending it in with a contribution.

"He's been one of our heroes but I think he's gone overboard," John says of Burnett. "He's lost patience. But if his magazine goes under we really don't have anybody left that's telling it like it is."

Chapter Four

He was supposed to be a priest, if mothers' dreams count for anything, and in most Catholic homes they do. His father was a strong-willed engineer who sold welding equipment and supplies and whose ethic emphasized the value of education and hard work.

Harold Suchak has the look of a high school math teacher. What remains of his hair is graying and flat on the top of his head. His moon-shaped face and metal spectacles bear witness to his own admission that in high school he was a nerd. He likes to wear plaid short-sleeved shirts with a pen in the front pocket. He is fifty-six, the same age as Allene. A flesh-toned hearing aid rests in his right ear, with little attempt made at concealment.

Suchak was the boy with the 5 A.M. paper route before school, the one who worked his way through college first as a houseboy and later, when he joined a fraternity, as the resident who paid expenses by working odd jobs around the frat house and serving food in the cafeteria.

He had few friends, no clique, little image. Once it became clear he would become a physician, Suchak chose a career in obstetrics because it promised to be "a happy profession." He knew that obstetricians rarely have patients die under their care; they can practice for months without having to treat a patient with a serious illness.

They bring life into the world and rarely preside over its exit. And along with the career Suchak discovered a persona.

In the first-floor hallways of Lovejoy informality reigns. Everybody is on a first-name basis—except Dr. Suchak. That is his title, that is how he insists he be addressed; he clings to it like an 1890s cowboy holding fast to his saddle and six-shooters, denying his own anachronism. The title of doctor is more than self-image, Suchak insists. It exalts him, protects him.

Suchak discovered the dark side of his happy profession while interning at Los Angeles County Hospital in the late 1960s. Abortion was illegal. L.A. County, like most public hospitals in large cities around the country, was the dumping ground for the patients with nowhere else to go. Often this translated into people whose medical conditions were exacerbated by a lack of previous medical care.

What Suchak most recalls about those years are the chaos and catastrophes. He remembers witnessing an unending procession of medical horror. The word that occurs to him is "destruction." He treated women who had put acid up their vaginas and others who had run coat hangers and knitting needles into their uteri in attempts to induce abortions. Most succeeded in that goal and many destroyed their reproductive systems in the process. Some died.

In his senior year at medical school Suchak married, and in 1969 he began his ob/gyn residency at the University of California, Irvine. That same year California legalized abortion. The hospital at which Suchak worked, like thousands of facilities around the country, suddenly had to confront a new aspect of obstetrical practice.

Suchak was one of four residents, one of two in their first year. The second- and third-year residents refused to perform abortions because basically, as a form of medical practice, abortions are less challenging and would keep them from working on a greater variety of cases. The other first-year resident was a devout Catholic woman. So Suchak, devoid of religious qualms, was told he would perform all the hospital's abortions.

Abortions were not a startlingly new procedure for physicians even prior to the *Roe v. Wade* era. For years simple first-trimester abortions had been available to women who knew which gynecologists to ask, and how. The doctor's terminology typically called for "a procedure necessitated by an incomplete pregnancy." In other words, a miscarriage had already taken place and the doctor was simply cleaning up after. The coat hangers and knitting needles were left to those who did not know about or could not afford a "therapeutic abortion."

For two weeks Suchak did little else but abortions, at the end of which time he marched into the office of the chief resident and said he would do no more. He even threatened to quit his residency. Suchak's was not a moral or emotional objection. He simply did not want to suspend his education while he spent the next three years doing nothing but abortions. The hospital soon hired someone else to take over abortions.

Three years later Suchak and his wife settled in Sandy, Oregon, the small town of their dreams and one with no ob/gyn of its own. Suchak's private practice grew quickly, his life attained the solidity and prosperity he had always sought.

Only occasionally does Harold Suchak wonder how or where he entered the storm that swirls around his life. In almost every decision he has made he has opted for the quiet, the conventional, the uncontroversial. Still, it sometimes seems as if life has presented him with a drama instead of the romantic comedy he thought he was dialing up.

Suchak knows *when* the change began. In 1985 his wife said she wanted him to move out. The couple had been married twenty years, their sons were sixteen and eleven. Three months later she asked for a divorce.

The divorce became final in 1987, and Suchak's midlife crisis began. Ironically, his life was following a path similar to Andrew Burnett's. He was searching for something different, not a natural condition for him. Typically, Suchak's search did not send him toward flying lessons or sailing to Tahiti. Working less seemed a logical way to start.

For years Suchak's private practice demanded sixty- to eighty-hour workweeks. In addition, an obstetrician's career can be guaranteed to make demands at all hours of the day and night; childbirth does not stick to a nine-to-five schedule. Suchak recognized that working as an abortion doctor is about the only way an ob/gyn can achieve regular work hours. There are few middle-of-the-night emergencies, since all surgeries are done by appointment; and at a facility such as Lovejoy, which pays its doctors on a procedure basis, there are always other physicians on staff willing to share the work if the patient load becomes too heavy.

Suchak began performing abortions at Lovejoy on Saturday and Monday afternoons while cutting back on his own practice. The memory of his early medical school days treating women who were victims of the wrong kind of abortions salved his conscience.

But basically it was the search for a more manageable, predictable life that led Suchak to Lovejoy. By the time he became medical director he had met Myra and her two daughters, his new family. As medical director, Suchak could set his own schedule, and by taking the more difficult and expensive second-trimester abortions he could manage a twenty-hour workweek and still earn over three hundred thousand dollars a year, considerably more even than Allene. Life was settling down again, peace was at hand for Harold Suchak. Even his insurance premiums were going down—malpractice insurers consider abortions a much safer risk than births.

On a Sunday afternoon three years ago Suchak was sitting alone in the family room of his spacious home. The lights were off as dusk began enveloping the house, that peaceful time of day when darkness makes its presence known but nothing yet is invisible. As Suchak walked to the downstairs bathroom he saw movement out of the corner of his eye. Picketers had taken up stations in front of the house. Then Suchak heard a sound from the back door, which opens into the kitchen. Moments later he saw a man standing in the kitchen. "What are you doing here?" Suchak shouted. The man scarcely moved, said nothing. Suchak called the police. By the time they arrived the invader and the other protestors were gone.

A year ago on a Friday night a school bus full of teenagers pulled up in front of the Suchak house. The kids, clearly under the direction of an adult, held a candlelight picket and vigil on the sidewalk. Later Suchak would call the local high school and learn a teacher had recruited the protestors from among his students.

Suchak says he mostly laughs at the protestors. His children ask if they can throw eggs. Neighbors, many of whose children were delivered by Suchak, have turned on sprinklers when protestors came within range.

But Suchak doesn't always laugh. For a period of six months a few years ago a man would take up a position at the fence in front of Suchak's house every morning at 5:30 A.M. He would hang a sign on the fence, stay for a short while, then leave. One morning Suchak, in bathrobe and slippers, confronted the man out front and took his photograph. In the days that followed the man began to follow Suchak's girls as they walked from their home to the bus stop every morning. Neighbors and occasionally the police began accompanying the neighborhood children to the bus stop. The man disappeared.

In his entire career Harold Suchak had never been sued until a case three and a half years ago. Tina came to Lovejoy for a tubal ligation—"tying tubes" in the vernacular—a simple surgical procedure that would keep her from conceiving. She hid the fact that she was a cocaine addict. During the surgery Tina went into cardiac arrest, probably a result of the cocaine in her blood interacting with the general anesthetic and changing the rhythm of her heart. She died. Her family sued Suchak for "wrongful death," possibly the worst and most devastating charge that can be leveled at a physician. The suit eventually was dismissed.

Suchak remembers sobbing as he left the operating room after Tina died. He also recalls breaking out champagne and cheering in the staff lounge when word came back two years later that he was exonerated. Suchak still thinks of Tina every time he walks into the OR.

"So how much are you using and what are you using?" Carye has the ability to sound nonchalant while discussing the most critical issues, when she must. This morning she must.

She is standing over Julia in the first-floor exam room, having administered an ultrasound. Five minutes before, they had talked in Carye's office. Carye thought the counseling session went well. Now she's not so sure. During the ultrasound Carye noticed needle marks on Julia's neck, a sure sign of a hard-core drug abuser.

"So what does it matter?" responds Julia. She is twenty-five but looks worn. Her teeth have rotted out, black and hollow, and her large breasts sag like those of a woman forty years older. The ultrasound reveals she is twenty-one weeks pregnant.

"Well, it means if you're using cocaine and you have an abortion and they put you to sleep, you can die," Carye says. What follows is a confession of sorts—a laundry list of drugs including cocaine, heroin, and methamphetamines—and a return to Carye's office for a second counseling session.

Julia has two children already, a four-year-old boy and a two-year-old girl. Both are in state-supervised foster care; they live with Julia's mother, a recovering addict. Julia describes her cocaine habit as two to three papers a week. Without asking, Carye mentally figures twenty units per paper, four lines per unit—a serious habit. It becomes even more of a potential problem when Julia admits that last night she injected twenty units of cocaine, enough to get a casual user through a week, or probably kill a non-addict if taken all at once.

Junkies are not uncommon at Lovejoy. Carye says she counsels two or three women each week who at first insist they do not use drugs, but confess otherwise when confronted with the dangers of mixing anesthesia and drugs. And those are just the two or three each week of which she becomes aware, who choose to reveal the truth. Proportionally these women represent a higher percentage of the second-trimester abortions. Their lives are out of control, their capacity for denial and self-deception well developed. Often decisions are postponed until they cannot be ignored any longer.

Now Carye must determine if Julia's drug use will make a safe abortion impossible and, if not, how an abortion can still be done. Julia has waited well into her second trimester. If she is to have an abortion it will have to be done under general anesthesia. Which means Julia's heroin use may not be a major problem. But cocaine and anesthesia don't mix: together they can result in dangerous heart complications, as Dr. Suchak well knows.

Carye is direct with Julia. They can get her through the abortion if she takes heroin, Carye says. There will be side effects, but they can be dealt with. But she must stay off coke and speed (methamphetamines) for forty-eight hours or risk dying on the operating table.

Julia earnestly nods her head as Carye talks. She says she is broke, with no stash of drugs and no money for more drugs. Then she launches into a convincing appeal: She is desperate to get her life together so that she can rejoin and parent her two children. This abortion is critical to her beginning to change. She is pleading. Carye is wavering.

Carye exits the room for a minute and comes back with Allene. Together they talk to Julia. Allene holds Julia's hand throughout. Have they been deceived? Carye doesn't think so. She is convinced of Julia's sincerity. And it isn't as if Julia has to go cold turkey, just no coke or speed. Julia leaves with an appointment with Suchak for the next morning. He will begin the procedure.

When Julia shows up Wednesday morning, Carye asks if she used drugs the night before. With a smile Julia says, "Only a get-well." Carye knows what that means—a small dose of heroin but no cocaine. The procedure is on track, the next stop Suchak's examination room.

Before Suchak leads Julia inside, Carye hands him her assessment papers and talks to him about Julia's drug history. Suchak's mind flashes to Tina, his nightmare come true. She had insisted she was not on drugs, had signed consent forms that certified that fact. A simple tubal ligation, for heaven's sake. Suchak watched as her heart began beating uncontrollably, faster, faster, faster, as if some outside power source were fueling its locomotive-like pounding. And then the line on the electrocardiogram (EKG) monitor went flat and there was nothing he could do. He was a doctor, trained to heal, turned into an observer. He was in the right place, an operating room surrounded by hundreds of thousands of dollars of the latest life-saving equipment. And he was helpless.

During his examination of Julia, Suchak reemphasizes the possibility that Julia might die if she takes cocaine or speed during the next thirty-six hours. After Suchak's exam Carye asks Allene and Suchak to join her in the back hallway, where the three of them discuss the case. The final word is Suchak's: They will perform the abortion.

A second-trimester abortion is actually a two-stage procedure. First, the patient's cervix must be widened by sliding dilators called laminaria into the cervical canal. These tiny depressors absorb moisture and swell from the size of matches to pencils, softening the cervix and helping its muscles relax. Generally two laminaria are inserted the first day; the patient returns the next day to have those removed and five more inserted as the cervix grows wider. A day or two after that the patient is ready for the actual abortion.

Julia is sent upstairs, where Suchak inserts the first two laminaria. The procedure takes about five minutes. Yet even now Suchak
is questioning his decision. He is not convinced Julia can stay off drugs
the necessary thirty-six hours before the abortion. He has dealt with
too many junkies and too many promises made by patients who would
tell him whatever he wanted to hear, experts at lying and manipula-
tion. He leaves the operating room still wondering if he is being
deceived.

The week before, Suchak had spoken about how others view
his job. He is aware that outsiders and even some staff members be-
grudge him the money he makes. Most abortions are not complicated
procedures. Nurses watch him at work and many feel they could do
as well. Suchak does not disagree.

"Anyone can do a blood test," he said. "I can teach anyone to
do a D & C ["dilation and curettage"—a first-trimester abortion
technique rarely used today]. The art of medicine is making judgments in appropriate circumstances and doing the appropriate procedure well."

The surgeon as artist, in Suchak's view, measures the medical, personal, and moral consequences of each potential action
before using his hands. Sometimes he thinks of the operation from
the patient's point of view, recognizing how the course of the
woman's life will be changed for the better. And occasionally he
forces himself to give first consideration to the perspective of the
fetus, imagining the life available to that child if it were to be carried to full term.

Legally an abortion can be performed at any time during pregnancy in Oregon, though past the twenty-fifth week a woman is
unlikely to find a physician willing to do it. Medically, a fetus may
be a viable being, able to thrive outside the mother's womb if given
access to the latest in medical support, somewhere around the twenty-
second to twenty-fourth week.

Suchak continually faces questions involving borderline abortions because Lovejoy is the only facility in Oregon that will consis-

tently perform abortions after twenty-one weeks. Because it is a fully licensed outpatient surgical center, Lovejoy's operating rooms are better equipped to handle complicated procedures and emergencies than most abortion clinics.

Suchak does not ignore the issue of viability. He is uncomfortable performing late abortions. Five to ten times a year he refuses to do an abortion at Lovejoy. Deciding which are to be among those few and which are not goes to the heart of what he sees as his art.

Every abortion doctor maintains his or her own perspective; the doctors are like painters working in different styles. Suchak says he knows Catholic obstetricians who will do abortions but won't prescribe birth control pills. He knows doctors who will perform abortions up to twelve weeks but not a week after. And he knows many obstetricians who simply will not perform abortions, some who once did.

"Everyone sets their limits," he says. But Suchak has found that for him it cannot be a simple matter of setting a limit and sticking to it. For him each case is original and unique. A few years ago Suchak had a twelve-year-old girl come in at twenty-six weeks. He performed the abortion. A year ago he refused a twenty-second-week abortion to a healthy twenty-six-year-old middle-class woman, a woman he felt was capable of mothering a child. But soon after, when a twenty-six-year-old junkie living on the streets came to him in her twenty-fourth week of pregnancy, Suchak went ahead with the abortion. "I don't want that baby born," he says simply.

There is a tension at Lovejoy exacerbated by the hospital's informality and also by the crossing lines of communication. The first floor belongs to Carye and to Allene, who is proud of the fact that roles are interchangeable, that if the receptionist is busy, she or Carye or any of the counselors will answer the phone, for instance. The second floor, the surgical floor, suffers from that lack of hierarchy. In Suchak's view, ultimately the doctors must be in charge on the second floor. His rationale is simple: The ultimate medical and legal responsibility is left with the doctor, so the doctor must be "captain of the ship," to borrow a phrase Suchak sometimes uses around Lovejoy. Nobody ever sues the staff, he points out. But at Lovejoy the doctors are a bit like hired guns, coming in for their surgeries but leaving the staff to manage the minute-to-minute details. As medical director, Suchak works the most hours of any of Lovejoy's surgeons, even at fifteen to twenty hours a week.

With a day to consider Julia's case, Suchak has begun to wonder if he was too quick to adopt Carye's perception of the woman's reliability. In fact, he decides Carye has been putting too much pressure on him to perform this abortion from the start. But he acknowledges the final decision was his. He has weighed the alternatives. He is certain that if he refuses to perform the procedure Carye will call the other doctors who work out of Lovejoy, trying to find one who will do it. Knowing it likely the abortion will be done anyway, Suchak decides he should be the one to operate. "I'm a better surgeon," he later will say.

Thursday's events do little to convince Suchak he made the right decision in approving Julia's abortion. Julia does not appear for her morning appointment to exchange laminaria, calling in and claiming she's having transportation problems. But Suchak is not a man who likes to be kept waiting. He decides to give her the rest of the morning, but he will call off the abortion if she does not show up today.

Just after noon one of Lovejoy's counselors reaches Julia, who offers explanations about her ride not showing. She promises to be in at 1 P.M. Suchak waits until 2 P.M. and then leaves for the day, but not without relenting a bit. He tells Carye that if Julia shows up, Carye can tell her to come in at 7:30 A.M. Friday. With the original two laminaria in place instead of the intended five, Julia may or may not be dilated enough for the surgery to take place. And he may or may not be willing to perform it.

Julia surprises Suchak when she appears Friday morning. But Carye is prepared. Rather than ask Julia if she has taken drugs in the last two days, Carye uses the pretense of needing to make necessary adjustments in the anesthesiology dosage. "So what did you use?" she asks. Julia admits she has continued her regimen of heroin, cocaine, and speed in the last thirty-six hours.

Upstairs Suchak is preparing for the operation. It is only 8 A.M. and already he is on edge. Earlier this morning he operated on another drug addict. He's wondering if taking on Julia might not be pressing his, and her, luck. And he isn't even aware of the latest development; Carye is taking the elevator upstairs to relate Julia's confession.

On the way up Carye is thinking of options. One possibility is to have Julia admitted to a hospital where she can be kept under surveillance for two days, long enough to assure she does not take cocaine or methamphetamines, then have the abortion performed there, if a willing hospital can be found. Dismissing Julia has its appeal, but refusing to do the procedure and sending her home is not so simple. Julia is dilated. In effect, the abortion was begun two days ago. With her cervix wide open, she has become a host for bacteria and other organisms that will not be flushed out unless the abortion takes place. These organisms might create an infection, causing a miscarriage, or worse.

An infection is only the most likely undesirable outcome. Years ago Tim counseled a patient who came in for a D & E at twenty-three weeks. After an ultrasound confirmed the date, the surgeon inserted laminaria to begin the procedure. That night Tim took a call from a hotel room where the woman was staying. And from what the woman described Tim knew what was occurring: She was giving birth, twins as it turned out. Tim called an ambulance, and the woman, with twins, was rushed to a hospital emergency room where doctors tried to resuscitate the babies, but to no avail.

If Julie ends up in a hospital emergency room because Lovejoy dismisses her, Carye knows, the Surgicenter could be held liable. When Julia admitted herself as a patient she became Lovejoy's responsibility. Now she is Lovejoy's problem, and a hospital or another doctor might not want to become involved. In an age when thoughts of legal liability are never far removed from any medical decision, no facility wants to become the receptacle for another's problem cases.

Carye finds Suchak in the upstairs hallway and starts talking. She knows the conversation is a mistake as soon as she begins. She should have asked that they meet in one of their offices. Now it is too late. Suchak drifts into the staff lounge. Most of the upstairs operating room staff is there. Carye follows Suchak inside, explaining what she has learned of Julia's drug use.

But the discussion between Carye and Suchak does not get far. As soon as Carye has related Julia's confession, Suchak's mind begins flashing through variations on this scenario. One case in particular occurs to him. About ten years ago, a frighteningly similar case, in fact. A local obstetrician had taken out a patient's laminaria but refused to complete the abortion. The woman was sent home and infection set in, which led to a septic abortion and eventually a lost kidney. The woman, he remembers, sued and won a very large malpractice award. This case is almost an exact duplicate. But the memory of Tina, who died on his own operating table, is even stronger.

Suchak interrupts Carye. "I'm taking her lams out but I'm not doing it," he says. There is controlled fury in his voice. All heads turn toward the two.

"I just want you to know this full history," Carye says. Again she is interrupted.

"I'm medical director here and I'm not going to have somebody die just so they can have an abortion."

Carye immediately turns away and walks back to her office downstairs. She will do exactly what Suchak expected. She begins to call other obstetricians who work at Lovejoy, hoping to find one who will check Julia into a hospital as a patient.

Ten minutes later she is still at her desk. Dr. Lane, her best hope, confirms that the potential liability resulting from starting a procedure and then stopping it is great. And he does not want to get involved.

Upstairs Suchak knows what Carye is doing. He also knows there are only three obstetricians in the state who will perform an abortion after twenty-one weeks. He is one of them, and Lane and Donovan, both of whom work out of Lovejoy in addition to their private practices, are the others.

But Suchak has come to another realization. Thinking back, he understands that Carye was not trying to push him into performing the abortion. He did not give her time to ask her intended question: What should we do? He hurries downstairs to apologize.

Finding Carye alone Suchak steps into her office and says, "Slap me."

"Not here," she responds. "I want to do it in front of the staff." She is not satisfied with his apology. In her mind the apology addresses only half his sin. By making his statement in front of the staff he has set up a situation in which she may well assume a reputation among the upstairs medical staff as a dangerous administrator, one trying to push a potentially deadly abortion on a reluctant and cautious physician, possibly exposing them all to litigation.

Suchak and Carye begin the discussion Carye originally had intended. In Suchak's mind this is still a tough call, but he has put a little distance between himself and Carye's latest report and he realizes again that there is risk no matter which path they choose.

If liability issues are never far from doctors' minds at Lovejoy, there is good reason. Suchak and his colleagues are being watched like no other doctors in this country. In many cities anti-abortion activists have used malpractice lawsuits as weapons to try to force abortion facilities to close or abortion doctors to give up the work.

Ob/gyns are accustomed to the environment. Legally, obstetrics is the most dangerous area of medicine even without abortions. The very nature of pregnancy and delivery, with uncertain outcomes even in the best of circumstances, make malpractice lawsuits inviting. Some women miscarry for no apparent cause. Some babies are born with defects and nobody will ever know the reason, be it the fault of the doctor or the patient, or simply an act of God. Nevertheless, lawsuits often follow.

And here Suchak is faced with a patient who has lied to him, who has admitted she has taken potentially lethal amounts of illegal drugs, and he is the one who must make a decision and take responsibility for its consequences. He considers the evidence on both sides of the ledger. First Suchak considers Julia's age, twenty-five. She is not a child incapable of being a mother. And the fact that the fetus is twenty-one weeks old, close to viability—another piece of evidence against performing the abortion. Then Suchak considers the total amount of heroin, coke, and speed Julia has taken in the last twenty-one weeks. He knows it is possible her baby would be born with severe birth defects or even addicted to drugs at birth. Coke and heroin are thought to lead to a variety of developmental and attachment disorders, but the medical literature is conflicting. Some children born to addict mothers exhibit little in the way of birth defects. And then Suchak considers Julia herself, the kind of mother she would be for this child, and his decision is made.

There is another option, and both Suchak and Carye know it—do the abortion, but not under general anesthesia. Use a local anesthetic with increased intravenous painkiller and sedation. It is not an ideal solution; in fact, it is rare in a pregnancy this far along. First, the procedure is usually considered too painful for a woman who is not unconscious by virtue of general anesthetic. Second, the operation will take longer, which means the cervix will be open and exposed longer, increasing the possibility of infection. Also, there is a danger the still-conscious patient might move about during surgery and risk perforation of her uterus by the surgeon's instruments. But Suchak and Carye agree it is the best solution available.

An hour later Suchak walks out of the operating room after giving pats on the back to his operating room team. His relief is apparent to all as he thanks them for their work. "We got away with one, guys," he says. The operation was a success, there is no evidence yet of infection.

Suchak considers the events just past. He would like to think his work today has enriched Julia's life, that now she is free to right herself. But he does not really believe that. At best, he thinks, he kept a drug-affected child from coming into a world where nobody was prepared to care for him. A junkie's world of overdoses, hepatitis, and AIDS. Suchak considers Julia one last time. He doesn't know which of the trinity will get her first but he thinks he knows her fate. "She'll be dead within a year," he says.

In the hallways and offices of Lovejoy, Allene Klass nearly always projects a composed, unruffled image. Even in the most tense situation she usually will offer the smile of a woman in complete control. Not today.

Fury has replaced Allene's calm visage. Returning from four days at her beach house she has learned of Julia's case. She is not upset at how events unfolded, she has no problem with the services Julia was provided. But when Suchak accused Carye in the staff lounge, he crossed a line.

Bad enough, in Allene's mind, is the picture of her medical director and director of counseling arguing out a case in front of the staff. But when Suchak made it appear that Carye was trying to force him to perform an abortion that might cost a patient her life, he risked dividing the loyalties of the entire second-floor staff. Whose side would the medical assistants be on next time? Would Carye lose her credibility among the medical staff?

Allene has spent twenty-five years hiding her own fears. She is certain that nobody on the staff would ever guess that Allene Klass has had sleepless nights. She is their protector. That, to Allene, is leadership.

But when the surgeon spoke of death before the medical staff, he was calling up a nightmare they have each considered and dismissed—that of healers doing harm. And an accidental death could land any of them as witnesses in a courtroom. In Allene's mind, there just isn't room for such doubts at an already-tense Lovejoy. Allene shakes her head, unable to rid herself of one thought: Suchak is not a leader.

The Suchak/Carye clash is nothing new. But what is new is the way Allene is framing the dispute today. She has begun considering life without Suchak.

Chapter Five

Some days Carye wonders if she's as savvy as she likes to think she is. If this morning's mail is evidence, her education is far from complete.

Carye is out in the hallway showing a letter to Allene. Last week a young woman called indicating she was a University of Oregon journalism major working on a class project. Would Carye consent to be interviewed for, say, thirty minutes? Carye was in the middle of a busy afternoon but she complied.

This morning's letter was the result of that interview—not a class paper but a three-page, single-spaced anti-abortion diatribe showing Carye the error of her ways. The writer begins by saying she lives in a cooperative house run by a local church. Across the back fence she stares out at an abortion clinic.

> *We are talking about life and death and prescribed eternal judgment for the things we do in this life. If you are counseling about another life, who is to be held responsible for yours? I do not mean for this in any way to sound like a threat. I am just concerned for your eternal soul.*

It isn't her soul Carye is worried about as Allene reads the letter. It's her judgment. How could she not have read the woman's intentions? Allene laughs and says she never gives telephone interviews. Carye must be working too hard, she says. "Normally we can smell them."

Maybe Allene's right. Late in the afternoon Carye storms out of her office even more agitated. Session over. She has just spent thirty minutes trying to counsel a woman with an eighteen-month-old baby. The patient had ignored the standard request not to bring in children. And Carye had discovered that trying to counsel a woman with a child on hand is a bit like trying to follow a television show when somebody keeps changing the channel.

This particular eighteen-month-old spent most of his time alternating between tugging on Carye's slacks and reaching for objects on her desk, with some success. The rest of the time the mother grappled with her child, trying to restrain him. And as if the distraction were not enough, Carye couldn't get a sense of the purpose of the session.

Finally, out of frustration, Carye said, "I have to ask you what you really want because I just can't tell."

"Oh, I want an abortion," the woman responded. "I just need to do it after eight-thirty on Wednesday. Is that okay?"

"That will be fine," Carye said, aware that she had just spent thirty minutes providing child care.

Looking in at her office from the hallway Carye points out the disarray. Cracker crumbs litter the floor beneath her desk. Carye hates the thought of cracker crumbs on her floor.

"Now you know why Carye didn't have children," says Allene, smiling.

"Yes, God knew what he was doing when he decided I couldn't have children," Carye responds, returning to her office. "But instead he gave me leukemia," she adds, over her shoulder.

Back at her desk Carye tries to focus on the speech she will deliver tomorrow before a committee of the state legislature. The committee is considering a bill requiring abortion facilities to involve parents in the decision-making process before proceeding with abortions for teenage girls. Currently state law requires parental notification for girls under fifteen. This bill would raise the age to eighteen.

As she reviews her testimony Carye's thoughts keep drifting to Tara. Carye might counsel eighty women in a busy month, but usually there is one whose role in Carye's life does not end with her counseling session. When Tara first stepped into Carye's office three weeks ago, there was little to differentiate her from many of the other sad stories that too frequently make their way into Lovejoy. She was another teenage girl from a small town carrying a big secret. She was also extraordinarily smart and perceptive, Carye recognized.

Sixteen-year-old Tara, blond, a scrawny little bird of a girl with an artsy look about her, was in her second trimester. Which means her abortion would require three trips to Lovejoy from her small-town home—two visits for a doctor to insert laminaria to dilate her cervix, and a third for the abortion itself. Week by week she had been growing larger as she bided her time and saved the money for three round-trip bus fares to Portland. She arrived at Lovejoy just in time, her twenty-fourth week of pregnancy.

Carye was struck by Tara's courage, haunted by her potential, and certain that if she had been forced to call Tara's parents—fundamentalist Christians whose relationship with their daughter bordered on the abusive already—the girl might well lose what little sense of home she had. Carye had no solutions to offer Tara, just support. In the end Carye felt she had taken more from Tara than she had given. Tara became a heroine in Carye's mind, a young woman who reminded her whom Lovejoy was intended to help, who reflected Lovejoy's ability to empower and also its limitations.

Tara had her abortion in the morning and returned home on a bus that afternoon after napping, eating a cup of microwaved noodle soup, and watching television alone in a back room at Lovejoy. And she left Carye believing even more firmly than before that an abortion is not the appropriate life event around which to try to bring together parents and children who have long been apart, that you cannot force a relationship that does not exist. Putting thoughts of

Tara from her mind, Carye looks back at the piece of paper on her desk and continues to edit tomorrow's speech.

Across the hallway Allene also is thinking about tomorrow's hearing. She sees the proposed bill as another in a series of attempts by abortion opponents to restrict women's access to the procedure. A conservative political action committee (PAC) is working on an amendment to the Oregon constitution to outlaw second-trimester abortions. There have been limits on federal funding of abortions, and in some states new laws require counseling intended to convince women abortion is wrong. To Allene it is all of the same cloth, woven by those who do not want women to choose for themselves. And most of the leaders of the organizations pushing these measures have little or no real interest in the welfare of the women who enter her facility or their fetuses, Allene believes. Maybe once they did. Now it is all about politics, about power, she thinks. But it is real, and she will accompany Carye to Salem, the state capital, tomorrow. She will not testify, but her presence in the hearing room will speak for itself.

Stick around the abortion wars long enough and you find yourself fighting the same battles over and over again, she thinks. Frustrating. Wasn't it just a few years ago they defeated another measure on parental notification? The wording changes but the purpose remains the same—make it more difficult to get abortions. This one is destined to pass, she figures, a bone thrown to the anti-abortion lobby by a suddenly Republican-majority legislature.

Two weeks ago she had driven to Salem to talk to a key Republican legislator at the request of the chief lobbyist for the pro-abortion forces. The legislator, a smiling, handshaking sort of man, had listened with great interest as Allene explained how things work at Lovejoy, from the counseling that lets clients know they have choices to the process intended to ensure they are not rushing into an abortion. When Allene mentioned the adoptions that Lovejoy has facilitated, the legislator fairly beamed. He left saying he was charmed. The next day Allene's grapevine reported the legislator was firmly committed to supporting the measure.

FRIDAY,   MAY   12

By the time Carye and Allene reach the capitol building the afternoon hearings are beginning. They quickly take seats to the left of
the center aisle, nodding and smiling at a few familiar faces. The
center aisle serves as more than a physical divide: On the left are those
who oppose the parental consent bill; and on the right, far fewer in
number, are those who support it. The first arrivals must have chosen the separation, and those after followed their instincts.

The dress on the left side is more eclectic, as typified by
Allene and Carye. Allene looks stylishly professional in her trademark short skirt and high heels with a designer jacket. Others
around her are dressed more simply and informally, like Carye in
a long peasant skirt from South America. The women on the right
side of the aisle easily could be attending a meeting of the PTA
in some suburban school. They are dressed primly, their hair styled
conservatively.

There are only three men among the approximately twenty-five
women in the audience, and they have the look of lobbyists in their
neat blazers and ties. At the front of the room the committee members, four men and three women, sit at a horseshoe-shaped table.

The first woman to testify approaches from the right side of the
aisle. She is blond, about thirty, and chewing gum, a fact of which
Allene takes note in a head-shaking aside to Carye. Her testimony
is compelling. She takes everyone in the room back to when she was
seventeen, in love, left pregnant and ashamed. Her parents were
against abortion, so she did not tell them of her predicament. She
dropped out of school, left home.

The woman says she made her way to an abortion facility
when she was twenty-four weeks pregnant. The counselor's only
concern was whether she could come up with enough money to
pay for her procedure. She claims she was sent into a basement
room with seven other girls who, like her, were to receive saline
abortions (which are rarely, if ever, performed anymore). The
women were lined up and a saline solution was injected into their

bellies. The solution induces abortion by burning the fetus and forcing miscarriage. Nurses came later with buckets to catch the miscarried fetuses as they were ejected from the women's bodies. Describing the cold, lifeless basement and the behavior of the nurses, the woman makes the scene sound eerily like the medical experiments performed in Nazi concentration camps.

As Allene listens to the testimony she looks across the aisle. She believes the woman is telling a story that never happened to her. More of the same, she thinks, more of the lies she has been hearing in testimonies and at protests for the last twenty years. The "antis," as she calls them, are bound together by their fundamentalist Christian doctrine, and at the same time by their loss of individuality. Some are dupes, lying as they have been told to, others are dangerous, even evil. Their belief that all men and women are sinners, inherently depraved, has cost them their humanity.

A week earlier, in her office, Allene spoke about Andrew Burnett. Someone wondered out loud what Burnett was like at home with his family, what kind of father he might be.

"You just don't understand," said Allene in a voice infused with a hard, angry edge. In her mind those responsible for twenty years of threats, of daily expressions of hatred for her and those around her, long ago lost their true souls, their uniqueness. They have become their dogma. Twenty years of warfare will force any soldier to objectify the enemy.

The testimony is over. The legislators begin their questioning, and it is clear some of them do not fully believe the story they have just heard. One woman asks if she could have the story's specifics; she would like to obtain the medical records. The woman who testified is not sure she can recall the name of the hospital. A man says she hasn't really addressed the question being debated: Would her horrible experience have been any better if she had been forced to tell her parents beforehand? He raises the possibility that she might have carried the baby to term, or been forced to seek a back-alley abortion, or ended up a teen suicide.

The interrogation completed, Carye strides to the desk facing the panel, her back to the audience. She leans forward, elbows on desk, and begins in the relaxed storytelling voice of someone experienced at this sort of thing, someone who knows how to assemble power without volume. It is as if the room itself has become instantaneously curious, and silent.

Carye speaks of her introduction to abortion as a freshman at a local Bible college, accompanying a terrified dormitory friend to a clinic, holding her hand through the morning. "I grew up in a fundamentalist Christian family where all issues are either black or white. By the end of my first term in college I had a new perspective developing. I face the gray daily."

She pauses, gaining momentum. "I have been counseling and advocating for women before, during, and after their abortions for seven years. I have listened to the stories of women who are in life situations that we—privileged with jobs, direction, homes, and support—think we understand, but can't. I can't forget sixteen-year-old Emily. She told me that she was late for her appointment because she had waited until her heroin addict mother was 'down' enough so that she could get the medical card out of her jacket pocket. At sixteen, Emily is her own parent. Confrontation with the reality of pregnancy is facing your beliefs, abilities, your dreams and desires. This bill places one more hurdle in the way of women who are at the highest risk, and instead of our state taking care of our own, we will see teens finding ways to get abortions outside of Oregon, further from their families and the follow-up care that is needed."

Carye describes the counseling practiced at Lovejoy. "Many of the anti-choice would like you to believe that a part of my job is to convince women to have abortions, to prevent them from talking to their parents. One-third of the women counseled at Lovejoy Surgicenter do not have abortions.

"I know that each woman confronting a crisis pregnancy feels a sadness about the loss of the potential—whether a grief about not feeling ready to be a parent, the protectiveness and resistance to adoption, or the fear of family or others finding out and showing disapproval, disappointment, or rejection. These women talk with the people that they trust. Women tell their parents when they believe there will be fairness and caring. No woman communicates because of a rule instructing her to do so, or a rule that tells her family to listen. Not all parents have that ability.

"This winter, sixteen-year-old Sandy came to Lovejoy; she had told her parents she was pregnant. Her parents told her that if she didn't have the abortion, they were done with her. Sandy doesn't believe in abortion, but she came to Lovejoy at the demand of her family. An ultrasound showed that Sandy was thirty weeks, far beyond the cutoff for an abortion. I have watched as Sandy finished her pregnancy in a shelter, not with the support of her family, but with the guidance of the Children's Services Division and Adult and Family Services. When her baby was born she sent out ten announcements, one of them to me. She told me she was working toward emancipation. Sandy is now a part of the epidemic in this state of teenage mothers. Her chances of finishing high school, having a job that pays above minimum wage, and being off state assistance are statistically bleak.

"I ask that each of you move outside the black and white. Do not make the young women of this state liars, falsifying age, going out of state. They will find ways to have an abortion rather than risk the ramifications of families that cannot communicate. Please trust that the young women of this state know their families better than we do. For the families that have trust, the communication is already there. If this is not present within a family, no mandate or law will bring it to be."

Finished, Carye looks up at the committee members. A conservative legislator leans into his microphone. "But what's the difference between telling a lie and living a lie?" he asks.

Carye asks him to repeat the question, which he does. Straight-faced she replies, "I'm a little oblique, but I still don't get the question." After another attempt the legislator gives up on his line of inquiry.

A woman legislator speaks. "I'm a little concerned that we continue to talk about women here," she says. She prefers the term "minor females" for the fifteen- to seventeen-year-olds the bill addresses.

The questions continue. "What do you do with a fifteen-year-old who is distraught but determined to abort?" Carye outlines Lovejoy's counseling process and the care taken in explaining to all patients the physical and emotional issues involved in an abortion—the controversial informed consent process. The legislator pursues: "What would you tell her if she is nearing twenty-four weeks?" "Wait," Carye firmly responds.

"Do you ever tell them to talk to other people before having the abortion?"

Carye explains that Lovejoy rarely schedules an abortion for the same day as an initial appointment and that she routinely advises women to find family and friends with whom they can share what they are feeling. In fact, Carye does not mention Lovejoy policy has been evolving; increasingly, first-trimester abortion cases are being counseled and performed the same day.

Carye knows that by state law a doctor at Lovejoy can call the parents of any patient under the age of eighteen without breaching the standard rules of patient/doctor confidentiality. The choice is the doctor's. In reality, doctors rarely exercise that choice with fifteen- to seventeen-year-olds. This bill would require that, just as current legislation requires them to contact the parents of girls under fifteen.

Testimony completed, Carye walks back to her seat. The committee chairman declares a recess, and Carye and Allene walk out together. Allene is still thinking about Carye's response to the question about a distressed fifteen-year-old. "You were great," she tells Carye. "But you should have said we would have brought in the parents."

Grinning, Allene says, "That woman, did you see her cheeks? They were growing pinker and pinker." Carye knows exactly who

Allene is talking about—the conservative legislator who insisted on the term "minor females." "She hated me," Carye says, laughing in relief.

They discuss the committee members and how each might vote. Carye researched the group last week and knows the vote is forecast to go four to three in favor of the bill. Her research did not result from idle curiosity. "I wanted to know who to look at," she says. During her testimony Carye's gaze was directed at those she knew supported the bill; she was hoping to find one face open enough to sway. A few days from now she will think back to those faces and wonder which one she might have influenced: One supporter of the legislation will change a vote, and the bill will die in committee.

During the fifty-mile drive back to Portland, Allene and Carye discuss the testimony and each of the legislators. Allene suddenly pulls her Jaguar into a Dairy Queen parking lot and the two women act like children let out of school early as they order Buster Bars, their affinity for the ice cream treats a long-standing bond.

Back in the car they discuss Lovejoy business, focusing on the doctors and their egos. Their identities are simply too tied up in their roles as physicians, the women agree. Consider Suchak, Carye says. Here is a man justifiably concerned about his well-being and that of his family. He has received death threats, his home has been surrounded by protestors, he wears a bulletproof vest to work, he refuses media interviews in order to remain as anonymous as possible. Yet the license plates on his Porsche, parked in the Lovejoy parking lot, read SIRGYN.

Carye says she talked to Suchak about the plates, and he told her that they were a gift from one of his children and that he would get rid of them as soon as they expired. "Let's hope they expire before you do," Carye told him, and she and Allene break out in laughter.

The conversation shifts to Tim Shuck, Carye's predecessor. It is obvious from the change in their voices that both love this man dearly. They agree he has been much better able to hold his concentration during his last few visits to Lovejoy. He seems clearer, Allene remarks, the hope evident in her voice. Carye relates a story Tim told her last week. Tim said he was in a restaurant recently, and as he waited for his food it occurred to him that he had completely forgotten what he had ordered minutes before. Rather than get aggravated at his failing faculties, Tim told Carye, he thought: Whatever it is I'll just think of it as a present. Carye leaned over and kissed Tim on the forehead. "Tim, that's how I'll always remember you."

Paul deParrie is overflowing with optimism. Andrew Burnett's second in command, editor of *Life Advocate* (Burnett is listed as publisher), he knows the magazine didn't come out this month because of a money shortage. Donations are down. Subscriptions are down. But deParrie is just naturally more effusive than Burnett, and today he's especially upbeat and positive. He's thinking strategy.

DeParrie is sitting in what once was a living room but now serves as the front office at Advocates for Life headquarters. A folding table that could seat eight for dinner is his desk. In back of deParrie, above a fireplace, six pink plastic models showing the stages of fetal development rest on a mantelpiece.

DeParrie, bearded, heavyset, wearing a tweed sport jacket, looks like a college professor waiting for someone to raise a hand. Where Burnett is likely to quote Scripture to make a conversational point, deParrie is likely to quote one of the history books he's fond of reading. A particular period of interest is Nazi Germany, especially the extermination camps.

DeParrie says he is sure that someday abortion will be discontinued in this country. But he doesn't think killing doctors is the tactic that will bring that day about. Anti-abortion forces will win, he says, because abortion is wrong and the people who do it know deep in their hearts it is wrong. DeParrie asserts this with an almost childlike insistence that right as he sees it will prevail. "I want to stop them from killing babies more than they want to keep on killing," he says.

Advocates' tactics will change in the year ahead, deParrie says, or rather, be refined. The first phase will be what he refers to as level two operations. The targets will be obstetricians around the state who perform abortions in their offices, often without the knowledge of their other patients. Advocates will go after this small group of providers in an attempt to make their lives so miserable that they give up performing abortions.

DeParrie is sure the methods Advocates for Life has perfected will work. For most of these obstetricians, abortions are not a big part of their business. They do them occasionally as a service, and because they can do them without attracting publicity. Exposure will encourage them to stop performing abortions, and once that happens only the major facilities such as Lovejoy will be left as abortion providers. DeParrie looks forward to the day when all the women in the vast rural, eastern half of the state will have to come to Portland for abortions, in some cases driving hundreds of miles. Many won't make it, he knows.

The second element of the new strategy is even bolder, targeting what deParrie sees as the weak link in the abortion providers' chain. Until now the "Nowhere to Hide" rallies have been limited to doctors' homes. In deParrie's estimation they have not been effective enough. That may change, he thinks, if the rallies focus on the staff. Most nurses and administrative workers such as receptionists are less dedicated to the abortion rights cause than are doctors, deParrie figures. Saturday morning rallies outside their homes, distribution of flyers with their names and pictures, should be very effective. "They don't get paid a lot," he says. "It isn't worth it to them. A lot of them are going to be saying, 'I'm getting ten bucks an hour and it just isn't enough for this grief.'"

And deParrie has no problem making the lives of these staff members hellish. "They're just as guilty as the receptionist at Auschwitz. What's the difference?" he asks rhetorically.

*

On a normal weekday morning at Lovejoy you will find two placard-carrying protestors. These are the regulars, practically institutions in the neighborhood. Most residents just refer to them by description, as in "the old guy with the lawn chair" or "the younger one who stares up at the sky all day."

The older one is Doc. That's what everybody calls him, and that's what he calls himself when you ask his name. He's been on this corner, with his lightweight folding lawn chair, for seven years, five days a week. Doc takes Saturdays and Sundays off. He is eighty-nine and confesses that lately he's had to cut back to just a couple hours each day.

Doc's hands are large and wrinkled, bushy gray eyebrows his only visible hair. Heavy folds of skin have overtaken much of his face, leaving two slits for eyes. His clothes hardly change from day to day—a worn blue sport jacket, striped tie, with white sneakers on his feet. Most of the year a green and white trucker's cap rests on his head; he wears a stocking cap beneath it when the weather is cool.

Doc is Advocates for Life's constant representative at Lovejoy. He lives in an upstairs room at the Advocates for Life house. The organization supplies the sign he holds high from his lawn chair perch. Sometimes it looks as if Doc is asleep in his chair, but the sign never wobbles. Black letters on white pressboard, it reads,

STOP MURDER

STOP ABORTION

SAVE THE CHILDREN

ADOPTION

Over the course of his lifetime Doc has farmed, logged, worked in a body and fender shop, performed odd jobs. He used to live in a small town about twenty miles outside Portland, toward the mountains. He never married. He never had children.

Doc has been arrested seven times for his anti-abortion activities. Five years ago he spent a month in jail. He's not sure of the total amount of money he owes as a result of the suits he has lost. He has no money to pay anyway.

Now he mostly sits in his lawn chair, letting his sign and presence speak for themselves. To passersby, Doc is the picture of harmless passivity—an old man who looks as if he can hardly keep up his placard. On a spring afternoon he appears asleep until two women walk briskly past and he calls out to their backs, "They kill babies there." The women continue into Lovejoy without pause.

Those working inside Lovejoy, especially those who have been there awhile, view Doc as anything but a kindly old man. He is one of the Lovejoy Eight, the group headed by Andrew Burnett who were primary defendants in the $8.2 million civil case. He was placed under house arrest for four months after helping block the entrance to the Surgicenter. According to court testimony, he used to yell at people that they would get AIDS if they walked inside. He has an injunction dictating what he can do and where he can go around Lovejoy. He can trace an imaginary line on the sidewalk in front of the building and past the hedge beyond which he cannot cross.

Although he is a member of Advocates for Life, Doc is equivocal about the shooting of abortion doctors. He thinks that strategy hurts the anti-abortion cause, paints the good guys as bad guys. As for the morality of shooting doctors, he simply says, "It may be justified, I don't know." Doc doesn't fancy himself a philosopher.

Doc usually is alone through his daily vigil, soaking up the sun in summer, fighting off the chilling rain in winter. Days can go by when he will talk to no one. Ask what keeps him coming back here each day and he will take a minute to think, then reply that once, about a year ago, a woman walked up to him carrying a baby and said, "Do you want to see a baby you saved?"

He can vividly recall the man and woman who, three or four years ago, approached Lovejoy on foot until the woman saw Doc and his sign and began crying. Doc watched as she stopped in her tracks, the man hugged her, and the two turned around and walked the other way.

And he remembers the woman who walked up to his chair one day, handed him a picture of a baby, and said her daughter chose not to have an abortion because he was there. And so he sits on, a community landmark, a man with purpose.

Hugh is the other regular in front of Lovejoy. His is the more compelling figure. Hugh is probably in his thirties, dark hair falling off the sides of his face, heavy black-framed glasses. Hugh carries a sign but he does not sit down. He stands stock still and stares up into the sky for hours on end. It can be an unnerving pose, though it may not be a pose at all. If you approach Hugh and try to talk you will receive no response. Hugh is in a trance, a world of his own making.

Hugh can also be found strolling around the neighborhood surrounding Lovejoy. He will stop frequently to stare back at the sky, or at a passing car, or seemingly at nothing at all. Frequently he will appear to be mumbling.

Occasionally Hugh will become lucid. He has told people he works in the lunchroom of a nearby hospital. Clearly he is unbalanced, and the sense around Lovejoy is that Hugh is basically a gentle sort.

Once Tamara, who works upstairs at Lovejoy, passed Hugh on the sidewalk in his customary skyward-looking pose. Not expecting an answer she asked, "What are you looking at, Hugh?"

"I'm counting the angels, the babies that have left Lovejoy," came the reply.

In the top drawer of a black hardwood dresser in Tim Shuck's bedroom a pile of letters is held together by a single rubber band. Most are cards, and many of them have flowers displayed on the front. Some are handwritten on stationery, a few typewritten. All are from women, letters to Shuck from grateful patients, and in a few cases, their parents. They are the sum of a life's work, and witness to its purpose.

> *Tim thank you for our talk and your friendly support. As I've told you once before, sometimes just knowing there's support close enough to reach is all I need. You're in a good place, Tim, keep hugging all of us "rattled" females, you help more than you'll ever know.*

Tim does not often read the letters, but every month or two he takes them out of the drawer, props himself up in bed, and settles in for a little reflection. For years he told Allene he would never leave. "They'll have to drag me out of here," he said on more than one occasion. They didn't. But now, Tim must drag himself back in.

Tim learned he was HIV positive in the winter of 1985. By January 1993 he knew he had developed AIDS. There could be no other explanation for the overwhelming fatigue that had begun to make each day a trial. By the time he visited his physician the diagnosis hardly had any impact. He is a gay man in America in the 1990s. He has watched friend after friend be buried.

In the months that followed, as his energy slowly left him like a sibling quietly growing apart, as the infections with no apparent source set in, acceptance came easier than Tim could have wished for, as if all this was expected. But as the realization of his beckoning mortality grew there was one idea Tim was unable to confront directly, one element of his life with which he could not fully make peace. When the time came, Tim was not ready to say good-bye to the Lovejoy Surgicenter.

It has been a year and a half since Tim left Lovejoy. But nearly every Wednesday of those eighteen months he has walked through the front doors with a collection of flowers—gladiola for the lobby and a generous assortment for Allene to take home that evening. His contribution for the week. Sometimes he notices a woman in the waiting room looking especially distraught and he will take a seat next to her. Inevitably, minutes later, you will find the two of them talking. Later he sticks his head in Allene's door and she invites him to sit down. They chat. Carye often comes in. The visits last no more than fifteen minutes as a rule. Allene is always looking for signs that the conversation is becoming a strain on Tim.

> *I realize I was a real pain in the "arse" but I want you to know that I did appreciate your tender care—your warmth and your help thru the deepest darkest lowest period of my life. Please except my apology—I'm normally a very nice thoughtful type person. . . . You were super—a real friend when I needed someone so badly.*

Tim needs those letters, needs them more than he ever thought he would. There are days when he needs help in remembering. He is ready for death, he can laugh at it if the punch line is good enough. He cannot laugh at what is happening at Lovejoy, or the pain he feels not to be a part of it. The letters keep him in touch with what his life has been about.

> *It was a delight and great comfort to have been helped through this ordeal by someone like you. (You ought to teach courses in empathy—others could benefit from your style and personality!)*
>
> *I'll always remember the kindness you showed me—and I'll always be grateful there are men out there with your kindness willing to help others.*

As if it were yesterday Tim can summon up a picture of a counseling session years ago. The girl was fifteen years old and accompanied by her father and mother. Tim recalls feeling vaguely uncomfortable at first as he watched the father and daughter in the lobby; they appeared too intimate. His suspicions were aroused a bit more when he invited them all into his office—the mother stayed in the waiting area while the father and daughter followed Tim. Halfway through the session the daughter, with no prompting that Tim could detect, raised herself from her chair and went over to sit on her father's lap. And Tim, not wanting to wrongly accuse or judge, could only manage, "I'm really uncomfortable with what's happening here." When the father went back to the lobby, the daughter broke down and told Tim the baby was the father's.

And there were the people who fooled Tim, worth a good laugh now. About a dozen years ago Allene hired a nurse practitioner to offer general women's health care such as Pap smears and advice on birth control. One of the nurse practitioner's regular customers was an elderly man with an especially gentle manner. Over the course of a few months he would bring in young women who looked like street kids and pay for their medical care. Usually he would sit and chat with Tim while the young women were being examined. Tim began to think the man a modern-day saint. In fact, everyone in the office grew fond of this grandfatherly figure.

One day the nurse practitioner asked Tim and Allene to join her for a conference. She was bothered by comments made by some of the young women the man brought in. When the nurse asked about their sexual activity, each girl would admit to multiple partners but offer no more information. That was enough to set off Allene's antennae. She called the police, who discovered the young women were part of a prostitution ring, and the old man was running it.

One patient more than all the others comes back to Tim in the quiet moments, the one sure to bring a smile to his face when he eases back into bed reading these letters. The one who forced Tim to reconsider the foundation of his counseling philosophy because she was the one who made him break a rule he had thought inviolate. Tim's philosophy allows him to share his feelings with patients, but not to take decision making away from them. Her name was Beverly.

Beverly was a nurse who came to Lovejoy for an abortion. Married ten years, she and her husband had agreed years before that they did not want children. She was at Lovejoy because their contraceptive had failed.

As Beverly spoke, Tim detected little equivocation in her words. She was straightforward about wanting the abortion. But a tremor in her voice told another story. What Beverly had described, when Tim thought about the words and voice together, was an ultimatum from her husband—terminate the pregnancy or divorce.

As Tim listened to Beverly a second voice kept at him. This inner voice told him Beverly's choice was wrong. Tim's work is helping women make choices, knowing that some of those women feel they are choosing between life and death. It is his job to ignore the voices that come from within himself. But this woman was telling him she could not kill flies or spiders; when she found them in her house she captured and released them outdoors. Beverly told Tim she had never been able to cut the flowers she grew in her backyard garden because she could not stand the thought of their dying. And here she was talking about ending an eighteen-week pregnancy.

Tim forgot about Beverly until he looked at his calendar one morning and noticed she was coming in for another counseling session and her laminaria. The morning passed quickly for Tim, as if he were working on automatic pilot. His mind was on Beverly all the time.

When Beverly arrived Tim greeted her with a smile and they quickly retreated to his office. They spoke briefly about matters of little consequence.

"So, what are you thinking?" Tim asked. Beverly's hands were clasped tightly together in her lap. She told Tim she was ready to proceed with the abortion. To Tim the words sounded wooden. It was not any strain in her voice so much as the lack of expression that pushed him.

"I don't think this is the right decision for you," Tim said. And even as the words spilled out of his mouth he was blanching inside, wondering if he had overstepped his bounds. But the two of them began talking.

Beverly decided to go ahead with her abortion and walked upstairs to the exam room for her lams. Tim, who promised to stay at Beverly's side, remembers her dress that day—blue, restrained, more severe than the outfit she had worn to their other session. He briefed the surgeon on Beverly's situation, sharing with Chandler the discomfort he felt. Tim watched as Beverly lay on the examination table about to be dilated, listened as Chandler leaned over her and said, "Beverly, are you sure this is what you want to do?" And Beverly began crying and uttering as if she were the child, "No, no, no," over and over.

"That's the right decision," Chandler said, and he hugged Beverly, who turned to Tim for an embrace.

Tim met with Beverly once more. He told her that he saw her facing a situation in which loss was inevitable. She could lose her child and keep her husband, or keep the child and lose her husband. But what he really saw, he said, was a potential for double loss, that if she had gone ahead with the abortion, it is likely she would have someday divorced her husband anyway. Or he would have divorced her. Then Tim arranged for Beverly to begin long-term therapy with a psychologist.

Three years after that, Tim went to see an orthopedist about a sore shoulder. As he walked into the doctor's office Beverly ran up to Tim and hugged him. She worked there as a nurse. And now she completed her story for Tim. She and her husband had divorced, but she had this wonderful three-year-old daughter around whom Beverly's world now revolved. There was nothing wooden in her voice as she spoke these words, just joy.

*

When Tim left Lovejoy he felt like a child moving away from home just when he needed it most. He and Allene still remain close, and when Passover or Thanksgiving arrives Tim will be at Allene's house. But it is not enough, never the same. "Coming to work was not work," he says. "It was an extension of a family unit that was created here." And that is why the Wednesday visits have continued. He wants to be around Allene, somehow. Like Carye, Tim talks of Allene's energy. "I do miss that," he says in a lowered voice.

Tim plays another role now. Allene needs to leave Lovejoy behind, he believes, and he does not hesitate to bring it up in conversation. Tim of all people knows how hard it would be for Allene to leave. But as the shootings and firebombings increase in number he fears for Allene's life. For years Tim hoped one of Allene's children would take over the business, but now he rejects the idea as too dangerous. He even tries nudging Allene toward a compromise: At least she should wear a bulletproof vest, he tells her. He knows she won't, but he's not above getting in a little commentary. "I don't think she'd look good in a dress with a vest," he says, laughing. "Allene's busty to begin with and she wears tight clothing."

On a warm April afternoon Paul deParrie made mention of Tim. Years before, during an Advocates for Life protest at Lovejoy, Tim stepped outside the building and the two men began a remarkably cordial conversation. Tim probably is the only person at Lovejoy who could do this; his gentleness and willingness to suspend judgment are that easily discerned.

DeParrie spoke of each of the people at Lovejoy and what he perceived to be their motivations. Suchak, he said, performed abortions for the money, was driven by greed. Allene, he thought, had made abortion "a sacrament." But Tim, deParrie felt, was different. Tim, deParrie was sure, had a place deep in his heart where he knew abortion was wrong.

DeParrie is half right. Tim has no time for unexamined ambivalence, no room left for denial. He has looked in his heart and confronted all the thoughts and feelings that hide in the deep places. In a quiet moment his words explain a lifetime.

"I have never denied that human life begins at conception," he says. "If I have a complaint about our society, it's that we don't deal with death and dying. Do we believe human beings have a right to make decisions about death and dying? Yes, we do, and those decisions are made every day in every hospital."

Years ago Tim made his own decision about dying. He asked Allene to help him when his disease enters its final chapter, to help him die with dignity.

On a cloudy Wednesday in early June Tim calls Allene after returning from a ten-day trip to Yosemite National Park. He is feeling a surge in energy—a gift, an unexpected bounty. Whatever its cause and however long it lasts, he wants to spend it at Lovejoy. Would counseling one afternoon a week be possible?

Allene is overjoyed. She feels as if one of her children is returning for an extended visit. They agree on Wednesday afternoons for a start. A few minutes later Carye walks into Allene's office and hears her boss exclaim, "Timmy's coming back!"

Welcome to Advocates for Life Ministries Action News for Friday, May 19. This hot line will not be updated until Monday, June 5. Please join us for our "Nowhere to Hide" picket on Saturday, May 20. Meet at 10 A.M. at the Advocates for Life Ministry's office. From there we will caravan to abortionist David Clark's house.

In case you have not heard, new reports out of China are that eating aborted babies has become the latest health food craze. Hospitals and clinics are selling them to people, or doctors and staff are taking them home to eat themselves. The report, in the highly respected Hong Kong newspaper the *Eastern Express*, quotes doctors saying, "They would just go to waste if we didn't eat them." Claims are that they keep your skin young and give vitality. One person even said that it cured allergies. Reports have staff members actually fighting over the little bodies. Sounds okay to me. Remember that ex–NOW chief Molly Yard approved of the Chinese forced-abortion policy. The pro-abortion forces want all opposition to their favorite sacrament shut down, as I'm sure it is in China. And next they'll want this health treatment available.

Then abortionists Jane Perkins and her tag-team abortionist husband James as well as David Clark, Sarah Meeley, Harold Suchak, and the rest of the gruesome gang can further enrich themselves in the latest health food frenzy. I wouldn't put it past any of them. Thank you for calling Advocates for Life Ministries.

In the last five years there have been at least twelve shootings of abortion doctors and staff in North America, from the day in 1991 when two workers were wounded at their Springfield, Missouri, clinic to John Salvi's mad explosion in Brookline, Massachusetts, in 1994. Salvi opened fire with a rifle in the lobbies of two clinics in suburban Boston ten minutes apart, killing two receptionists and wounding five other people. In 1993 Dr. David Gunn was killed outside his Pensacola, Florida, clinic, and Dr. George Wayne Patterson was killed in Mobile, Alabama. The year 1994 saw Dr. John Bayard Britton and an escort killed in Pensacola. In November 1994 Dr. Garson Romalis was shot by a sniper while eating breakfast in his Vancouver, British Columbia, home. The victims have included doctors, administrators, nurses, and patients. The assailants, at least those identified, were all men.

And then there is Shelley Shannon. Andrew Burnett is Allene Klass's enemy, but Shelley Shannon is her nightmare, a woman over the edge for whom violence is the only justifiable option. Whether that edge is one of madness or simply philosophy Allene can only speculate. Today, in her dimly lit office, Allene is working at that puzzle along with Carye and Cheryl Glenn, special agent for the Bureau of Alcohol, Tobacco and Firearms.

Ostensibly Glenn has asked for this meeting to explain to Allene and Carye events that will be unfolding this afternoon in a federal courthouse downtown. Shelley Shannon will be entering a plea agreement, basically accepting somewhere between ten and twenty additional years in jail in return for an admission of guilt. The exact length of her jail term will be decided by a judge two or three months from now.

In August 1993 Shannon drove from Oregon, where she had been protesting with Andrew Burnett outside Lovejoy, to Wichita, Kansas. As far as anyone knows she was alone. She had a gun, a .25 caliber handgun. Shannon took up a position outside the office of Dr. George Tiller. When he appeared Shannon shot him four or five times, hitting both his hands. Two months later Shannon was convicted of attempted murder and sentenced to ten years in prison.

In time federal agents discovered that the shooting of Dr. Tiller was merely the climactic act in Shannon's career of anti-abortion violence. Beginning with information they were able to pry out of her while Shannon was in prison, they pieced together a trail of anti-abortion crimes stretching over four months in 1992, prior to the Tiller shooting. That is what ATF agent Glenn is here to discuss today.

Glenn is a serious and intense woman, a dedicated, hard-working, hard-to-pin-down-her-age type somewhere in her thirties who has made Shannon the focus of her career. She is leading one of the few conversations in Allene's office that is not punctuated by laughter. Even when Allene and Carye have discussed subjects as painful as Allene's father, slowly slipping into senility, or Tim's graceful decline, they have used humor to deal with their pain. Not today.

Shannon will likely receive a fifteen-year sentence to run after her ten-year sentence for shooting Dr. Tiller expires, Glenn explains. She will be somewhere in her sixties before she becomes eligible to leave prison. "By that time we think the hormones will not be raging anymore?" Carye suggests.

Allene, sitting behind her desk, looks concerned, intent. The door to her office is closed, a rare occurrence. She knows that getting Shannon to confess to more crimes is of secondary importance. Everyone feels that Shannon had help. Someone had to teach a meek and unassuming Grants Pass homemaker and mother of two how to make firebombs, plot strategy. Somebody had to teach her how to shoot and where to get a gun, and each of the women in this room had hoped an accomplice or better yet a conspiracy would be discovered. Each of them is also aware that Shannon was frequently in the company of Burnett outside Lovejoy before and possibly during the period she committed her crimes. But nine months of investigation and two grand juries leave that an open question, Glenn confesses.

"Shelley is not your average criminal," Glenn says. The ATF agent has been working on Shannon's case in such a personal, career-staking way that the idea of calling her subject by a last name does not even occur; to everybody in this room for a long time there has been only one Shelley.

"She wouldn't give up anyone," Glenn continues. "For her, it's not ratting off her friends, it's ratting off God, and she's not going to do that."

Glenn outlines the crimes to which Shannon will plead guilty later. Basically they include a string of firebombings at abortion facilities along the West Coast, including a 1992 firebombing at Lovejoy. So today's report closes that case for Allene. No more will she have to listen to anti-abortion spokespeople claiming she set fire to her own clinic in order to lay blame at the feet of protestors.

The bombing spree actually is quite remarkable. Clinics in Eugene, Oregon, and Reno, Nevada, both torched in one day. Chico, California, the next. Six in all were attacked by Shannon.

"How the hell did she get to all these places?" Carye interrupts. The idea of an undiscovered conspiracy, of an opportunity lost, haunts this conversation like a spectre. Nobody feels this more than Glenn; she and other federal authorities have been convinced for years that at minimum some sort of network exists among the splinter groups and individuals in the radical anti-abortion movement. Shannon might have been their witness in proving a conspiracy, but that is not part of the bargain that has been struck. So today's news really is a compromised blessing.

Glenn does not need to remind Allene of the other spectre, the one they are all pleased to avoid as part of this bargain. Shelley Shannon is already in jail, so adding fifteen years to her sentence matters little to Allene. But without a plea agreement there would be a trial, a long, drawn-out trial that would bring to Portland and Lovejoy the national media circus fresh off the O. J. Simpson trial. The national curiosity could now turn its attention toward Shelley Shannon, mild-mannered homemaker turned firebomber and gunwoman. And following behind, eager to get a piece of the spotlight, would come every anti-abortion activist in the country, and maybe one or two of the gun-toting crazies as well. A show trial would also provide Andrew Burnett a focus for his desperate fund-raising efforts. Today's good news is that there will be no trial.

It doesn't feel like enough. Maybe, Allene is thinking, they've missed their one chance to get Andrew Burnett. Shannon was with him shortly before she went to Wichita, after all. And who else is out there?

Glenn reveals that authorities have an idea who might have mentored Shelley in the ways of violence. She calls the man "the Mad Bomber" but does not reveal his name. They are tracking his movements but so far haven't gathered a single bit of evidence against him.

As for Burnett, Glenn thinks he and Shelley are not on the best of terms. Glenn has spent countless hours talking with Shelley, and she's convinced Shelley views Burnett as all talk and no action, lacking the nerve to carry his philosophy to its natural conclusion as she has.

"That's how I feel," Allene says. "Were Shelley and Andrew ever friends?"

Glenn says probably not.

"She's the mad Oregon housewife," Glenn says, painting a picture of a shy and bored small-town homemaker with children soon to leave home, a woman ripe for a cause, for something to lend purpose to her life. Her husband had no idea Shelley was torching buildings and shooting doctors.

"She's even likeable," Allene interjects. "If she got out today, she'd start up all over again, don't you think?"

"I don't know," Glenn responds. There is no doubt, Glenn says, of Shelley's continued commitment to the anti-abortion cause. From prison she continues to correspond with other radical anti-abortionists. In fact, Paul Hill came to visit Shelley in prison shortly before he killed Dr. Britton and an escort outside a Florida abortion clinic months ago. But Shelley hasn't completely cut herself off from the rest of her life. Glenn says she convinced Shelley to accept the plea agreement by telling her that if she did not, the only way she would ever be able to see her grandchildren would be through prison Plexiglas.

Carye wonders out loud if Shelley was motivated to take the plea bargain by a desire to stay in prison, to play out a role that she perceived as her destiny all along.

Glenn has been thinking along the same lines. "Life in prison for a martyr for the cause is not significantly different from being a bored Grants Pass housewife," she says.

Allene asks Glenn about Burnett. She calls him Andrew. Could he be pushed over the edge to the point where he would become a shooter?

Glenn answers with a Burnett quote that ran in the local newspaper recently: "If you really believe abortion is murder then you may have a right, or even a duty, to consider killing an abortion doctor as a last ditch defense of those you see as defenseless—the unborn. . . . I can't live with the knowledge of people being killed all the time without going crazy."

"I think he's a person who could snap," she says. "He's wound pretty tight. But I think we have at least fifteen years before his kids are grown and gone, before Andrew picks up a gun."

"There hasn't been a fire in a long time," Carye says.

"Do you think we're going to have one?" Allene asks, her eyes on Glenn.

Glenn reminds Allene that Shelley has confessed to only six firebombings. Shelley insists two others that were thought to be part of a pattern were not her work. "There's still a bomber out there," she says.

Glenn's words appear to focus Allene's concern. Her eyes narrow as she leans forward, chin on hand. Her free hand is playing with the gold ring on her finger. Carye is kneading a palm-sized rubber heart that she once gave Allene as a desktop ornament.

"Do you think we should do anything about asking for extra surveillance tonight?" Allene asks.

In a prison cell that has yet to confine her passion or her sense of humor, Shannon mulls over the question of regrets. Recently she became upset with guards who wouldn't answer from the hallway when she called. Luckily she had a brown paper bag in her cell, a remnant from a sack lunch. She blew up the bag and then popped it, and sure enough the guards came running, certain that Shelley Shannon, the crazed bomber and shooter, had struck again.

Would she do it again? Shannon, straightforward, polite, answers as best she can. She hopes so, but she's not sure. The reality of twenty or thirty years behind bars is beginning to exact its toll. She misses her family, the Oregon mountains, the organic garden she so lovingly tended. She prays every day, but God's voice is becoming harder to hear above the prison noise. "I might wimp out," she says. She just doesn't know.

Two days later Carye takes a call from the National Clinic Defense Project of the Feminist Majority Foundation. The Mad Bomber, Shelley Shannon's possible accomplice, has been spotted outside an abortion clinic in Kansas City.

SATURDAY, JUNE 17

Paul deParrie is moving about the Advocates for Life headquarters like a stage mother just before the curtain rises. He's psyched, ready for battle, full of pent-up energy and purpose. Even the threat of rain on this gray Saturday morning does not diminish his animation.

Andrew Burnett is gone, halfway through a summer drive around the country. Burnett, wife, and five children are pushing hard in the family Chevy wagon, thirty-eight days, nine thousand miles, home visits and barbecues with supporters—a combination traveling ministry and family vacation.

Burnett left believing this summer and fall represent a critical period for Advocates and for the entire anti-abortion movement, from which he is becoming increasingly isolated. The forces of politics and compromise are winning the battle for the hearts and minds of those who oppose abortion. Andrew Burnett stands for rejection of compromise.

Anti-abortion members of Congress are pushing legislation to outlaw certain late-term, or partial-birth, abortions. The proposed bill would send to prison any doctor found practicing the procedure—for three years. To Burnett this represents exactly the type of incremental approach to fighting abortion he cannot endorse. Abortion is murder. You do not give a three-year sentence to someone con-

victed of murder. Burnett has angered potential allies with his re-
fusal to support the bill.

The summer tour of the country provides Burnett an opportunity to talk to his people, to buttress those who may be falling prey
to doubts, to the seduction of political compromise. At the same time
Burnett is assessing just how isolated his organization has become.
Advocates for Life desperately needs more support, financial as well
as moral. In his heart Burnett knows they cannot continue unless
more solid financial footing can be established.

So Paul deParrie is in charge now. For weeks the Advocates hot
line has been touting his new "Shame Campaign." DeParrie has
planned every element of today's action, right down to the maps he
has meticulously put together showing the route to the protest site.
All he needs are troops.

When deParrie arrived at headquarters at 10 A.M. he was met
by Bill, a thirtyish man with a trimmed beard, aviator sunglasses, and
a green camouflage jacket. Bill joined Advocates a few months ago.
He says he is here with a perspective different from the others. He is
not a fundamentalist, does not even attend a church. "I lost a child
through an abortion," he says, explaining that his girlfriend had an
abortion without consulting him. He sits by himself in the front office as deParrie hustles about. DeParrie's sleepy-eyed twelve-year-old
daughter lounges near the front door.

DeParrie is dressed in black—black pants and T-shirt covered
by a dark wool sport jacket. Dark blue Nike running shoes complete
the effect of the man in protest. The small turnout, the passing minutes do not deter him. Advocates supporters operate on pro-life time,
he says, and that means late. He peeks out the front door and looks
up the street.

Last week deParrie sent a fax about today's activities to the
Portland police intelligence officer who has been charged with
monitoring the abortion clinics. But the fax did not say where the
protest would be held. Sure enough, deParrie spots the officer's gray
surveillance van facing the Advocates headquarters from a side

street. DeParrie crosses the four lanes of Sandy Boulevard and walks straight to the police van. He and the plainclothes officer exchange friendly greetings. In the van's passenger seat another man holds on his lap a camera with a long telephoto lens. He doesn't speak. DeParrie hands the driver one of his maps and heads back to the Advocates office. The man beside the police officer, he says, is an FBI agent.

The police presence does not bother deParrie. In fact, it buoys him. "I want the cops there," he explains. "It's in everybody's interest they feel assured we're not trying to do anything illegal. And I also like more people there. If we can get cops out there in riot gear, that's a lot of fun."

DeParrie is reveling in the attention and in the power of leadership. Putting together his video equipment, assigning tasks to his daughter and Bill, even reminiscing about major protests of the past, he sounds like a general preparing his soldiers for military maneuvers. With glee he recalls the afternoon in 1994 when he was shot at while sidewalk counseling in front of a New Orleans abortion clinic. Anything might happen today, he cautions his people.

A smiling gray-haired man walks into the office wearing a golf hat that proclaims I LOVE JESUS. He greets deParrie and Bill and settles off to one side of the room. Bill will handle the video equipment, taping every moment of the day's events, possible evidence should today's work lead to a court proceeding. Bob, the older man, volunteers to distribute the day's printed message, a flyer exposing Allene Klass. With undisguised satisfaction deParrie tells the group that while they are picketing Allene Klass's home today another Advocates supporter will be handing out the same flyer to neighbors at Klass's beach house. She has been outflanked.

Fifteen minutes later two more supporters arrive. Shirley, a fiftyish mother of six, obviously a regular, has brought with her a clearly reluctant son of about twenty-five. The young man alternates between trying to gain acceptance as part of the group and making it clear he would rather be at home, first greeting everybody and making a halfhearted attempt at small talk, then complaining about the chances of rain and arrest. Mostly he is ignored.

DeParrie announces it is time to go, and the group of six takes to two cars and heads to Klass's house twenty minutes away. The police surveillance van has beaten them to the spot and waits inconspicuously up the street. The house sits in a development that borders on the rural—no sidewalks and no parking lane at the side of the road. Nobody is sure where to park. Finally the two cars settle on a gravel spot about a hundred yards short of Klass's driveway, next to an ominous set of NO TRESPASSING signs running parallel to the road along Klass's front yard.

DeParrie opens the trunk of his car and gives Nikki, his daughter, the first choice of signs. She grabs one that says ABORTION KILLS CHILDREN. DeParrie takes another with the message FREEDOM OF CHOICE? A picture below the words shows a forceps holding the head of an aborted fetus. DeParrie and Nikki begin walking up the street. Over his shoulder deParrie carries a camera bag. As he reaches Klass's driveway he takes out a camera with a telephoto lens and begins shooting pictures of the cars in Klass's driveway. He is the birthday boy at a party to which almost nobody has come, but he is playing every one of the games and enjoying himself nonetheless.

Bob has collected his flyers and begun canvassing the street, placing the material on cars and in doorways. Bill has taken up a post across the street from the Klass house and is videotaping events. Nikki, alternately smiling and bored, is picking out stones from the side of the road, looking for smooth rounded ones that might be good for skipping on water this afternoon.

Carrying signs, deParrie and Nikki begin walking back and forth in front of Klass's property like tin ducks in a shooting gallery. Klass's long curving driveway and the tall bushes planted in front keep the house mostly obscured. There is one patch of about ten yards where the house is visible from the street, and each time deParrie walks past he pauses and looks in toward the house for a few seconds before resuming his patterned stroll.

The deParries are joined by Shirley, wearing a long purple rain-coat and white sneakers, and carrying another sign showing a fetus. This one reads STOP ABORTION! HE SHOULDN'T DIE FOR YOUR SINS; JESUS ALREADY DID! A drizzle has begun. Shirley's son, taking note of the police van, is hanging back near their car.

The street is quiet, as usual in this neighborhood. Nobody walks by, nobody leaves the homes, which are set well back from the street. One or two cars have driven past the miniprotest without anybody inside taking notice. The only interested people are in the surveil-lance van up the street. But deParrie's enthusiasm never wanes. He tells the others that somebody is looking out at them from behind the curtains of the Klass home.

Allene's daughter, Leah, exits the front door and walks across the driveway to the house next door without acknowledging the protestors. Seconds later she returns home with one of Bob's flyers in her hand.

A man comes out the front door of a house across the street and takes a flyer off his car's windshield. He glances at the flyer, which reads YOUR NEIGHBOR IS AN ABORTIONIST! Beneath the words are two grainy, photocopied pictures of Klass, one front and one side view, like mug shots.

"You people ought to go home, you know," the man shouts.

"I'm just practicing my First Amendment rights," deParrie re-sponds. "It's fun. You ought to try it."

A small-scale shouting match develops. From his front porch the man tells deParrie that Bob is trespassing by coming up the drive-way with the flyer. "You ought to respect somebody else's right," he says. In a feeble attempt at intimidating deParrie he makes a show of walking over to the two Advocates cars and taking down their license plate numbers.

As the neighbor heads back into his house deParrie shouts, "Get the baby killers out of your neighborhood, and we won't come back!"

Twenty minutes later, the protest completed, the group of six jogs back to the two cars as the day's rain begins. DeParrie is exuberant. He has done what he intended to do, and like Burnett he refuses to be dismayed at the lack of support.

The next day's Sunday *New York Times* encourages him even further. The front page displays the headline CONSPIRACY IS AN ELUSIVE TARGET IN PROSECUTING FOES OF ABORTION. The dateline is Portland, Oregon. The story continues to a full page inside, with a two-column picture of Andrew Burnett across the top. The *Times* reviews the case of Shelley Shannon and her upcoming sentencing and discusses theories of conspiracy involving the powerful "militant" leaders of the anti-abortion movement, Burnett foremost among them. There is no mention of the previous day's six-person campaign. There is only image and publicity and an opportunity Andrew Burnett and Paul deParrie could not invent.

But the weekend also crystallizes the paradox confronting Burnett. He knows that every move he makes is critical to his organization's survival. In America, where the media define reality, Burnett's power and influence increase with each shooting at an abortion facility because he is perceived as a leader to those who would shoot. Even Burnett reluctantly acknowledges he is becoming "bigger than life." But with each shooting he loses popular support, becomes distanced from many Americans who are opposed to abortion. Burnett is staking his ministry on the idea that he can continue to lose the political battle but win the war over abortion with the help of the national media.

"Don't send a hearse," Carye roars into the telephone. The sight of a hearse being loaded with a plastic bag full of fetal tissue at Lovejoy just might send a few of the patients in the lobby scurrying home. "And no van with funeral lettering," she adds before hanging up.

Upstairs Dr. Lane has just removed a twenty-eight-week-old fetus from the womb, a fetus with anencephaly. No brain. If the pregnancy had continued, the baby most likely would have been dead

on delivery. If not, it might have been hooked up to the most advanced forms of life support available, consigned to existence as a
nonconscious, inert being until the decision was made to discontinue
artificial support. But the mother never wanted an abortion, does
not believe in it. "Did she have a choice?" Carye wonders.

It is Carye's belief that most of the women who walk through
Lovejoy's doors are victimized by a feminist political dogma that
makes it appear as if a buffet of alternatives is available to them—
they merely have to choose. Carye hates the phrase pro-choice. The
phrase has nothing to do with the world in which she works. Many
of her patients, by the time they reach Lovejoy, are not choosing
abortion any more than the woman upstairs, who has asked that her
abortion be treated as a death. Many of them fear abortion like they
fear death. And most of them will never find the ceremony or the
ritual to guide them past their actions. But not in this case: Tomorrow in Portland there will be a funeral for a child never born.

Chapter Six

In the downstairs hallway just a few feet from Allene's door, Harold Suchak takes a moment to collect his thoughts before deciding to continue walking. He has just come from the first-floor exam room.

For the last few days Suchak has considered talking to Allene about ultrasound policy. He believes every patient at Lovejoy should have an ultrasound performed before being sent upstairs to see a doctor. The Surgicenter's policy is that ultrasounds are done if a woman believes her pregnancy has advanced beyond twelve weeks, if she has a history of problem birth or pregnancy, or if her counselor, after talking to the patient, feels uncertain about the date of conception. About 40 percent of Lovejoy's patients receive ultrasounds downstairs.

Suchak views the ultrasound policy as another in a series of shortsighted cost-cutting measures instituted by Allene, but abortion doctors around the country are divided on whether ultrasounds should be mandatory. Some abortion clinics ultrasound all patients as part of intake. At Lovejoy every woman sent upstairs for surgery is given a pelvic exam by her doctor, another method of determining the size and gestational age of a fetus. If the doctor's impression conflicts with the estimated age in the counselor's notes, the doctor has the option of using the upstairs ultrasound machine before beginning a procedure. Some doctors at Lovejoy use the upstairs machine on every patient; Suchak does not.

Counselors at Lovejoy know that what patients tell them can be less than reliable. A few years ago Tim counseled a woman who insisted she had been pregnant less than twelve weeks. A pelvic exam upstairs and a subsequent ultrasound showed she was less than a week from delivering a full-term baby.

A pelvic exam can often be misleading about gestational age, especially for an obese woman or a woman whose uterus is unusually positioned. But the exam gives the surgeon valuable information about the position of the uterus. And Carye fears that with mandatory ultrasounds in hand, some doctors might forgo the pelvic exam. Also, the information a downstairs ultrasound provides is limited because it is performed by Lovejoy's counselors, not doctors who are trained in the nuances of deciphering the pictures the ultrasound produces. One final consideration: The simplest ultrasound is billed at $40; for many of Lovejoy's patients, that can be a lot of money.

Ultrasound policy is on Suchak's mind because of a case one of Lovejoy's other doctors handled this week. The patient, a heavyset woman, was so certain she was ten weeks pregnant that no ultrasound was performed by her counselor. Upstairs, the doctor's pelvic exam failed to indicate anything different. The woman was given the standard painkillers, and a simple tab local was begun. As the doctor tried to aspirate the fetus, the woman complained that it was hurting too much. She was given more Valium.

A tab local should take five to ten minutes but the doctor could not seem to remove the fetus, and the woman had now spent nearly twenty minutes on the operating table with only local anesthesia and Valium to dull her pain. The head of the fetus was stuck—clearly it was larger than the head of a normal ten-week-old fetus. The doctor set aside his suction device and attempted to use forceps, but even this failed to remove the fetus. Ideally the patient would be dilated further, increasing the opening for removal of the fetus, but that would be too painful for a woman who was not under general anesthetic. It was becoming obvious, painfully to the patient, that this procedure could not be done as a tab local.

A flurry of telephone calls went out for an anesthesiologist and an operating room team. An ultrasound was performed that revealed the patient was sixteen weeks pregnant. After a wait of an hour the woman was taken into the operating room for a full D & E. There were no further complications, but Suchak thinks the episode could have been avoided if the woman had been administered an ultrasound downstairs. Still, he has decided not to bring the subject of routine ultrasounds up with Allene. She wouldn't listen to me, he thinks, continuing through the hallway and back upstairs.

FRIDAY, JUNE 30

Allene is poised behind her desk. She has hardly moved from her seat the entire afternoon. It's good to know that even after twenty years this day can have me on edge, she thinks. Just like the job. June 30, the end of the fiscal year. The day when she proves again, to herself, her worth as a businesswoman. And in recent years that has been an increasingly difficult proposition.

Across the country fewer and fewer abortions are being performed. Portland is no exception. What is different about Portland is that the number of facilities doing abortions refuses to drop.

Throughout the day Carye walks into Allene's office updating the daily and monthly patient count. Traditionally they wait until this day to add up the numbers, though Allene keeps a running monthly count in her head all year. Allene prefers it this way, and the sense of excitement and relief she feels as the numbers come in remind her why. It has not been a blockbuster year, but satisfactory? Yes. Definitely.

Throughout the day, too, Allene has asked a few of Lovejoy's medical staff and bookkeepers in to her office for meetings, informal performance reviews, actually. Payroll, especially, has become a problem. Lovejoy is not doing a precise-enough job tracking who works what hours. That has always been an issue. Upstairs nurses and assistants often complain they've been working in surgery seven hours without a lunch break on shifts when patients all show up at once. Other days, when the patient load evens out or is light, those same assistants might take a series of extended breaks outside smoking cigarettes, or in the staff lounge. The staff sign-in sheet, behind the receptionist downstairs, is often ignored. But mostly the problem is with the bookkeepers, who have resisted a new accounting program, and Allene has a lecture or two to deliver this afternoon.

The numbers look good. Lovejoy has performed almost 200 more abortions than the year before, reversing a declining trend that characterized the last few years. The Surgicenter has, in effect, beaten the national statistics. Allene considers the reasons. The numbers, though still incomplete, tell most of the story—180 more tab locals this year. Tab locals are Lovejoy's most competitive market because all abortion facilities are prepared to do these simpler, early operations. A large percentage of the city's second-trimester abortions, especially the more difficult cases, will always come to Lovejoy because it is set up as a full outpatient surgical facility. Allene wonders if Planned Parenthood is going to open an abortion clinic in Portland, as they have proposed. And why. Planned Parenthood has the greatest name recognition in the abortion field; they could drive one or more of Portland's providers out of business. But not Lovejoy.

More answers. Lovejoy has maintained its cash price this year for a first-trimester abortion—$230. But for the same abortion billed to an insurance company, for which Lovejoy almost never will receive the full billed amount, they have raised the rate, from $430 to $530. And the fee they pay their doctors for that abortion remained the same this year—$75. Which means for each insurance-billed tab local Lovejoy has profited $100 more. And they've done this while increasing market share.

Tab locals have always led the way to profits. Second-trimester abortions demand more equipment, including the general anesthetic and the anesthesiologist, who gets paid on a per case basis. A tab local patient usually will be seen by a doctor only once. A second-trimester D & E patient will probably see a doctor four times—twice for insertion of lams, once during the surgery, once for a two-weeks-after-care appointment. And every extra minute a doctor spends with a patient instead of on another case translates into lower profits for Lovejoy, as well as reduced income for the doctor.

Doctors get $600 for each D & E they perform at Lovejoy; at some of the other facilities in Portland they make much less, Allene knows. And Lovejoy has the volume, so a doctor such as Suchak can perform up to thirty D & Es a month, add a few tab locals and tab gens each week, and make $300,000 a year. With that kind of clout I should be able to reduce the physician's take from each D & E, Allene thinks. Something to consider for next year.

Carye walks in and takes a seat across from Allene's desk. More figures. These show an increase this year in welfare abortions. Carye estimates welfare cases must now be 15 to 20 percent of all abortions at Lovejoy. A few years ago the figure was around 3 percent, Allene notes. Increasingly Lovejoy is becoming the place for women with little money of their own. More women with cash are going to the Downtown facility, and Carye tells Allene she thinks she knows at least one reason: Downtown, run as a cooperative, is doing a better job at holding the line on doctor's fees.

A doctor at Downtown gets just $130 for an early-second-trimester D & E instead of the $600 doctors are paid at Lovejoy, Carye says. On top of that, Allene points out, Lovejoy gets the majority of the most difficult and least profitable cases, the late-second-trimester abortions. A second glance at the statistics sheet shows a decrease over the previous year in the easier twelve-to-fifteen-week tab gens. Those are probably going to Downtown, Carye says.

Carye produces a chart showing annual abortion numbers for each year over the last decade. There's a blip in the numbers, 1990, when 5,719 abortions were performed at Lovejoy, their single biggest year. She points out that 1990 was the year of the Lovejoy Eight trial, with constant reporting in the newspapers about violent protests outside the facility. She and Allene puzzle out this seeming contradiction. Has the competitiveness of their business overshadowed any societal stigma or personal fear among patients? Has it gotten to the point, as it seemingly has for Andrew Burnett, at which any publicity is good publicity? Allene says she doesn't think so. She remembers too many calls that year from women asking about the protestors, women worried they would not be able to make it inside the building or deal with the emotional trauma.

Next they consider tubal ligations, Lovejoy's most frequently performed surgery other than abortion. Down from 139 to 107, Carye reports. Allene has an answer. Start putting pressure on Kaiser, the health maintenance organization (HMO), for a contract to perform all their tubals. Allene and Carye have been discussing this strategy for weeks, since Kaiser announced it was closing down Bess Kaiser Hospital, where the HMO has performed most of its surgeries.

Lovejoy's problem is its notoriety as an abortion facility. For those who might forget, there are Doc and Hugh and the others to remind them. Even so, Lovejoy would be a natural contractor for Kaiser's tubals, Allene says, since they already perform all of Kaiser's abortions. Now they just need to convince administrators at Kaiser that the protests are mild enough that patients requiring tubals won't mind coming to Lovejoy.

Plastic surgeries are down about two a month, Carye announces. Only two local plastic surgeons are willing to work out of Lovejoy. One has begun cutting back his practice and the other is using a hospital closer to his office. At this point there's not much chance of luring plastic surgery business to Lovejoy, Allene says, so let's not spend too much energy on it. Besides, there's little profit. A tubal ligation generally takes about thirty minutes and is billed at $1,115, of which Lovejoy keeps $400. A face-lift ties up one of the surgical rooms for six hours, for which Lovejoy might only get $550, while the surgeon makes up to $4,000.

Carye exits Allene's office and returns with the day's patient count, and thus the year's final tally. Today 21 women have had abortions at Lovejoy, bringing the monthly count up to 384 and the yearly total to 4,045, an increase of 168 over the previous year. Both women smile.

Allowing themselves a little dream time, Allene and Carye speculate about someday bringing in arthroscopic surgeries. They know that as long as Lovejoy is identified as an abortion facility that scenario is about as likely as Carye and Suchak kissing at the office Christmas party. But the protests have been scaled down of late.

Throughout their conversation Allene has alternated between looking directly at Carye and filling out checks from the company ledger on her desk, annual bonuses for each Lovejoy employee. Outside, in the hallway, members of the Lovejoy staff have been milling about. The last of the day's patients has gone. A birthday celebration for one of the medical assistants is about to begin in the staff lounge, as soon as Carye and Allene arrive. Her head still down as she signs the remaining checks, Allene with nonchalance hands one over to Carye and says, "Carye, I love you more than life itself." Carye looks at the check and begins weeping. Last week she told Thom that if this year's bonus was $1,000, the two of them would go to Italy together next spring. The check is for $5,000.

Before the two women head out the door to the staff celebration Carye mentions that she took a call this morning from the Feminist Majority Foundation. The foundation is interested in buying Lovejoy's $8.2 million judgment and pursuing the collection.

Screw this, Carye thinks, setting down the telephone. The thought passes, the momentary anger fades. Time to get creative.

She has been speaking with Marissa. Marissa, nineteen years old, a single mother already, trying to raise her own child while working as a nanny for $1,600 a month. And $450 of that goes for child care while she works. Not that the government cares, Carye thinks. Carye is well aware of the numbers that matter. In this case Marissa is making $37 a month too much to qualify for state health care. She is, as they say in Oregon, over the line. And most nannies don't get health insurance.

Marissa first called last week from one of the city's other clinics. The ultrasound showed her at twenty-one weeks, and they weren't willing to do an abortion beyond twenty weeks. They suggested she call Lovejoy. But first the clinic was charging Marissa $100 for the ultrasound and a doctor's exam. Which led to Carye screaming at the clinic's administrator over the phone: "You're sending me this patient, and she had $800 and now she has $700?"

The clinic dropped the $100 charge, which did little to solve Marissa's basic problem. She's been able to save the $800, but an abortion at twenty-one weeks will run her $1,200. And if she waits until twenty-two weeks, the price will become $1,300. At twenty-three weeks it's $1,400.

Oregon offers one of the country's most progressive state health care plans. In an attempt to approach its goal of having every citizen of the state medically insured, it lowers income barriers and rations services. In essence the state formulated a list containing every conceivable medical procedure and then went through the arduous process of ranking the procedures in a sort of societal cost/benefit analysis. Pre-natal care—more important or less than heart bypass? Each year the legislature decides at what level it will fund the plan, and depending on the amount of money available, a line is drawn on the list. All procedures above the line will be paid for by the state, and those below the line will not. Assuming your earnings are below the qualifying requirement.

Abortions have always been above the line, so when the Oregon Health Plan went into effect two years ago extending coverage to more Oregonians, it changed the way business was conducted at every medical facility in the state. Previously at Lovejoy about half the patients who came for abortions without private health insurance qualified for state assistance. Now nearly 90 percent of them do. Marissa, at $1,600 in earnings a month, is one of the unlucky few.

Marissa told Carye she could pay Lovejoy $700 now and the other $500 out of her paychecks over the next few months. Carye reads her as honest and responsible. She also knows that once an abortion is performed with the patient promising later payment, the money rarely materializes. Part of the reason certainly is financial. Some of it may be that once a woman has an abortion she wants to leave the experience as far behind her as she can as quickly as she can. For someone with a bleak financial picture to begin with, these bills are easy to dismiss. So Lovejoy shouldn't count on the $500. But Carye schedules an appointment for Marissa to begin her procedure in two days.

Carye recalls her days at the city's nonprofit abortion clinic. When presented with women such as Marissa she would send them to Lovejoy, knowing they would get their abortions even if they could not pay. Now she's at Lovejoy and it's not so simple. Allene is willing to give away about one abortion a month, but Carye knows before she takes a case to Allene she had better first have exhausted every other alternative. And this would be a big one to give away. The $700 Marissa can pay will just about cover the cost of surgical supplies, staff time, and Lovejoy's insurance, Carye thinks. The basic overhead, which doesn't even include the surgeon's fee—$600.

Carye considers which doctor might be willing to waive his fee. Suchak hasn't had a freebie in a while. She thinks she will approach him first, then see Allene about discounting Lovejoy's charge. If Suchak refuses to take the case on, she will go to Dr. Lane, who has never refused her. But Suchak should be first—he's making the most money out of Lovejoy.

About twice a week Carye is faced with a patient who wants an abortion but cannot afford one. For most she can find an administrative solution. But Lovejoy is not a collective or a nonprofit feminist organization. There may still be room for some clever maneuvering with Marissa, however.

Carye has already told Marissa to call NARAL, the National Abortion Rights Action League. The local chapter maintains a special fund and sometimes will give a woman $100 toward an abortion. And Carye urged Marissa to go after her ex-boyfriend for the $500. She even provided a strategy.

The ex-boyfriend said he didn't want to be involved. Carye explained to Marissa the state's policy requiring fathers to pay for child support. When the child of an unmarried mother receives public assistance, the state often pursues paternity testing to determine the father, who can then be required to make monthly payments for child support until the child reaches age twenty-one.

"Tell the boyfriend you can't afford the abortion," Carye says, "but don't let him know you might be able to have it done anyway. Put it this way: He can pay $500 now to help you get the abortion or force you to have the child. Then he can wait twenty weeks and risk paying $450 a month for the next twenty-one years. I think it's up to him to see if he takes the bet."

Carye doesn't know if Marissa will take her advice. But meanwhile she plots her own strategy. She makes a mental list of her friends with extra cash and decides she will call one or two of them before asking Allene to give away the procedure. Which still leaves the problem of the surgical team. Doctors aren't the only ones in the operating room. Anesthesiologists also get paid on a per case basis, and they are notoriously more reluctant than surgeons when it comes to forgoing a fee.

Anesthesiologists maintain a more anonymous relationship with a patient than surgeons. In many cases they do not know anything about her, even her name. They are technicians who often view time as their only marketable commodity.

Carye recalls approaching an anesthesiologist about a freebie a few years back. The patient was a Russian immigrant who had been raped. When Carye made her request, the anesthesiologist told Carye, "What's the point of coming in to work if I'm giving it away?"

So both a doctor and an anesthesiologist will have to be convinced to care for Marissa free of charge. Difficult, but not impossible. Another option occurs to Carye. Years ago in a similar situation she contacted the Religious Coalition for Abortion Rights, an organization of religious groups trying to counter the anti-abortion work of their more conservative brethren, and they helped out. It might be time to try them again.

Rising from her seat, Carye slowly walks over to Allene's office. She mentions Marissa's case and the possibility of Lovejoy providing a discount but she does it in an almost hypothetical way, not pressing Allene for a commitment, just letting her know it's out there. Only as a last resort will she ask Allene to give the procedure away, and she knows how she will do it if all other options fall through. She will have Marissa come in one day and introduce herself to Allene. If Allene meets the woman, she's practically taking her home, Carye reflects. Over the years many patients who made their way to Lovejoy but had no place to sleep ended up in Allene's house overnight.

Returning to her office Carye muses on the many ways that money drives the machine that is Lovejoy. Yesterday she saw Tom Donovan, one of Lovejoy's surgeons, walk through the doors of the operating room to the snack machine in the second-floor lobby. Still dressed in surgical garb he used a key to unlock the vending machine, removed the handfuls of coins that had been deposited, and filled it with new cans of soft drink and packets of crackers.

Donovan runs a snack machine distributorship on the side and last year convinced Allene to let him install a machine at Lovejoy. But the sight of a doctor going straight from surgery to loading soft drinks while patients looked on was too much for Carye. "If I ever again see you out there servicing the vending machine in your scrubs, I'm going to kick you until you're dead," she told Donovan.

*

Lauren, admitting at the front desk, has only Lovejoy's steady stream of patients to service today, and she's not enjoying it. Her job has her alternating between receptionist and bookkeeper, and she much prefers the latter. Lauren is a businesslike twenty-eight-year-old who came to Lovejoy earlier this year. She is also the single mother of a three-year-old boy. She has fashioned a distinctive look with retro sixties-style eyeglasses and short hair, and she presents a matter-of-fact countenance that keeps conversations rolling.

A few minutes ago she was upstairs in the business office when Jami, the receptionist, asked her to help out with a patient at the front window. Now downstairs, Lauren is confronted with a blond, seventeen-year-old girl, the girl's mother, and a complicated billing problem.

The family is from Washington state, just a few hours away. Because she lives at home the girl is covered by her parents' insurance. But that insurance comes courtesy of the United States government—Dad works at an air force base. And with conservatives controlling the national political agenda, the insurance plan for the armed forces, Champus, does not cover abortions unless the mother's life is threatened.

But this is no problem, the girl explains. As backup she holds a card for state medical insurance. Lauren is well aware that Washington state, like Oregon, pays for abortions. The only concern now is the additional paperwork. Lauren explains that she must first bill Champus. When Lovejoy's bill is returned to the family with a denial of coverage, they should send it to the state, which will pay for the abortion.

The flaw in that plan, the girl says, is if they bill Champus and the denial comes back in the mail, her father might see it. Dad doesn't know anything about this pregnancy.

Lauren says she has no choice. Washington will not consider the bill unless first notified that the family's primary insurer has denied coverage. "Basically, you'll have to guard the mailbox," she says.

The girl's mother reassures her daughter. "Oh, that's not a problem," she says.

Lauren returns upstairs and calls Champus to verify that the government is still not covering abortions. While there she glances at the Washington welfare coupon the girl has provided and notices that it does not indicate full medical coverage. Intended as backup because the state recognizes the limitations of Champus coverage, it can be used only for family planning. And that, Lauren knows, means it does not cover abortions. Which means the girl has two medical coverages and neither will pay for her procedure.

Back downstairs Lauren explains the situation. Exasperated, the girl says, "Can we pay cash for the procedure?" Lauren has to fight back a wince when she explains they may not even be able to do that—paying cash for a medical procedure when you are already covered by the state might be fraudulent. The state's policy as interpreted by Lauren is that if you have the cash to pay for an abortion, you shouldn't be getting state-assisted family planning.

The paradox would be laughable if this girl were not standing in front of her with a look of disbelief. Lauren is beginning to feel like Scrooge as she explains one more time why the family's insurance won't pay, the state welfare system won't pay, and Lovejoy cannot accept cash. Out of solutions, she suggests they proceed with the paperwork today and that the girl meet with a Lovejoy counselor on the assumption something will be worked out. She is even willing to schedule an appointment for an abortion next week. In the meantime, Lauren says, the girl needs to go back to her caseworker and explain the situation and ask for basic state medical coverage, which would pay for an abortion.

"What if she's not eligible?" asks the mother.

Lauren doesn't have an answer. And she wishes she were not so familiar with a system so unfair. She represses a desire to tell the girl that she is raising her son with no child support, that she makes $9 an hour at Lovejoy and that Lovejoy's medical insurance requires her to co-pay $220 a month, a sum she simply cannot afford. She does not qualify for state insurance. So Lauren and her son have no medical coverage at all.

Lauren has thought out her own plan of action in case her child should face a medical emergency. First she will go to the Oregon Health Sciences University, the hospital of choice for Oregon's indigent. She will insist the hospital bill her husband, from whom she is separated. Six months ago he lost his job and with it their medical insurance, but at least the problem will be his.

Bookkeeping at Lovejoy exposes all sort of strange situations, Lauren knows. Earlier this morning a dark-haired twenty-seven-year-old woman came into Lovejoy for a pregnancy test and counseling from Anneke. The test showed a first-trimester pregnancy, and the woman chose to make an appointment for a tab local. Anneke asked Lauren to verify the woman's insurance coverage, and when Lauren made the call she learned the woman's policy pays for 80 percent of billable expenses and carries a $250 yearly deductible, of which $66 had already been met.

Hanging up the telephone Lauren figured out that if Lovejoy billed the woman's health insurance, she would end up paying 20 percent of $530, which is the rate at which Lovejoy bills insurers for tab locals. The woman would also pay an extra $184, the balance of her yearly deductible. The total came to $290. On the other hand, if the woman simply paid cash for the abortion, it would cost her a total of $230. So sometimes medical insurance doesn't help all that much anyway, Lauren thought.

Lovejoy's two-tiered billing procedure is fairly standard throughout the medical industry, which prospers on a series of administrative winks and turned heads. When Lovejoy bills an insurer $530 for a tab local, it includes $200 for the doctor's fee and $330 for Lovejoy. Rarely will the $530 be paid in full; Lovejoy can expect payment at somewhere between 50 and 80 percent. The cash price of $230 breaks down to $75 for the doctor and $155 for Lovejoy.

This morning Lauren decided she would not keep silent. She explained the billing procedures and advised the woman to pay $230 cash for her abortion, then take the itemized statement from Lovejoy and submit it to her insurance company for reimbursement. The insurance company will probably send her a check for $46—20 percent of the $230—and her deductible will have been paid off for the year. The savings should amount to $106.

The woman reacted to this helpful information with disappointment. She had medical insurance, and yet she was being told it would cost her less to pay cash. And she did not have the cash with her today—Lovejoy accepts only cash, credit cards, and money orders, not personal checks—which meant rescheduling and coming back later in the week. But she could not dispute Lauren's math.

Lauren considers what she would do in this patient's situation. She doesn't have an extra $230 lying around. In fact, two years ago Lauren became pregnant and wanted an abortion that she could not afford. Privately she asked one of Lovejoy's doctors to help her out, and he performed the surgery in his office outside Lovejoy for free. Only a few of Lauren's close friends at Lovejoy and the doctor know.

As the Washington woman and her mother leave Lovejoy with an appointment for next week, Lauren surveys the rapidly filling lobby. This will be one hectic day, she recognizes. But extra help has arrived. Tim appears shortly after lunch in a crisp white shirt, perfectly creased slacks, and black tasseled loafers. His face and posture do not match the relaxed professional look. His cheeks are flushed, and as he walks down the hall he shuffles his feet. Clearly he is dragging. In addition to general fatigue, Tim's fluctuating temperature has been an indicator of his overall health. For weeks it will remain steady, then soar and drop as a wicked reminder that his disease is inevitably progressing. He reports to Allene that yesterday his temperature was 102 degrees.

But he has made it in today and he is needed. Just his presence energizes Allene. It is three weeks since Tim called and said he wanted to work again. As if AIDS has a devil's sense of humor, shortly after that call the weakness overtook him again. In the last week it has seemed to abate a bit.

Tim's first patient of the day provides an easy transition back to work. She is nineteen years old, mature for her age, Tim thinks. She has been living with her boyfriend for a year. Six months ago she decided to stop taking her birth control pills because of the side effects: She had been moody and bleeding more than usual. She and her boyfriend agreed to use condoms but during intercourse one of the condoms broke, so here she is.

The woman and her boyfriend both attend college and intend to get their degrees. She seems sure of herself and Tim does not see the need to counsel her much about the seriousness of abortion. Instead he spends about fifteen minutes educating her about birth control. They decide a diaphragm might be a sensible option. As the woman heads off for her tab local, Tim thinks counseling is a bit like riding a bike, especially with patients such as this.

Reading his second patient's intake form, Tim anticipates a bit more of a counseling challenge. Any twenty-one-year-old experiencing her sixth pregnancy must have more than a few issues, he thinks.

Just like old times, Tim has been taking his patients into the office directly across the hall from Allene's, now Carye's. When he goes into the lobby to call the patient's name, he falls back on an old habit of trying to figure out which woman she is and what she looks like before he called her name. Often, he thinks, he learns more from observing the lobby scene than from what patients actually tell him in their sessions.

In this case he notices the woman is accompanied by a man, probably a boyfriend, who looks pleasant enough. As he announces the woman's name he sees the man start to rise to accompany her, then return to his seat. Tim wonders if this reflects a tension between the two, but he is also aware that many men simply don't deal well with being at Lovejoy and talking about abortion. Tim looks for signs of anger in the man's posture but finds none.

"You're welcome to come back," Tim tells the man, who complies. Back in Carye's office Tim asks, "Are you two doing okay?" The man explains he has trouble dealing with medicine and hospitals. The woman begins her story.

She is raising a five-year-old son by herself. She delivered her child when she was eighteen. She has had five abortions since. She recently started taking birth control pills but her breasts began hurting, so she stopped. From the way she conveys this information, Tim surmises that the fact that she could then become pregnant was not a concern. The woman exhibits little emotion throughout the session. An abortion apparently is not something to get excited about.

So Tim steers the conversation to birth control. "Are you planning on having any more children?" he asks.

"Absolutely not."

"Have you thought about having your tubes tied?"

"Can I have it done here?"

Tim knows the answer, but he also takes a moment to consider the evidence. Five abortions by age twenty-one and the woman's attitude weigh in heavily on one side. Still, she is just twenty-one, and he wonders if someday she might want another child and regret having had her tubes tied.

Basically the decision is not his, so Tim decides not to spend time on the topic. Besides, there is a fail-safe: The tubal cannot be done immediately. First the woman has to deal with her pregnancy. She is on welfare but federal funds will not pay for a tubal. The Oregon Health Plan will cover the operation, but a state law requires that she not be pregnant when she signs the consent form for the tubal. Also, she must wait thirty-two days after signing the form before she has the operation.

A privately insured woman in a similar position would have the abortion performed and her tubes tied as part of one operation and under one anesthetic. In this case all Tim can do is schedule the woman for an abortion, have her sign the consent form the day she leaves Lovejoy after her abortion, and hope she returns a month later for her tubal. Considering the woman, he's not sure if she will follow through. As he leaves her at the front desk scheduling an appointment, he heads out the back door to join Carye and Lauren on the bench for a smoke.

A few minutes later Lauren is back at the reception window. Anneke is sitting behind her; the small self-contained area serves as a general lounge area for counselors and downstairs staff taking a break. Sign-in sheets, a bulletin board, and a coffee pot are scattered about; a bathroom and storage area lead off the back of the room.

Anneke, having just finished a counseling session, is filling out her paperwork. Her head is down and a young woman, about Anneke's age, walks through the front door a few feet away. The woman is short and nervous-looking with curly blond hair. A few steps into Lovejoy she looks around, begins to walk back toward the reception window, stops, continues a few more steps to where Lauren waits, then hesitates again. "Can I help you?" Lauren asks. The woman turns around and walks back out the front door without replying.

Behind Lauren, Anneke had lifted her head for a moment when the woman first walked in the front door, but she had returned to her paperwork as the woman performed her little waiting room dance. Head still down, she whispers to Lauren, "I know her."

"Who?" Lauren asks.

The woman has disappeared.

"Did she leave?" Anneke says. "Oh no."

Anneke hurries out to the lobby and sees the blond-haired woman rushing down the street. Anneke pauses to consider the appropriate action, which provides the woman time to get into her car. By now Anneke knows what has occurred. The woman, an old college friend, was surprised to see a familiar face when she came in for an abortion and Anneke, that familiar face, scared her away.

Anneke and Lauren check the appointment book and find the friend's name. She is scheduled for a second-trimester D & E.

"She needs to come in," Lauren says.

Anneke is distraught. She decides to ask Carye what she should do—call and explain to the friend that what happens at Lovejoy is confidential, or maintain the cloak of impersonality and leave the woman alone.

For the next hour Anneke moves about between counseling sessions like a ballplayer during a rain delay, anxious but with no field on which to play. Both Tim and Carye are busy with patients. Finally Anneke cannot wait any longer for advice. She calls the friend and leaves a guarded message asking the woman to return her call—guarded because the woman may have roommates who don't know their friend is halfway through a pregnancy.

Back behind Carye's desk, Tim is wondering if the woman facing him has been raped. She's twenty-one years old and this is her fourth pregnancy. She is raising a sixteen-month-old child, and she has had one previous abortion and a miscarriage.

On her intake form, under "Why are you terminating this pregnancy?" the woman has written, simply, "Because of how it was conceived." Twice now Tim has tried to maneuver the conversation to ascertain her motivation but the woman is sticking to a pat answer: "It's the circumstances of this pregnancy." Each time she delivers this reply with an emphasis that makes it clear she will not further discuss the topic.

Tim asks her about birth control. This time the woman replies, "Abstinence," and finishes with the same dead silence and direct stare that make it clear her part of the conversation is over. At the end of fifteen minutes Tim recognizes he knows little more than when he started, and he is beginning to wonder if his counseling skills might not be a little rusty after all.

The woman is nearly nineteen weeks pregnant, and Tim silently questions why she waited so long before coming in. He asks if the decision to abort was a difficult one.

"No, I didn't know exactly how far I was until last week," the woman replies.

Tim looks down at the intake form; sometimes it can offer more mystery than education. The woman admits to multiple sexual partners and IV drug use. She has brought a friend along, another woman. Concerned about the combination of a general anesthetic and drugs, Tim asks how recently she has taken drugs.

The pregnant woman turns to her friend and asks, "When was the last time I did drugs?" The friend answers, "January." The two explain that they met at an Alcoholics Anonymous meeting in January and have been in treatment since then. Their use of AA terminology convinces Tim they are telling the truth. Ten minutes later Suchak has inserted lams, beginning her three-day procedure.

Meanwhile, Tim relaxes on a seat outside Allene's office. He says he's been a little nervous today, but it is the kind of buzz he has missed "because you don't know what's going to walk in the door, and that's what keeps you here." He looks more energetic than when he walked in that door three hours ago.

Carye and Allene surround him in the hallway and the three drift into Allene's office. The two women are making no attempt to conceal their glee at seeing Tim back at Lovejoy; their smiles tell all.

Tim is describing his day's patients. His voice has a distinctive way of turning falsetto when comically emphasizing a word or phrase at the end of a sentence. "I just never thought it would happen to me. 'Help.'"

Suchak, passing by Allene's office, pokes his head in. "It's so nice to have you back here," he says to Tim.

Tim and Carye wander back to Carye's office, their office today. Carye points out the brass box with Tim's business cards behind the paper clip holder, still in place though this has been Carye's desk for three years. The woman who cleans the offices was going to take the box away one night but Carye, working late and surprised at the force of her own voice, yelled at her to put it back.

LOVEJOY

Tim's cologne and old azidothymidine (AZT) prescriptions remain in the desk's bottom right-hand drawer, along with his old telephone messages. Carye never felt the need to assert her control over this office, and her heart never wanted to.

The day is near an end but Tim says he will take one more patient, a tab local. Carye heads out the door as Tim sits opposite an attractive blond woman and her boyfriend. She is thirty-two years old, divorced, a waitress with a five-year-old child, and she and the boyfriend appear very middle class to Tim. Early in the conversation Tim takes note of her easy sense of humor and he relaxes. "Finally," he thinks. "A normal one." He likes this woman.

Then the session takes a turn. Tim asks the woman if she would consider taking birth control pills.

"I can't take the pill because I have a brain tumor," the woman says. She's too young for that, Tim thinks. He feels his heart sinking.

The story follows. Six months ago this woman was told that she had a brain tumor and that she probably would live another year or two. She began radiation and chemotherapy. She and the boyfriend were careful about birth control, using condoms and spermicidal foam. Then came a weekend at the coast with the condoms forgotten at home, a romantic evening during which they got carried away. Now she is six weeks pregnant and certain she wants an abortion. If she can beat the cancer she might someday want another child, but this is not the time, she says.

"She's okay with it. She's gone through her stuff," Tim thinks. Certainly he knows all about the stuff. And he finds his own spirits uplifted. He and the woman end up comparing experiences with insurance coverage and Social Security—lifelines for the terminally ill—a thirty-two-year-old waitress and a forty-six-year-old abortion counselor with more in common than they ever could have thought possible.

At five P.M. Tim is at Carye's desk while Carye talks to Anneke just outside the doorway. Anneke still is upset about her friend's departure. Carye tells Anneke that her friend's situation could end up better this way. If the woman gets over the shock of seeing Anneke here, she will return, knowing a friend will be present to help her through the ordeal. But Anneke cannot see beyond the facts: Her friend is twenty-one weeks pregnant according to the appointment book, and if she doesn't come back within the next couple of weeks, she is going to end up with a child she doesn't want.

Carye points out that her friend undoubtedly was conflicted before she came into Lovejoy. Otherwise she would not have waited until twenty-one weeks before making an appointment. Experience has taught her that women who wait that long either are practicing denial or their lives are well out of balance. "There's a reason she's a D & E," Carye says. Anneke still looks sad as she prepares to leave.

An unusually busy day is nearly over. Carye walks into her office and asks Tim, "If it gets crazy tomorrow, can I call you?" Tim, still seated behind her desk, says yes, but admits that he is very tired. He had hoped to get out the door by 4 P.M. based on a long-held theory of his: The most "messed up" patients tend to schedule toward the end of the day as a symptom of their ambivalence and general emotional problems. But here he is at 5 P.M., and both he and Carye have fallen prey to fatigue.

Forced to vacate her office while Tim counseled, Carye finds herself behind on the day's paperwork. Her gaze shifts from desktop to Tim. "Get away from my desk," she snaps. She has surprised herself. Laughing, she says, "I must be getting possessive. I've never done that." Tim yields the seat.

Carye cannot outlast Tim. She wants to go home, but Tim has come home. Well past 5 P.M. he's in the front lobby throwing out last week's gladiola, changing the water in the vase, putting in the new flowers he has picked up at the wholesaler and arranging them just right. Tim and Carye leave together, turning out the lights and arming the security system as they go.

*

Two days later Carye takes a call from Marissa, who wants to reschedule her appointment. She explains that her pregnancy has caused her to miss a few days of work and her reduced hours this month might bring her earnings low enough to qualify for the Oregon Health Plan. If she qualifies for state assistance she can have her abortion free of charge within forty-eight hours. Last week Carye suggested Marissa keep her check stubs for just this possibility, but now Carye wonders if it was sound advice. Marissa was twenty-one weeks when she first called and she is taking a big gamble in delaying her abortion.

Chapter Seven

When she turned twenty-seven, Carye and Thom decided to confront the question that had silently plagued their lives for the three years of their marriage. Carye could not conceive as a result of the leukemia she had suffered as a young woman. But at various times during their life together each had expressed a desire for a child and adoption seemed the natural alternative.

After months of discussion Carye and Thom decided to adopt. They spent weekday evenings filling out the endless forms required by adoption agencies and attending eight weeks of adoption classes. A social worker came to their house for a home study, the final step in the approval process. They were placed on waiting lists and told their time would come.

One morning soon thereafter Carye answered the phone and listened to her sister, Joanne, explain she had cancer. Carye agreed to nurse her in the final year of her life. Through the succeeding months Carye's desire for a child somehow lost its intensity. Starting a family went from a concrete goal to an abstract idea for the couple. Had you asked Carye during that stressful year if she still wanted a child, she probably would have answered yes. But her answer would not have been the same yes as months before.

Joanne died in January 1991. By that time the answer was no longer even yes. Carye felt drained and knew she did not have enough nurturing left in her to parent as she would like. It was two years before she and Thom sat down and finally decided to give up on the idea of children. By then, though, silence and inaction had spoken loudly enough.

Carye adores children. She loves to listen to other people talk about their children's latest playground breakthroughs and potty-training travails. Friends depend on her for baby-sitting, and as their children have aged, more than a few have sent Carye their adolescents for a week. Kids listen to her, maybe because she never learned to talk as a parent. But she knows now that she will never raise her own. There is an empty spot in Carye's soul.

Three days after the close of Lovejoy's fiscal year Heather arrives for an abortion. Close to six feet tall and strawberry blond, Heather has managed to hide her pregnancy from everyone in her life. Heather, twenty-two, has long limbs and big bones but she is not heavyset. In fact, she is very athletic-looking and played tennis on her high school team.

Heather lives in a small town east of Portland. Her father runs a bowling alley, and her mother, a housewife, has often told Heather abortion is a sin.

Two days earlier Heather suspected she might be pregnant, so she went to a physician for a pregnancy test. The test was positive. Instantly Heather knew abortion was her only option. She also knew she would have to have it quickly and keep it a secret, which meant she could not use her parents' medical insurance. The next day Heather rushed out to the state office building in a town near her own and applied for state medical assistance. The day after that she came to Lovejoy.

It is mid-afternoon when Carye heads out to the front lobby to meet her next patient. Retreating back to her office with Heather in tow, Carye is thinking that this young woman does not look pregnant. Rather than begin with a counseling session Carye leads

Heather straight back to the exam room for an ultrasound. Might as well find out what we're dealing with before beginning the discussion, she thinks.

As Heather leans back on the examination table, Carye's eyes drift to her stomach and she knows Heather has made a mistake on her intake form—she is beyond twenty-one weeks. As a rule of thumb, when the expansion in a woman's belly begins at the belly button the woman is about twenty weeks pregnant, Carye knows. Heather's bump is well above her belly button.

Without comment Carye proceeds with the ultrasound. Casually she asks, "How long have you known you were pregnant?"

"A couple months," Heather answers. A tremor in Heather's voice makes Carye wonder if the young woman is starting to confront what must be becoming obvious to her. In fact, Heather has been praying during the ultrasound, praying that she is indeed only twenty-one weeks pregnant.

Carye looks at the ultrasound picture and sees a fetal head down by Heather's pelvis. Ultrasound pictures are fuzzy and people unaccustomed to reading them rarely can tell what they are looking at. Heather sees nothing troubling in the picture. But Carye, still silent, has paged Suchak, who is upstairs performing D & Es.

Suchak is rushed; patients are waiting upstairs. Immediately Carye hands Suchak the ultrasound picture. Heather is still on her back, unaware that this is not standard procedure. Suchak, equally unaware of Heather's situation, takes a glance at the photo and says, "Oh my, it can be any time."

Heather's head jerks up and toward Carye with the wide-eyed look of a nocturnal animal caught out in full daylight. Turning to Suchak, Carye says, "I just needed a reality check." "Good luck," Suchak offers as he breezes out the door, leaving Carye wondering for which woman the comment is intended.

Ultrasounds are inexact, Carye says, but Heather is around thirty-six weeks pregnant.

"Well how far along is that?" asks Heather. "Is that like five months?"

"No," Carye says. "You're there." Anywhere from thirty-nine weeks on is considered a full-term pregnancy, but a child three or four weeks premature will usually survive outside the womb with no problem.

Heather begins shaking her head back and forth. "No, no, no," she says.

"Let's go back to my office and talk," Carye says in the gentlest voice she can muster. As soon as Carye's office door is closed behind them Heather says, "I feel so stupid."

Before responding Carye silently invokes a personal reminder— not to bring her own feelings into this session. She is amazed that this seemingly responsible young woman can carry a child she does not want to full term and then end up here, but there is no room for judgment now. And certainly no time. She forces her voice to go flat, to eliminate any tone or nuance that might indicate to Heather that she is being judged.

"Have you known you were pregnant awhile?" Carye asks. Her strategy is to first assess the depth of Heather's denial. Did she truly not know she was pregnant for thirty-six weeks?

Heather begins talking dates, a safe topic. Also an easy one. Heather does not have a boyfriend. She has had sex only two times in the last year, both unintended events with a longtime friend. The last time was Valentine's Day, twenty-one weeks ago. The other time she and her friend got carried away was way back in October—Halloween. About thirty-five weeks ago.

Carye couldn't have scripted a better opening for lightening the mood. "Do you, like, have a thing about holidays?"

"We have two options here," Carye continues after a pause. "One is we have to talk to your family. And the second is we can talk about an adoption if you feel like this is something you can't do."

"I . . . can't . . . have . . . this . . . baby," Heather says. Carye can tell from her measured, subdued tone that this is not an open question.

Heather explains that when she first learned she was pregnant, two days ago, she immediately thought of one of her best friends, who had become pregnant two years ago. Heather's mother would not even let Heather's girlfriend in the house. Heather, with little money and a middle-class future in sight, still lives at home. If her parents discover her predicament, she likely will have to leave. That would mean finding a job with which she could support herself, dropping out of community college, and mortgaging the future toward which she has so steadfastly been working.

Quickly Heather and Carye begin discussing adoption. Heather's primary concern is hiding the pregnancy from her parents. Carye is amazed she has managed to do so up to this point. Friends, coworkers, parents—nobody has noticed. But secrecy will be harder to maintain now, Carye points out. Maybe impossible. In the weeks ahead Heather's pregnancy will become staggeringly obvious to those around her, Carye insists, not only as Heather's physical shape changes, but also as she begins to feel more of the effects of late-stage pregnancy. Even if Heather somehow could maintain her illusion, Carye says, where will she live when she is recovering after giving birth? The only silver lining Carye can see is that at least Heather is in her eighth or ninth month of pregnancy and will not have to continue her charade for long.

Repeatedly Carye asks Heather for the name of someone she can talk to about this. Heather insists she can tell no one. When Carye tries to talk about the pregnancy and its circumstances, Heather insists her Halloween/Valentine's Day confusion satisfactorily explains why she is sitting in an office at an abortion center thirty-six weeks pregnant.

The session has developed a rhythm; more practical details are discussed. Carye tells Heather of an attorney she works with in adoption cases. And she briefly mentions Jim and Carla, a couple she knows who have been desperately hoping to adopt a child. They are close friends of one of Lovejoy's nurses. Heather can be shown the couple's portfolio at the attorney's office, and she will be introduced to other couples if she desires.

Carye is taking a big step. She has never before tried to steer a patient toward putting a child up for adoption with someone of her acquaintance. This takes her out of the role she is accustomed to as counselor and places her in the role of baby broker. She has spent many hours considering whether she should or could do this, knowing it divides her loyalties. Though she is not a close friend of Jim and Carla, they are far from strangers. Whether she wants to or not, Carye will be looking out for their welfare as well as Heather's. This is not a comfortable position for her. Carye would prefer to focus on helping one person—Heather—through what she knows will be a difficult process. But Jim and Carla have been searching for a child for two years and Carye believes they would make wonderful parents, so she decided a few months ago to help them if she could. She reminds herself that the chances are good that Heather will not even choose Jim and Carla as the adoptive couple, and that's assuming Heather follows through with her decision, made just moments ago, to put the baby up for adoption. Still, a sigh passes through Carye's lips as she considers the possible emotional and personal fallout that could result from the worst-case scenario in a private adoption—the birthmother changing her mind after giving birth.

Discussing the adoption process has jolted Heather from her focus on keeping her secret. "How will I know when it's happening?" she asks.

Carye considers the question for a moment and realizes they are getting into territory with which she is not familiar. She has attended thousands of abortions, but she has never given birth. "I don't know," she answers. She asks Heather to wait in her office a moment.

Across the hallway Carye finds Allene at her desk poring over financial records. "I have a patient who is thirty-six weeks and I was hoping you'd talk to her," she says. Carye hurriedly explains Heather's situation to Allene, then brings Heather in.

Allene does not take Carye's kid-gloves approach. She is very direct. She is not a counselor for this woman, she's the voice of experience, the woman who gave birth to five children.

Heather says she does not understand how her mother has not noticed the pregnancy. At the dinner table last night her shirt began moving up and down as the baby bounced about. She looked at the faces of her family members but nobody had seen a thing.

"Your mother doesn't look at you," Allene says. As she speaks the words she knows how hurtful the idea must be, but how important it is that Heather begin to grasp the reality of her life.

"Now that you aren't able to be in denial anymore about this, you're going to know your body," Allene says by way of addressing Heather's original question. Then Allene describes labor, and the kicking feet and breast swelling Heather has already begun feeling.

Allene starts talking about her childbearing experiences. She tells Heather her first labor took only three hours and that she chose to have four more children. Her tone is matter-of-fact, conveying the idea that childbirth is the most natural of occurrences. Later in the afternoon, alone with Carye, Allene will say with a knowing tilt of her head, "What I didn't tell her was, in my other labors, it took a while longer." By the time she leaves Allene's office Heather appears to be adjusting to her new reality. And she has an offer of a temporary place to live after the birth—from Allene.

Back in her own office Carye asks Heather what she's looking for in an adoptive couple, and Heather answers, "A stable income. That they really really want it. Not that they figured they need a baby to go with their two cars and garage." Secretly Carye is pleased at this response. Heather is not Becky.

Becky is another young woman who came in too late for an abortion, a brassy, savvy, effervescent seventeen-year-old heroine just waiting for her role, still stuck in the life of the streets with drug-dealing parents and no place to turn. She came to Lovejoy in February. Carye counseled Becky, befriended her, helped arrange her adoption, saw her once a week throughout what remained of her pregnancy as counselor, confidante, and friend. Carye kept silent as Becky chose an adoptive couple Carye did not like. When she relinquished her child, Becky suffered the greatest emotional pain Carye has ever witnessed in a human being.

Heather returns to Lovejoy two days later. She has met with the attorney Carye recommended and decided to give her child up to Jim and Carla. But Heather insists she does not want to meet them. Carye resists confronting Heather about this. She knows it is a common first reaction for a birthmother, Heather's new identity in the lexicon of social workers and counselors. Carye wonders if this is a form of self-punishment, as if the birthmother is telling herself, "I don't deserve to meet them." But Carye knows that soon, if Heather is like the other birthmothers she has counseled, curiosity about the adoptive family, and eventually heartfelt concern for the welfare of the child, will take precedence. Then Heather will ask for a meeting.

Yesterday Dr. Donovan examined Heather at his private office and confirmed that she was at least thirty-six weeks. Heather has maintained her secret—nobody outside Lovejoy knows she is pregnant. Carye wonders how long Heather will be able to conceal her pregnancy from her mother and father. When she gives up on that lie, Carye thinks, it will be a sign that her wall of denial is finally starting to show some cracks. Then again, maybe she can carry the masquerade through.

Today Carye and Heather talk about the crucial questions that are addressed in all modern adoptions. Long gone are the days when social service agencies took newborns away from birthmothers and dismissed them. Today the power of choice is with the biological parent. The two women discuss a birth contract. Would Heather like this to become an open or closed adoption? Does she want any visitation rights after the child is relinquished? Annual updates with pictures from Jim and Carla? Carye prefers her birthmothers choose to have some contact with the child after the adoption is finalized, something on the order of a visit or two during the first year. Her first concern here is Heather's welfare, and she thinks such contact makes it easier for birthmothers to get on with their lives. Heather is not so sure.

Toward the end of this second session Carye asks, "Do you want to talk to them on the phone?"

"I want to meet those people," Heather responds with newfound certainty.

A meeting is arranged. Carye hands Heather a pad of paper and a pen and asks her to begin a list of questions for Jim and Carla.

Heather begins. "What would you do if the child is born disabled?" "What would you do if your child became pregnant someday or if it's a boy that impregnates a young girl?" "What would you do if you discovered your child uses drugs or alcohol?" The questions of a teenager, Carye muses, responding to her own life in a rigid family. Heather continues. "How did you get together?" "What do you do when you're not working?" "What are your families like?" Carye is smiling inside, pleased at the insight Heather's questions show. She's getting involved in the process, Carye thinks, past the denial. She cares.

The next day Heather and Carye meet after work at Fuddrucker's, a large self-service restaurant in the suburbs, as anonymous a place as can be found. They take seats at a table in the rear. Heather is wearing an oversized rugby shirt and gym shorts, clearly not dressing up for this meeting. Outside the temperature is over ninety degrees. When Jim and Carla arrive there are smiles all around, but there is little connection. Four Pepsis sit on the table in front of them, but nobody chooses to eat.

"Look," Carye begins. "Everybody's nervous. So we're just going to pretend that everyone's nervous."

Jim and Carla are in their early forties, both successful in business, childless. Three years ago Carla became pregnant and delivered a stillborn child. They are affectionate, occasionally holding hands beneath the table.

Carye is silently comparing Jim and Carla to the couple who adopted Becky's child four months ago. Even at a first meeting Carye did not feel comfortable with them. She saw two people who wanted a baby so much that they would do anything, including lie, to get one. But Becky was impressed by their affluence.

Carye wonders if Jim or Carla will ask Heather whether she uses drugs or what kind of grades she has gotten in school. That would be a tip-off, Carye thinks, that they are the wrong couple, at least the wrong couple if it were Carye's child to adopt out. Are they looking at Heather as breeding stock instead of as a person? she wonders.

But Heather is the one asking questions this afternoon, and the decisions are hers to make. Carye's role here is ill-defined at best. Counselor? Friend? Intermediary? Matchmaker? Conventionally in meetings of this sort Heather would be accompanied by her attorney.

The meeting eventually attains a relaxed atmosphere. Heather asks the first question on her list: Will they take the baby if it is born with a major defect? Jim and Carla give the question a moment's thought and say yes, up to a point. They admit that they would not feel capable if it should be a defect as major as, say, Down's syndrome. Carye interjects that if Heather delivers a baby with Down's syndrome, the baby will be placed somewhere. She knows that, in fact, there are waiting lists of families willing to adopt such babies. Heather's eyes indicate she is comforted by this bit of information.

As Jim and Carla learn more about Heather's predicament, they offer to serve as Heather's birth coaches and to let her live with them and the baby while she is recovering from the delivery. At the end of the meal Heather asks them in a voice with more than a bit of little girl showing through, "Did you really mean that?" And that is when Carye knows that a match has been made.

An hour later Carye and Heather are shopping at a local mall for maternity clothes that emphasize concealment.

J U L Y   1 4

While Tim is convinced that the most difficult patients arrive at the end of the day, some of the staff at Lovejoy hold to a similar theory that the most unreliable patients tend to make their appointments for Friday. Nobody can cite any evidence, it's more intuition based on years of occasionally chaotic Fridays. One explanation is that women who wait until the last day of the week to come in are more likely to have been postponing any action. Their indecision could be a symptom of an inner turmoil, and it usually makes their experience at Lovejoy that much more difficult for everybody involved.

Behind the receptionist's desk this morning Anneke is still trying to reach her old school friend, the young woman who bolted last week when she saw Anneke at this same spot. Anneke's calls have not been returned, and the young counselor has been disturbed by thoughts that she might be partly responsible for an unwanted child being born. And she has been thinking of her friend, probably very frightened and distressed by now. Anneke cannot help but remember that when her friend came into Lovejoy she was alone.

Carye, too, has been conducting a fruitless telephone search. Marissa, so desperate to find a way to pay for her abortion, has disappeared, and now she has waited too long if an abortion is really what she wanted. But Marissa does not stay on Carye's mind as she settles in behind her desk. Heather has taken over her life.

When Heather walks into Carye's office Allene is behind the desk in her own office, the door open as usual. All but the most sensitive conversations in Allene's office take place with the door open. These most private discussions are often held at a neighborhood restaurant because Allene is concerned that her closed door would alert the staff that something critical is being decided, and rumors and anxiety may result. Also, Allene likes to be able to look out at the front lobby from her chair.

Concern etches Allene's face as she watches Heather walk by. Allene has seen this happen before, seen Carye become absorbed in the mothering and counseling that are so naturally needed by women giving their children up for adoption. Something about these adoption cases releases Carye from her normal role of abortion counselor and it has to stop, Allene thinks. This is not her job.

Today Heather is wearing a pretty blue ribbon in her hair and pink plastic earrings that look like bows. She is another in the seemingly endless procession of Lovejoy patients who are making adult decisions but whose dress and sometimes manner cry out "little girl." More than many of those others, though, Heather is an intelligent young woman, directed and industrious. She works as a cocktail waitress and occasional cook at a local tavern—5 P.M. to midnight Monday through Friday and 11 A.M. to 3 A.M. on weekends. On top of that she attends community college two days a week. Still, she is here and thirty-six weeks pregnant.

Carye begins by showing Heather the forms that John, the attorney, has sent over. They are consent forms; once she has signed them after the birth, Heather will have no recourse—the baby will no longer be hers.

The papers also include the agreement that Heather has worked out with Jim and Carla stipulating visitation rights in the first six months and annual letters and pictures tracing the child's progress. Carye notices how anxious Heather appears while wading through the document's legal jargon.

"John and I both are working for you," Carye says. "These forms are to make sure that if you're changing your mind or having any problems . . ."

"Then you'll slap me," Heather finishes with a smile.

Exhaustion shows on Heather's face. Her work and school schedule would be demanding enough without the added toll of a thirty-six-week pregnancy. The pressure of keeping her secret from everybody in her life adds to the fatigue—she can never let down her guard. Heather has not yet missed a work shift or a day of school. Another waitress at the tavern was fired last week and Heather's boss has asked her to work extra hours. Even Carye inadvertently adds to the demands when she advises Heather to try to get ahead with her school work, because when she is recovering from the delivery Heather will probably miss a week of classes.

Work is on Heather's mind. "I feel like an asshole leaving them short of help," she says.

"I don't think you have a lot of options on this one," Carye responds.

Once again, Heather is finding it easier to talk about her elaborately camouflaged life than the larger issues involved in her pregnancy and relinquishment. Carye is almost certain Heather will go through with the plan and give up the child. But she is concerned that Heather hasn't tried to anticipate what giving birth and surrendering the child will feel like, that Heather is allowing her secrecy and ruses to fully occupy her mind. At some point, Carye knows, Heather will see that the secrecy is secondary. But when will that realization hit her? Today? In the delivery room at the hospital? A week later, when the child is gone?

Heather hardly appears to be considering the emotional impact of adoption. Carye, however, is silently doing that for her. Carye has counseled thousands of women who have made all sorts of pregnancy-related choices, but one of her rock-solid convictions, confirmed by her experience with Becky, is that none of them suffer as much as the ones who surrender their children for adoption. When, occasionally, someone tells her, "I could never be so heartless as to put up my baby for adoption," she has to restrain herself from an angry retort; in Carye's experience, women who relinquish their babies are going through an experience she compares to having their hearts ripped out of their bodies.

Still, Heather says she is most afraid of losing her job and Carye suggests maybe Heather can talk about that with somebody at work, perhaps another waitress. Heather insists she cannot. But some excuse will be needed for Heather's disappearance during and after delivery.

"So what you can tell somebody is that you're having cysts on your ovaries, and they're going to have to monitor them and you might need surgery," Carye suggests. "That's the oldest one in the book."

The two women consider the dates involved. Heather's parents will go on a week-long vacation shortly. The timing is fortuitous, especially since Dr. Donovan, the obstetrician, is willing to induce labor so that Heather can deliver and recover while they're gone.

Carye reiterates her own invitation for Heather to stay at her home for a week after the delivery. But Heather keeps coming back to her job—she can't miss a week.

"You're going to have to tell them. You can't work fifteen-hour days. Physically, Heather, you can't. At some point you're going to have to stop."

"I can't do that, no way."

"I don't think you're going to have a choice. We can tell them it's an emergency surgery, so it's not like a flakeout."

Heather has crossed her legs and adopted a casual position in the chair at the side of Carye's desk. She is wearing beach sandals, white socks, shorts, and a T-shirt. It appears as if her emotional denial is affecting her physical appearance: She does not look at all like a woman about to give birth. Her face has taken on a quiet, downcast look. Unconsciously she begins rubbing together her thumb and index finger.

"They want to know if you can come and visit next week," Carye says, changing the topic to Jim and Carla. "She wants you to get to know them."

"Why does she want to do that?" Heather responds with a hint of teenage petulance.

"She wants you to like them."

"I'm waiting for it all to explode," Heather says, petulance replaced by exasperation. Carye thinks she means the camouflage, but she could just as easily be talking of the entire scenario she has created, including giving up the baby. "I don't stop long enough to really think about it."

"Have you come close to telling anybody?"

"No. Because I'm single, because they'd figure out who the father is and he'd find out and that would ruin that friendship."

In fact the father, this friend, has another girlfriend. Heather sees him around their small town every few days and he does not suspect.

"I keep hoping it's going to work itself out, and it can't," Heather says.

"I really believe some way we're going to work this out," Carye says consolingly. "This is going to come together."

"I wish someone would say, 'We're going to cut you open, take it out, and that's it.'"

Heather is not as sure of herself as last week. The complexity of her ruse is beginning to take its toll. The details of hiding her life from her parents and her friends at work, trying to hold on to her job, remain in school, find somewhere to stay, explain her absence, and prepare for childbirth have begun to frazzle her. She has become the juggler on *The Ed Sullivan Show*, spinning plates on poles. The longer the plates spin the more frantic the juggler becomes, running from one pole to another, forgetting one over here, another there. Heather cannot keep up with the juggling act that has become her life, and part of her wishes somebody would step up to the stage and give her help. That's when she wonders, as she does now, why nobody has noticed how she has changed.

"The reason people aren't noticing is because you aren't drawing attention to yourself," Carye says. "We've just got to figure out a short amount of time to get you away from both, from your parents and work."

Heather, ever elusive, tries to explain how she failed to realize she was pregnant. She has always been prone to weight fluctuations. When she gains weight it always shows the most around her stomach.

Dr. Donovan gave her a book entitled *What to Expect When You're Expecting*. Each night, Heather says, she reads a chapter before bedtime. But she finds the book upsetting because it continually refers to the role played by the husband or partner in supporting a pregnant woman. Heather does not have a partner, not a husband or a boyfriend, not even a supportive mother. She does not have a birth coach or somebody whose hand she can place on her womb to share the wonder of the baby's movement. That book was not written for her.

Last week Heather was having lunch with her girlfriends when one of them mentioned another girl from their school who had just discovered she was five months pregnant. "Someone said, 'If you don't know you're five months pregnant you're pretty stupid,'" Heather relates. "And I'm sitting there thinking, 'Well, some people aren't quite regular.'

"When you're in this town that's so focused on what everybody else is doing . . ." She leaves her sentence unfinished, with a drop and a shake of her head.

For a third time this morning Carye swings the conversation to Jim and Carla. She is not usually this persistent, but she figures that if Heather won't meet them again, it may be a sign she is not completely sure of her decision to have them adopt her baby.

Carye knows that in the week or two left before Heather's delivery she will not be able to crack through all the elaborate denial Heather has constructed, but if she can't get Heather to face a little more emotional reality, there is a greater chance that she will not be able to follow through with the adoption. And Carye is certain this is what Heather wants, and probably is what is best for her.

"What do you think about getting together with Jim and Carla?" Carye asks. "Do you want them at the birthing class?"

"If they want to be there, that's fine."

"What about next Friday morning? Saturday?"

Heather looks down at her hands. "Friday, I guess." A sigh punctuates her reply. She begins picking at her fingernails with a paper clip from Carye's desk.

"What does the doctor say about it?" Heather asks.

"He says everything's fine."

"He just doesn't talk to me," Heather says.

Carye suggests they compile a list of questions to ask Donovan at Heather's next visit. She takes out a pen and a clean sheet of paper. Heather begins.

"How painful will the delivery be?" "How long before I can leave the hospital?" Another concern diverts Heather: "I don't want my name in the newspaper."

Yesterday Heather found herself reading the birth announcements in her town's newspaper when it occurred to her that the paper probably received the notices from the hospital.

"If I get to that point and it all falls apart, I'm going to be mad," she says. The thought of such an irony causes both women to smile. Carye suggests lunch and they call a local restaurant for two orders of Thai food.

"Do I have to bring an overnight bag?" Heather asks.

When Carye says she does, Heather adopts a little girl's falsetto pout. "I don't want to stay there overnight." But the joke is on her. Her eyes begin to water.

Carye asks if Heather wants to spend any time with the baby in the hospital. Heather says no.

"When I have the baby I just want to see it. It sounds like I'm heartless but I'm not. I don't want to have a chance to form a real bond."

"I don't know if holding it is a real big thing with changing your mind," Carye says.

"I'd like to hold it because it's been really wild," Heather says. "But I just want to see it.

"I need to get on with my life because it's going too fast. It's their baby now, and it will be that much easier to get on with my life if everybody's not coming around, bringing it around." Heather's voice quivers with uncertainty; Carye suggests they wait before making any more decisions.

"Everybody's opinion is I'm going to want to spend a lot of time with the baby," Heather continues, not elaborating on who comprises everybody. "That's why I'm giving it up, so it can have a better life. It's not like I don't want it."

Carye wants to prepare Heather for what she anticipates will be a heartbreaking day at the hospital. She suggests Heather spend some time this week playing out in her mind the hospital scene in all its potential variations, including worst- and best-case scenarios.

"You need to give yourself as much mental honesty as you can in your thoughts," Carye adds.

In a voice equal parts anger and hurt, Heather says, "If I was telling people I had an abortion, I'd be bad. I'd be killing something. But if I tell people I'm putting it up for adoption, it's worse. It makes me mad."

"Nobody should have to do what you're doing," Carye says.

Carye takes out a package of birth control pills and Heather begins removing a week's worth from the month's supply and throwing them in a nearby trash can. "Now if my mom says something I can say, 'Yeah, Mom, then how come I've got birth control pills,' and I can show them to her. I've become such a good liar."

Heather is brightening. She shows a true smile for the first time today. The mood does not last for long.

"I've always thought if I was pregnant and couldn't have an abortion, I'd kill myself," she says.

Carye has no more answers today. She and Heather hug, and Heather heads away. Carye is left in her office trying to understand why she can't back away from Heather. Conventionally she would turn Heather over to her lawyer, who would take care of the adoption arrangements and set up counseling with an outside therapist, paid for by Jim and Carla. Carye knows why. Becky again.

Becky is who Carye sees in fleeting moments of anguish when Heather is sitting in the chair next to her desk. "I'm watching Becky fall apart," Carye says with her own mixture of hurt and anger. "I'm watching her get a job as a stripper. I'm watching her dye her hair black and putting on heavy black eyeliner. I'm watching her date three different guys since she had her baby in March. I'm watching her become promiscuous and that's a word that doesn't even fit into my vocabulary."

Becky gave up, Carye thinks. Or was worn down. Carye saw potential in Becky. She was going to change her life and she was smart enough to do it. She must be smart, she had Carye fooled. Even now Carye hasn't let go. She still sees Becky for an afternoon coffee or a shopping trip every few weeks.

Allene talked to Carye last week about becoming too involved with these women. She thinks Carye's pent-up maternal instincts take over in adoption cases. Allene may be right. But it probably goes deeper than that. Heather reminds Carye of herself, too, with a mother so distant. Maybe, Carye thinks, Heather can be the antidote to Becky. Maybe this time it can turn out right—the baby in a good home, Heather able to deal with her loss and begin a happy life.

From her office Allene watches Heather and Carye hug and Heather depart. I've got to toughen her up, Allene thinks.

Chapter Eight

Heather has a beeper now. Carye needed some way to reach her without having to continually risk vague telephone conversations with Heather's mother and father. And that's not all that's changed, Carye thinks. Heather is beginning to show her anger. Last week Heather told Carye that when she walks down the street in her hometown, walks among people who either do not know about or do not acknowledge her pregnancy, she wants to scream at passersby, "Are you stupid? Don't you see this?"

And Heather is making decisions, exerting some measure of control over her life. Both positive developments, Carye decides. It's just too bad I'm the only person to whom she can vent that anger.

Carye knows she, too, is suffering for Heather. She has found herself recalling her own teenage years and how she sometimes could make herself invisible when her mother and sister began screaming at each other. She has been short-tempered of late, though her own life appears free of major conflicts. Carye doesn't want to scream at strangers; she might, however, relish a confrontation with Heather's parents.

Again Carye's musings about Heather bring her back to Becky. Becky can say, "I have a son." Years from now, when Becky finds herself among women talking about their first birth experiences, she will not feel she must stay silent, keep her memories or her tears on the inside. Dark secrets exact a lifetime toll. At least once Heather gets through this episode in her life, she probably won't be willing to be invisible ever again, Carye concludes.

Heather's mother now believes her daughter has a thyroid condition, which explains the weight gain. Heather talks with Carye every two or three days and has decided she will live with Carye while recovering from the birth. If the timing works out Thom will be out of town for two weeks right after the birth. And timing is not completely out of their hands, since Dr. Donovan is willing to induce the birth.

Explaining the post-birth absence will not be so easy. In preparation Heather has told her mother she has dropped out of school but will return next semester. Knowing her mother would ask for the tuition money the school should have refunded, Heather asked Jim and Carla for $140, which she gave to her mother to complete the ruse. In truth, she is maintaining her schedule of attending community college during the day and working nights at the tavern. All the groundwork is laid, as long as she doesn't need a cesarean section. There is no way Heather can conceal three or four weeks of recovery time.

For no apparent reason Carye recalls the day she learned about Bradley, Allene's first child. Carye had been working at Lovejoy for three months and was counseling a couple with a problem pregnancy. The husband and wife were in their forties and had been trying to conceive for years. Tests showed the baby would suffer from Down's syndrome and severe hydrocephalus and might not live even if the pregnancy continued. Carye had no words for them, no way to ease their pain as they arranged for the abortion.

After the couple left, Carye wandered into Allene's office and related their predicament, now the counselor looking for comfort, for the right words.

Allene, without any show of emotion, looked at Carye and said, "I had a baby. His name was Bradley and he died. And today is the anniversary of his death." And Allene started talking about Bradley, who was born with the two lobes of his brain unconnected; how she bathed and fed and held him until he died after three and a half years, and how he would lift himself up on his knees and bounce across the room whenever he saw her. And Carye began noticing tiny tears forming in the corners of Allene's eyes, and without saying anything Carye stood up and went to hug Allene, who released a torrent of tears while comforted in Carye's embrace.

Searching for distraction Carye considers Debbie, who had a D & E today. Debbie came in Tuesday, straight from Kaiser, where an ultrasound had confirmed her pregnancy. While her mother waited in the lobby, Debbie explained her predicament.

"Well, I'm getting married in ten days," Debbie said. "Kaiser told me I was twelve weeks up until today, when they did the ultrasound. Now they say I'm at sixteen weeks. I can't have this baby. I really screwed up."

Debbie said the pregnancy was the result of a one-night stand with an old boyfriend who just happened to be passing through town. Debbie's fiancé just happened to be in the middle of a six-week out-of-town business trip at the time. Until the ultrasound, Debbie figured the pregnancy resulted from sex with her fiancé. But if the pregnancy was sixteen weeks instead of twelve, the baby was the ex-boyfriend's.

Carye tried to calm Debbie. She explained that ultrasounds are approximations, nobody could be sure who was the baby's father. If Debbie could live with the secret, why not have the baby and let the doctor help her obscure the exact date of conception?

"That won't work," Debbie responded. "My boyfriend is six foot five and has blond hair. This guy is five-six and has black hair. In fact," Debbie said with a pause, "he's black all over."

With this Debbie began giggling. She couldn't help herself. Neither could Carye, who joined in. Finally, through unrestrained laughter Carye blurted out, "Oh my God, Debbie, I have no idea what to say."

Regaining composure Debbie said, "My boyfriend would not understand." The two women considered what could be done. Debbie's fiancé knew she was pregnant; in fact, he was looking forward to the birth of the child. So simply telling him she decided to have an abortion wouldn't work. Miscarriage sounded like the best explanation. But because Debbie was going to need a D & E, she would have to visit Lovejoy three times. The boyfriend might become suspicious.

A plan was developed. Debbie told her fiancé the first day that she was having a few tests at the ob/gyn's office. Wednesday she said the doctor called with results that might indicate a problem pregnancy. And the third day, today, Debbie had her D & E, explaining to her fiancé that she miscarried and was taken to the hospital.

Debbie's waiting mother was more than willing to join in as coconspirator and back up Debbie's story to the fiancé, complete with the appropriate maternal condolences and concerns.

So Debbie has carried out her plan, and now will have her own secret to live with. Carye leans back in her chair and wonders what she would have done in Debbie's situation. She knows she could never make Debbie's choice because she could never be so deceitful with Thom. And she would never risk setting him up for the anxiety Debbie's fiancé is going to feel the next time Debbie becomes pregnant and he suffers through nine months wondering if she is going to miscarry again. But Carye is stumped trying to figure out another option that would work.

FRIDAY

By mid-morning Carye is in Allene's office, the two women trying to get hold of a phantom. In the last few weeks protestors outside have become bolder. Three times they have initiated physical contact with arriving patients. In other social situations the type of contact exhibited might not be so replete with significance—an overly aggressive salesman reaching for an elbow, a sensitive nurse placing her hand on top of a patient's hand. But outside Lovejoy these actions speak volumes, crossing an invisible but critical line and sending a signal that Allene and Carye are trying to decipher.

Neither woman can identify a reason for the increased hostility. There has been no unusual media publicity about Lovejoy or abortions. No shootings have taken place at other clinics, no lawsuits against protestors have raised stakes. Just these minor incidents. The latest occurred Saturday. A tiny woman, no more than five feet tall, was trying to get past a knot of protestors and into the building. She was accompanied by her tattooed and tank-topped boyfriend. She refused the pamphlets thrust her way by protestors. A middle-aged woman grabbed her arm and tried to force the patient to take a pamphlet. Carye, observing, hurried out of the building and asked, "Did she grab you?"

"Yeah," the patient answered.

Turning to the protestor Carye said, "Big mistake." She hustled the patient inside, explained that the protestor's action was illegal, and asked if the patient wanted to call the police.

"Yeah, that's what I want to do," the patient said.

Fifteen minutes later two police officers unfamiliar to Carye, a man and a woman, arrived. The patient met them outside the building, pointed to the protestor who had touched her, and said, "I want her arrested." The woman police officer responded by asking, "Did they tell you inside you have to do this before you can have an abortion?"

Carye and Allene are more upset about the attitude of the police than the incident. Carye's attempts to talk to others in the chain of command have been met with a disinterest that is a marked change from the sympathetic reception she has received over the years. In the last year a new lieutenant has taken over their precinct, and previous talks with him have led Carye and Allene to think that Lovejoy's relationship with the police is changing with the changing guard. Monday morning Carye called the lieutenant to discuss

Lovejoy's problems with security, and he mentioned that Portland police officers could be rented for overtime work at $42.54 an hour, including uniforms and patrol cars. This was not what Carye hoped to hear.

Carye suggests to Allene that the police might feel less involved with Lovejoy's problems because Lovejoy hasn't followed the security recommendations the police have provided in the past. Over the years the police urged Allene to build walls at critical places inside Lovejoy, which would prevent an intruder from rushing straight back to Allene's and Carye's offices. But those walls would destroy Lovejoy's informality, erecting barriers between the patients and the people who worked there, and between the employees themselves. No longer would Allene know to pick up the ringing telephone because she could see from her office that Lisa, the receptionist, was swamped.

Allene disdainfully speaks of the battle zone mentality at one of the city's other facilities, which has installed a permanent lock on the front door; patients, viewed by a security camera, must be buzzed in before entering. "Everyone there is scared to death," she says. "I'm not going to turn us into a fortress. We are not a battlefield. Women have a right to come in and feel warm and welcome and cared about."

In Allene's mind Lovejoy still is a surgical center, not an abortion clinic. And surgical centers don't have these concerns.

The problem, Allene says, is the new lieutenant, Dave Austin, who hasn't been around long enough to recognize the real danger at Lovejoy. Allene knows that if police officers are called to the facility too frequently, they begin to feel they're used as Lovejoy's private security force, and they don't like that. In her mind Lovejoy has scrupulously tried to keep the police uninvolved, only calling them as a last resort. Austin doesn't seem to know this.

"He's too arrogant, and I'm going to have to sit him down and give him a little history," Allene says.

Leah walks in. Leah is using Carye's office to counsel a woman who began sobbing moments ago when Leah told her the ultrasound showed she was thirty-six weeks pregnant, a few weeks short of giving birth.

"What do we do?" Leah asks her mother.

Allene doesn't hesitate a beat. "Give her the Boys and Girls Aid Society number," she says, looking at her daughter. Then Allene's gaze shifts to Carye, seated across from her. Carye is looking down at the carpet between her feet. She does not say a thing.

WEDNESDAY, AUGUST 2

Both Carye and Allene have known the utter sadness that comes with nursing a family member who is dying. Allene's experience was perhaps the worst that any human being can endure because the family member was her child. Allene was twenty-two when Bradley was born, and by the time he died three and a half years later she had two other children. She never gave in to her anguish, never once considered abandoning her full-speed-ahead approach to life. Within a year of Bradley's death Allene's fourth child was born and she had begun working evenings as a nurse to help put her husband through medical school. Allene was, and remains, an indomitable woman.

The year Carye's sister succumbed to cancer probably helped define Carye in a way Bradley's death did not change Allene. Carye felt transformed to the point that she was certain she must look different to those around her, as if a large scar hung over her eyes, visible to all.

Carye's sister was thirty-four when she learned of her illness and thirty-six when she died. As children, Joanne and Carye would put together puzzles and perform the dance of most siblings more than a few years apart. Carye would trail after Joey, as she called her, who would write spicy entries in her private diary knowing Carye would read them all the way to the end, where it would be revealed that Joanne had set up her nosy sister from the start.

During Joanne's last year Carye spent every other evening with her sister, who had returned to their parents' home to live. The last few months Carye would head straight there every day after work to help hold Joanne up as she showered, read to her, talk. Often Carye would stay the night and head back to Lovejoy without having been home to Thom.

One thing Joanne's death did not do that it might have done was destroy Carye's inclination to empathize. She did not learn to keep other people and their troubles at arm's length, to protect herself with distance. She did not learn to separate herself from suffering. Carye feels that the year of grieving made her more sensitive to the little conflicts that cause a hurt, and the little understandings that can help the healing.

Last night Heather came home from work early, in pain. Her mother said it was probably heartburn. Heather just smiled, then left home and drove to Portland. Before she had gone fifteen miles the contractions were coming every three to four minutes. With each contraction Heather's foot would involuntarily press down a little harder on the gas pedal, accelerating the car. She pulled over at a highway rest area about halfway to Portland and called the hospital to alert them she was coming in. The trip took just over an hour, about the same time as the labor. By the time Heather made it in, her delivery was so advanced it took a total of nine pushes and the child, a boy, was out, at a little past 1 A.M.

Twenty minutes after the delivery Heather signed the relinquishment papers. The next afternoon she returned to work at the tavern.

Carye heard about Heather's baby fifteen minutes after the birth. She awoke from a deep sleep, picked up the telephone, and heard a crying newborn boy: Jim and Carla had put the telephone right next to the child and dialed. Then Carye briefly talked to Heather. "Are you okay?" she asked. "It's amazing," Heather responded. And Carye smiled as she returned to her slumber.

Carye took another call this morning, after she reached Lovejoy. This one came from a state social worker. The baby was still in the hospital and needed a hernia operation. Apparently its intestine had descended into its scrotum.

While the baby was being prepped for the hernia operation, the hospital followed standard procedure by drawing and analyzing his blood. The test showed methamphetamines in his system. The social worker was insistent when Carye expressed disbelief—Heather must have taken the drugs in the last few days of her pregnancy. And state regulations are clear in such matters: The Children's Services Division would now investigate the case to ensure the child's welfare was not compromised by the mother.

Carye called John, the attorney who helped make arrangements for the adoption. Between the two of them they explained that the child was being adopted. If he received drugs through Heather, it was irrelevant to the care he would get when he went home with the adoptive parents. The social worker agreed not to pursue the case.

After speaking to the social worker, John reminded Carye that until the adoption papers are filed in court he is the child's legal guardian. According to the social worker, the baby probably will have to go through some sort of withdrawal to rid himself of the drugs in his system. And the greatest concern, though this John doesn't need to tell Carye, who has already begun to obsess about the possibility, is that Heather was taking drugs throughout her pregnancy and the baby could be severely affected.

Putting down the telephone Carye takes a few minutes to assemble the facts with which she has been bombarded. She is nearly distraught, cannot fathom how this could be. Not Heather.

*

Jim and Carla have now spent almost a full day at the hospital with the baby. Somebody has to break to them the news of the drug test. Because they are not legal guardians, the hospital staff will not have told them.

Carye considers their situation. She feels reasonably sure they will go ahead with the adoption, especially after a day of bonding. But Carye's main focus throughout this ordeal has been Heather, and that is still where her concern is drawn. This could certainly change Jim and Carla's feelings about Heather, and the supportive relationship the couple has forged with her.

One more time Carye tries to figure out the puzzle she has been presented. She simply cannot conceive of Heather taking methamphetamines during her pregnancy. Carye has spent enough time with drug users to be able to recognize one. In fact, in the past Carye has claimed she is practically telepathic about drug use. And as Heather's confidante these last four weeks, she has gotten beyond any camouflage that might have been constructed.

Allene steps into Carye's office and Carye launches into a summary of the news. "No way," Allene says. "That kid is not a drug user."

After Allene leaves, Carye allows herself another moment before returning to work. Maybe there's something I just don't want to see, Carye thinks. Then another thought pushes the first aside. Diet pills. Maybe Heather foolishly has been taking diet pills to help conceal her pregnancy—losing weight to compensate for her increasing size. Diet pills are a form of methamphetamines, speed. Maybe that's the explanation.

Heather has not called Carye since the birth. Carye knows she left the hospital early this afternoon. So it appears Heather has changed her mind about staying with Carye during recovery. Another thought hits Carye, that Heather doesn't even know about the blood tests. Nobody has talked to her since she left the hospital. Carye picks up the phone and tries Heather's beeper. No answer.

Putting thoughts of Heather aside, Carye rises and walks out to the lobby. This is a Wednesday. There are twenty-seven women to see today and no time to think it all through.

But there is one thought that cannot be banished so easily. As she scans the room full of waiting women, Carye is stung by the notion that Allene was right, she should not have involved herself in another adoption case. They just accumulate too much baggage. Too much sadness.

Throughout the day Carye badgers Dr. Lane for studies on the effects of fetal exposure to methamphetamines. The doctor knows that the two most often cited effects are moodiness and impaired sucking ability. Carye wants more details. Carye also leaves messages at Heather's house throughout the day, asking Heather to please give her a call.

"Don't reprimand her," Carye reminds herself as she dials. And yet, she wonders why Heather did not think she could tell Carye about her drug use, if that's what it was. Did Heather need her approval that much? Carye thinks back to a scene two weeks ago, the one time her antennae told her something was not quite right. Heather was acting coy during one of their talks, evasive. She remembers now wondering why Heather wouldn't look at her. But when pressed, Heather insisted everything was fine and the questions were soon forgotten.

By the end of the day Carye is telling herself there probably is no good explanation. Heather must have been taking drugs.

THURSDAY, AUGUST 3

Still no word from Heather. Carye is fighting a growing sense of betrayal but so far managing to keep conviction at bay. Getting ready to leave for an empty home, Thom having begun a trip to visit family on the East Coast, she dials Heather's home number one more time and is surprised when Heather's voice comes back through the phone. Trying to exert self-control Carye begins by asking, "Heather, how are you?" and manages about fifteen seconds of small talk before giving in to a blunt tone she had hoped to keep out of her voice.

"Heather, one of the blood tests was positive, so I need to know if you've taken any medications," Carye begins.

Heather says she has been taking medication for back pain, nothing more.

"Then what about Sudafed or something for your allergies?"

Heather says last Sunday at work her boss gave her two twelve-hour cold pills. Twelve-hour cold pills taken Sunday should not show up in the baby's blood Tuesday, Carye knows. Carye also knows that cocktail waitresses are notorious for their use of methamphetamines, often putting the drug in their own drinks. Maybe somebody at work mixed up her drink with Heather's.

"And nobody would slip anything to you without your knowing it?"

Heather doesn't think so. Carye suggests they get together Sunday morning and Heather agrees. Carye knows Heather's different moods, and she can sense that at the first mention of the blood test Heather was assuming a quiet defensiveness. Now Heather is beginning to relax just a little bit, knowing she is not being accused by her one ally.

Heather confesses that before she found out she was pregnant she occasionally snorted crank, the street name for methamphetamines. Maybe once or twice a month. That means at least through the first six months of the baby's gestation, Carye thinks, because Heather came to Lovejoy so late.

With her confession Heather becomes silent. Carye waits for her to continue but Heather does not. Carye can practically feel her despair through the telephone line.

"Are you okay?" Carye asks. After a pause she switches the topic to Jim and Carla. Carye says they have been desperate to talk to her. Carye knows Heather cares deeply about their opinions of her, knowing that whatever Jim and Carla think is what the child will hear about his birthmother in years to come.

"Heather, they're not mad at you," Carye says. "This is what we've been dealing with all along. We've got to make sure that on this end there are no more secrets."

More silence. "They're not calling you to interrogate you about your private life," Carye continues. "But to some extent it ain't that private anymore. Because now they have the baby and that's their first responsibility now."

As she speaks into the phone Carye begins pouring water into a paper cup from a squeeze bottle she keeps at her desk. Reaching into a drawer she removes a small bottle of herbal tincture and puts a few drops into the water. The potion is reputed to relieve stress. Carye wants to get home, to sort this out away from Lovejoy. She promises Heather she will call again this evening.

Checking the building's doors and lights before closing up, Carye is bothered by the thought that if Heather could tell her about her crank use now, maybe she didn't do such a thorough job of asking the right questions earlier.

At home, after dinner, Carye again calls Heather, who obviously has been brooding over their earlier conversation. "I guess I should go out and shoot myself because nothing is working out," Heather says. But she tempers those words by saying that right after the birth, when she saw Jim holding the baby at the hospital, she wondered how she could ever have thought about an abortion, and was thankful she did not abort.

Carye cannot decide if Heather is serious about suicide. She can hear despondency in Heather's voice, so she makes an effort to keep the conversation going awhile. Carye also asks Heather to promise she will call her before doing anything impulsive. Heather agrees. Carye sighs as she replaces the phone, knowing that Heather is going to need a lot of help and that she has refused all offers of standard post-adoption counseling. Which means Carye is involved with Heather for the long haul.

*

WEDNESDAY, AUGUST 16

Hostility is so commonly expressed around Lovejoy that the people who work there do not react to it as might people who rarely confront such raw humanity. It is there in the threat represented by the protestors and sometimes in women who come to Lovejoy but would give everything they own not to be there.

This morning Tim called in and Carye told him the schedule was light, he would not be needed to counsel. But Tim comes in anyway, dressed in an old sweatshirt and sneakers to drop off the week's supply of gladiola and a second bundle of flowers for Allene to take home. He watches from the lobby as a patient vents her anger on every staff member who approaches. The patient, a burly compact bulldozer of a woman, shoves her papers in Lisa's face. She demands to use the office telephone. She pushes her way to the telephone and shouts epithets at everyone within earshot.

With Carye talking to a doctor upstairs, Anneke is the only available counselor. But Anneke says she won't go into a counseling session with the woman.

"I'll take her," says Tim, materializing as if drawn by a magnet. Nobody at Lovejoy can match Tim's calming presence, the gentleness that so obviously is not an act but a way of being. Before introducing himself to the woman, he heads to a back room for a surgical top to place over his sweatshirt.

Once inside Carye's office Tim finds he has met his match. The woman finally has a captive audience for her anger and she's taking full advantage. Her face screws up as if someone is twisting her tongue inside her mouth. She has had four state-financed abortions already and one miscarriage, she tells Tim, who is reminding himself how badly this woman does not want to be here, and that this diatribe is her way of letting that go.

Tim's hands begin shaking uncontrollably. As his disease has worsened, this is one of many new symptoms that have come to inhabit his body like squatters in a decaying building.

The woman bursts out of the room. Finding Anneke near the reception area she shouts, "What's wrong with that doctor? Is he a crack addict or something?"

Anneke knows what she must do. She calls Allene, briefly explaining the series of events. Allene is out of her office in seconds, marching up to the patient.

"I hear you think Tim is a crack addict," she begins. She does not need to shout to command attention, the force of her presence does that. "First of all, he is ill, but he is not a doctor. If you don't change your attitude, you can go somewhere else. Four people have dealt with you and four people have had very bad hits. I will be very glad to make an appointment for you at any number of other places, but if you want to stay here, you will have to change your attitude."

The woman, so imposing a moment ago, shrinks like a chastened child. She returns to Carye's office with Tim. She explains her fear: She is in her first trimester but desperately wants to be under general anesthetic for her abortion and she knows the state will not allow that, since it is the state that is paying. She offers to wait a few weeks until she has passed the twelve-week cutoff for locals.

Tim, and everybody else at Lovejoy, would be only too happy to oblige. Nobody wants to deal with this woman in a conscious state any more than necessary. He asks the woman to wait while he walks over to Allene's office and presents the situation.

"Give her what she wants," Allene says in a laughing "Are you kidding?" tone of voice. "It's far better to do that than upset the entire floor."

The next day Tim arrives dressed in a perfectly tailored suit. A local television newscaster is putting together a show on Andrew Burnett. Tim and Allene are being interviewed ostensibly to provide balance, but both are growing uncomfortable as the reporter's questions turn increasingly hostile.

Allene knows that she is courting danger just by appearing on the show. She risks refocusing the ire of Burnett and those who follow him, and she becomes ever more visible to the lone gunman out there looking for a target.

Carye thinks that even a show such as this represents a marketing opportunity. Women will see Allene and hear the name Lovejoy Surgicenter and when they need an abortion Lovejoy will come to mind.

By now any woman coming in for an abortion expects to navigate past pickets, Carye figures. What she has noticed is that after a major protest outside Lovejoy makes the news, business often increases. Carye is sure that the marketing benefit of simply getting the Lovejoy name out is greater than the effects of increasing fear and anxiety in potential patients.

Allene refuses to believe that bad publicity encourages business. Her primary reason for doing the interview is to provide a strong voice to balance Burnett's. She's not giving an inch of ground to the man.

Last night Carye spent two hours with Heather, who had driven up to Portland. Two days ago Heather began questioning the women she works with at the tavern, and one confessed she had been spiking Heather's drinks with methamphetamines as a practical joke. The friend, of course, did not know Heather was pregnant. Able to relate that news to Carye, Heather's outlook improved. She began asking questions that represent her first open curiosity about the baby. She asked how he is sleeping and eating, how Jim and Carla are adjusting to parenthood. Then Heather told Carye she thinks her mother has known about the pregnancy all along. Last night Heather's mother came into Heather's room, uncharacteristically hugged her daughter and said, for no apparent reason, "I love you."

"I think Allene was right," Heather said, referring to a discussion two weeks ago. "I think my mom and me made a silent agreement about this, and she knows I'm taking care of it."

Soldiers say that after enough time in the field they develop a sixth sense, becoming aware of incoming artillery a moment before it is seen or heard. Some emergency room doctors in inner-city hospitals say they acquire a similar prescience, knowing their theatre is about to explode with damaged and decimated bodies before the screaming ambulances arrive with their payloads.

Alarms are sounding in Carye's head this morning, even as she is trying to convince herself that random coincidence is at play.

Ginger was the first to arrive, at 5:45 A.M. She had been designated to open the building and prepare for admitting the day's patients. Ginger is a short-haired woman of twenty-six whose casual, loose-fitting skirts and Birkenstock sandals belie a no-nonsense approach. She has been working in both billing and admitting since she was hired eight months ago. But Ginger's key wouldn't fit into the front door lock. At first she assumed somebody had changed the locks on the building and forgotten to tell her. Bending down for a closer look she saw the lock had been sabotaged; somebody had filled it with quick-setting glue. It did not take Ginger long to recognize the tactic because it had been used before at Lovejoy. A quick check of the building's other entrances showed the saboteur had been thorough—all the building's locks had been glued.

Ginger walked two blocks to a pay telephone and called Carye with the news. Carye called John, Lovejoy's maintenance man. By the time both reached the building the 6:30 A.M. patients had begun to arrive and mill around outside. Ginger, Carye, and John began searching the outside of the building, looking for a window left open a crack the night before. John found a crow bar in the trunk of his car and has spent the last twenty minutes trying to pry open the front door. The day's patients, observing all this from out front, clearly are becoming unsettled. Watching John work the door, Carye consciously fights off a growing paranoia.

With one last push John frees the front door, and the patients and staff rush into the lobby, setting off the threatening blasts of the building's security alarm.

Entering the building Carye is aware of the excitement that has charged everyone in the Surgicenter, patients included. This is not the atmosphere that encourages an efficient day of surgeries, she thinks. And then Carye notices something else that sets off her personal security alarm. Picketing outside the building on this Friday morning is Ron Norquist, one of the defendants in the Lovejoy Eight trial, an insurance salesman turned full-time anti-abortion activist.

Norquist is hard to miss out on the sidewalk; at six feet four inches he stands a head above the rest. Ten years ago he was earning close to one hundred thousand dollars a year at State Farm Insurance, raising horses and enjoying a more than comfortable life with his family. He began attending protests and rescues in 1989, thinking the worst that could happen to him was thirty days in jail for criminal trespassing, a price he was willing to pay. His height and heft—he weighs about 215 pounds—made him a natural point man during rescues at Lovejoy; Norquist would put his back to the seam of the two front doors and brace his feet against the opposite railing. Fellow protestors would gather around for a more than formidable blockade.

When Lovejoy filed suit Norquist found himself one of eight primary defendants, along with Andrew Burnett. The judge told defendants they had to sign a document promising they would obey the court's injunction limiting their activity at Lovejoy or stay in jail indefinitely. Norquist chose not to sign and spent seven months in jail. He was released only after the trial was over, and by then he owed Lovejoy six hundred thousand dollars. In the interim he had been dismissed from his insurance job.

Now the suburban house is gone, as are the horses. As an anti-abortion organizer, occasional tree cutter, and substitute teacher, Norquist earns minimum wage, knowing anything he makes over that can be garnished.

Today Norquist is accompanied by four other protestors carrying picket signs and observing the morning's activities. But what bothers Carye is that Norquist usually shows up on weekends. And she has never seen him outside this early in the morning. Maybe he's more than an observer, she thinks.

Carye doesn't have much time to reflect on the matter. More surprises await. As the staff rushes about trying to ready the Surgicenter for admitting and surgery, to retake some of the lost time that already has them behind schedule, word comes to Carye that the gas cannisters used for anesthetic and oxygen in the operating rooms are unavailable. The cannisters are kept in a small storage shed in back of the building, and the locks to the shed have also been glued shut. Half an hour later John has used a hacksaw to cut the locks off the shed. The first of the day's four general surgeries starts about forty minutes late, locals to follow.

As the morning settles down into something approaching routine Carye thinks back over the last few days, her brain sorting out what have seemed like random occurrences until now. On Monday a padded manila envelope bearing a Palm Beach, Florida, return address arrived in the mail. Lisa and Anneke, who were seated in the reception area when the mail was delivered, opened the package. Inside they found what at first glance appeared to be a metallic green plastic handgun. But closer examination revealed this to be a gun with a difference: the cylinder was a curled-up fetus. The hammer was frozen in the cocked position. No written message accompanied the gun; none was needed.

The gun bothered Carye only a little bit. At the time, what most unnerved her was that two members of her staff had completely ignored established protocol and opened the package in the first place. If the package had contained a letter bomb, it would not have been Lovejoy's first; seven years ago one had been sent but intercepted by postal inspectors alerted by the police.

South Florida is home to perhaps the most active and violent anti-abortion movement in the country. At least two abortion doctors in that area have been shot and killed. "That's like being in Israel and opening a package from Beirut," Carye thinks.

By late afternoon on Monday the FBI had returned Carye's call and told her the name of the man who sent the gun. Lovejoy was not the only recipient; similar packages had been sent to a number of abortion clinics. The man was now under surveillance.

While Carye reviews the week's events, unknown to her a commotion has developed in the lobby. Firmly planted in a seat near the front door is a dark-haired woman who appears to be in her mid-thirties. She is wearing a filmy white dress and a colorful headband that looks like it might have come from South America. In her lap rests an open Bible.

Using a conversational voice the woman is talking to nobody and everybody in the lobby, in the manner of a sidewalk preacher on a busy corner downtown. Amazingly, nobody on the Lovejoy staff has noticed.

"Who is that woman preaching to us over there?" a patient asks Ginger at the admitting window. Ginger walks out to the lobby and sees the woman alternately praying and speaking to the patients nearby, who are doing their best to ignore her.

"Are you a patient here or are you with a patient?" Ginger asks.

"I think you should tell these people not to kill their children," the woman responds, her voice firm with conviction. The woman then tells Ginger she once was a patient here herself, and then she begins crying. The other women in the lobby are looking at the two with a measure of attention rare here; most patients awaiting admission make an effort to keep their eyes averted, as if pretending they are alone in the lobby.

"You need to leave," Ginger says.

But the woman does not leave, makes no move to rise. Ginger matches her patience and stays in place, then makes the request again.

"I'll get up with the strength that Jesus gave me," the woman responds, turning her gaze from Ginger and resuming her preaching. Her soliloquy now centers around "saving the children." Ginger doesn't move. Her presence finally takes effect. The woman rises, continuing her speech. She walks the few steps to the front door without acknowledging Ginger. As she nears the door, without turning around she says, "Thank you, Jesus."

"You're welcome," comes a voice, Ginger's, from the back of the room.

The woman finally turns her head. Speaking over her shoulder as she walks out the door, she shouts, in an angry voice that contrasts sharply with the gentle tone she has maintained until now, "You're not Jesus!"

Learning about the incident a few minutes later, Carye feels as if another brick has been added to a load she had not expected to carry. By now Carye recognizes all the regular anti-abortion protestors who visit Lovejoy, as well as the faces in the rogues' gallery notebook that she and other abortion providers have received from authorities. The book includes pictures of anti-abortion extremists around the country who are at large. But the woman is unfamiliar. Even more worrisome, she sat in the lobby for ten minutes before Ginger became aware of her. What if she had carried a gun or a bomb? Carye wonders. Concerned that more than coincidence is at play, Carye calls the police to report the morning's events.

After lunch a fax from the National Abortion Federation spills out of the machine in the reception area.

Late Wednesday, August 16, the FBI arrested Robert E. Cook, an anti-abortion extremist living in the Milwaukee area, after receiving information that he planned to kill an abortion provider sometime before next Tuesday, August 22. The arrest followed a year-long federal investigation into Cook's activities. He will be arraigned within the next few days in Federal Court in Milwaukee on bank larceny charges, stemming from the robbery last year of $260,000 from an armored car company for which he worked. News reports indicate that the robbery was intended to help fund an "army" for a war against abortion providers. . . .

Authorities apparently seized multiple weapons and ammunition from Cook's home, including an AR-15 assault rifle and a Glock pistol. According to an affidavit filed against Cook, he had traveled to Portland, Oregon, on August 9 and 10, and told friends there that he planned to kill a doctor before next Tuesday.

Within an hour the morning vandalism, the fax, and the tres-passing preacher will be forgotten as minor incidents in a day with much more alarming developments.

Chapter Nine

A surgeon shouldn't be frightened of blood. Harold Suchak is terrified. And the feeling of helplessness only compounds his anxiety. But Suchak has never had a patient bleed like this.

Suchak has just rushed back to Lovejoy but he knows there is little for him to do—Tom Donovan is in charge now. Suchak reviews the morning's events. Four generals, and all had seemed to go well. After finishing his work Suchak had left the operating room to Donovan, who would perform the day's locals. On the way home Suchak stopped to pick up his clothes from the dry cleaner. Two blocks from home his beeper went off. The last surgery of the day had not gone so well after all.

Her name is Chuan, he recalls, a tiny sparrow of a thing, sixteen years old, from Thailand. Suchak had been reluctant to take her on when shown the chart, which included an ultrasound, on Wednesday. Patients think doctors and nurses can look at a picture of a fetus on an ultrasound and just intuit its gestational age, but in fact the age is estimated by measuring the diameter of the skull, called a biparietal. In advertisements and over the telephone, people are told Lovejoy will consider abortions in cases where the fetus is up to 23.5 weeks from the date of the woman's last period, which translates into 5.3 centimeters, exceptions made on a case-by-case basis. Chuan's ultrasound showed a biparietal of 5.4 centimeters. Suchak knew he was dealing with a fetus between 23 and 24 weeks gestation, a judgment call.

Carye, who had counseled Chuan, told Suchak that the girl was a good student still in high school. She had a future. The counseling notes said she hoped to return some day to her native Thailand. Suchak decided to take the case.

Nothing that occurred during surgery had caused Suchak any concern. Removing the fetus he had examined the feet, generally a more reliable indicator of gestational age than the ultrasound. The fetus was further along than they had thought—his best guess was between 24 and 25 weeks. With the weekend beginning, Suchak had left the building a bit quickly perhaps, but he had no reason to do otherwise.

And then came the call to his beeper. Chuan, still resting in the recovery room, had gotten up to go to the bathroom and started bleeding. Suchak, just driving away from the dry cleaner, headed his Porsche back to Portland, knowing that by the time he arrived events would be well out of his hands. If Chuan was hemorrhaging, she would need urgent care immediately, and it would take Suchak at least thirty minutes to return to Lovejoy. Suchak knew he had just passed on a problem patient.

Back at Lovejoy, Tom Donovan is on the receiving end. Three minutes ago he completed a tab local, his eighth of the day, three more to go. He took a seat at the desk in the second-floor hallway, just outside and between the pre-op and recovery rooms. Donovan feels hyperfocused during surgery and he uses these short breaks to relax.

Life has been anything but relaxing for Donovan of late. Donovan, thirty-six, is a tall man with a mop of brown hair cut short and the beginning of a paunch. He looks a bit like an oversized Tom Sawyer, which is appropriate. With his everpresent hint of a smile, he indeed appears a man who has not completely outgrown his childhood. Everyone at Lovejoy is at least vaguely aware that Donovan has undergone personal trials in the last few years, and some know details of the cocaine abuse and divorce. There is, nevertheless, a bit of mystery surrounding Donovan. But his easygoing manner and able hands keep him in high regard with most. His informal style with patients presents a vivid contrast to Suchak's old-school approach.

Carolee, the downstairs counselor who is assisting June, the recovery room nurse, rushes out into the hallway to the seated Donovan. "We have a patient of Dr. Suchak's who's a D & E, and she's bleeding more than usual," she says, a note of urgency underlining her words.

In five quick steps Donovan is at Chuan's side. The girl is lying on a gurney, still as a department store statue. A pool of blood beneath her testifies that she is real and in grave danger. Even Donovan can hardly believe how much blood she has lost, how much blood can come out of one human being. The blood has already saturated the sheet as well as the two blue absorbent pads that were placed beneath her buttocks. With the sheet and pads full, a pool of blood at least a quarter of an inch deep has formed around the lower half of Chuan's body, from her knees up to her navel and all the way to the edges of the gurney. Clumpy pancakes of coagulated blood, clots, break up the pool like stones in a waveless pond.

Donovan is jolted by a random thought: That's a Robie Unit. During Donovan's residency one of his professors, Dr. Robie, was performing an abortion when the patient started bleeding, and her blood nearly filled a bucket that had been placed between her legs. That quantity of blood became fixed in his mind, and in the minds of other astonished observing residents, as a Robie Unit.

Donovan notices Chuan's IV needle has already been taken out. She must have been preparing for discharge when the bleeding started, or the IV would still be in place. That IV is going to be needed, he thinks, picking up Chuan's wrist to check her heart rate. He has to count fast to keep up with the beats. Making a quick calculation after fifteen seconds he estimates her rate at 120 beats a minute, which means Chuan probably is going into shock.

"We need to get an IV started right away," Donovan says, the words coming out at the same time the thought is formed. He begins a hurried examination of Chuan as June begins inserting a needle and hooking up the IV.

Chuan is awake, though she has not said a word or made a motion since Donovan arrived. Her dark Asian complexion is strikingly pale. "Are you having any pain other than cramping?" Donovan asks, looking directly into Chuan's eyes to judge her alertness. Chuan's eyes are focused but anxious as they stare directly back at Donovan.

A simple "No" comes through Chuan's rapid breaths. There is fear in her voice, but control as well.

The reply is a clue. The most likely cause of the bleeding is a perforation during surgery, some puncture or laceration of the uterus. But if Suchak perforated Chuan's uterus during the abortion the girl should be feeling shoulder pain in addition to severe abdominal pain, Donovan knows. The perforation would cause leaking blood to send nerve signals that the brain would misinterpret and send back as shoulder pain.

A second possibility could be retained tissue—say, part of the placenta left in the uterus because it was not completely removed during surgery or flushed out by uterine contractions at the end of surgery. The remaining tissue would keep the uterus from contracting; those contractions normally stop the bleeding that takes place after an abortion or a birth.

Donovan knows Suchak has left the building. "Is Marion still here?" he asks of the day's anesthetist to no one in particular. Donovan has treated emergency cases before. He knows his words will be heard and acted upon.

"She's left," he hears.

"Page her and Dr. Suchak. Stat."

Donovan knows this is not the ideal setting to perform an examination. He also knows there may be no time to set up the

surgical room and wheel Chuan over there. The rest of the recovering patients have been shielded from Chuan's gurney by a
curtain pulled across the room, and Carole, a medical assistant,
has gone over to comfort them. Donovan places his hands on
Chuan's stomach and presses down at various points, actually feeling the uterus from the outside. If the uterus feels soft or mushy,
the problem may well be uterine atonia, insufficient contracting.
If it feels firm, he will need to keep looking. Firm. And Chuan is
still bleeding.

Next possibility is a cervical laceration. Only one way to check
for that. Donovan asks for gloves and quickly puts them on his hands.
It is possible that the upper part of Chuan's uterus is firm but the lower
half is not contracting because it is filled with blood clots or leftover
tissue. Donovan places his right hand inside the uterus and his left
on top of Chuan's stomach. He begins feeling around the inside of
Chuan's cervix and uterus, seeking something, anything abnormal.
Near the edge of the cervix something feels distorted, not perfectly
round. Maybe a tear.

Two minutes have elapsed since Donovan entered the recovery room. The cervical tear may or may not exist, and it may or may
not be contributing to the hemorrhaging. But there just seems to be
too much bleeding for that to be the only cause. He considers other
possibilities—amniotic fluid somehow leaching into blood veins
could do it. The fluid contains agents designed to resist coagulation,
and in blood they can initiate nonstop bleeding. Placental accreta is
another possibility, the placenta growing into the uterus during pregnancy, some of it remaining behind, stuck to the uterine wall. A
second fetus undetected outside the womb, growing in the uterus,
could be responsible.

"Go ahead and call an ambulance," Donovan says, again direct-
ing his words to the recovery room as much as any individual. His
voice remains calm. Then, "Let's take her back to the OR and see if
we can put a stitch in this tear."

The anesthetist, Marion, arrives. She had gone out for coffee when her beeper sounded.

Donovan helps June wheel Chuan's gurney into the operating room. Marion places a blood pressure cuff on Chuan's arm, and then a pulse oximeter clip on her finger to measure the oxygen content of her blood. Finally, Marion places an EKG pad on Chuan's back, with four leads connected to the monitor.

Blood pressure is low but stable. The first positive sign they've had, Donovan thinks. He notices another: Chuan's bleeding has slowed.

Marion has already started an IV solution into Chuan's arm, so Donovan tells her to add forty units of Pitocin and an injection of 0.2 mg. Methergine in an attempt to induce the uterus to contract and control the bleeding.

Next Marion prepares an IV general anesthetic. Within thirty seconds Chuan is unconscious. Adron, a medical technician, swabs her pubic area with antiseptic. Now she is ready for surgery.

Donovan places Chuan's legs in stirrups, uses a speculum to open the vagina, and peers into Chuan's cervix. He sees the spot where he thought he felt a tear before. Sure enough, there is a tear about three-quarters of an inch long. Within a minute Donovan has made one long continuous stitch to repair the tear. But there's no sign of bleeding from the tear, so Donovan still isn't convinced he's found the source of Chuan's problem. The tear just doesn't seem severe enough to cause that much bleeding.

Using a cannulat Donovan resuctions Chuan's uterus in search of blood clots that may be preventing contractions. But looking at the metal bowl where the suction has deposited the contents of Chuan's uterus, he knows blood clots are not the problem. The bowl is nearly empty. And Chuan's bleeding has accelerated again, not at its earlier pace but still too much. Worse, there are absolutely no clots in her blood now, which means her body is not taking measures to stall the bleeding. Chuan has now entered into disseminated intravascular coagulation (DIC). Basically, her body has used up all its blood clotting factors, leaving the blood without the ability to clot itself. But DIC is just a medical description, not an answer; it can stand for a cause or an effect.

Donovan guesses Chuan is the victim of some clotting abnormality, something she may have carried with her long before she came to Lovejoy. But her chart made no mention of any disease or abnormality, and if she had a blood disorder, by age sixteen it is likely she would have been aware of it. The cause of Chuan's hemorrhaging is of secondary concern now, Donovan knows. Without plasma she could die. And Lovejoy does not have blood or plasma for transfusions.

Donovan has the staff wheel Chuan back into the recovery room so that she can be more easily monitored until the ambulance arrives. Blood pressure is close enough to normal but her heart rate is still greatly accelerated, like a metronome gone haywire.

Suchak arrived while Donovan was operating. One look at the blood-soaked sheets told him everything. Now Donovan talks to him in the hallway, keeping his remarks as brief and specific as he can. Both know Chuan is Donovan's patient from this point on. He has undertaken the exploratory surgery. He is more familiar with Chuan's condition. And there's a third reason. Suchak does not hold privileges at any of the local hospitals. Chuan is going to be rushed to an emergency room, and a Lovejoy doctor will need to go with her; Suchak cannot go. Suchak will stay behind and finish up the day's surgeries.

In order to obtain privileges at a hospital a doctor must pay an annual fee. Suchak has resisted over the years, knowing all his work was abortions, which almost never demand he work at a hospital. "Almost never" has just arrived. And Suchak is helpless, helpless and afraid. He fears for Chuan's life, and that this is all due to some mistake of his.

With Chuan's condition appearing more stable, Donovan leaves the recovery room and joins Suchak in a hurried trip downstairs. They enter Allene's office and close the door behind. Quickly Donovan explains the situation. Before he can finish, a call comes down, and Allene picks up the phone. Chuan has resumed her heavy bleeding.

"Transfer her," Allene says, not knowing Donovan called for the ambulance while upstairs. The doctors rush back upstairs. Donovan finds his jacket and heads out to the parking lot.

Within minutes a fire truck streaks into the parking lot, which fronts the second floor. A dispatcher's error. As two emergency technicians rush in, Ginger stops them and says a mistake has been made. "We need an ambulance," she says. A few minutes later the ambulance arrives. June and Carolee help the ambulance technicians wheel Chuan's gurney out the door. Spotting the ambulance technicians, Donovan jumps in his pickup truck and beats the ambulance out of the lot.

As the ambulance speeds away, siren blaring and lights flashing, Suchak is left alone. The few remaining surgeries took only a few minutes. He prepares to return home, from where he will call the hospital for regular updates. He considers the work of the staff this morning and is thankful they handled the situation so well. Still, another twenty minutes, he thinks, and it would have been a hearse, not an ambulance taking Chuan away.

Allene notices Suchak wandering in the hallway before departing. She senses he is remembering the last time he saw a scene like this—Tina, who died. He's scared, Allene realizes, and he really cares. Suchak just might be growing into his job, she thinks.

The parking lot has become a vacuum, its kinetic energy sucked out by the ambulance now out of sight. Carye walks over to Chuan's parents, who appear to her incredibly tiny and fragile people, terrified and until now forgotten. They know little more than the fact that their daughter, whom they brought in for an abortion, has suffered complications, and Carye, using one of their other daughters as interpreter, tries to comfort them without providing detailed in-

formation. She does not want to panic the family, so she explains
that Chuan is bleeding more than normal, then leads the threesome
to their canopied pickup truck, which holds four more young children in the bed, and says the family should go to the hospital.

Carye, now alone, takes a moment to reflect on the effect this
morning will have on Lovejoy. She knows she will get calls this week
from other patients who saw the ambulance take Chuan away and
now fear that their own abortions were more risky than they were
told. Minor post-surgical pains will become unnerving to them. And
Carye knows the staff will go home tonight equally upset. As much
as various staff members might find themselves at odds during a normal workday, a patient ill or injured unites them in sorrow and in
fear. It is possible that many of the staff members feel most connected
to and proprietary about Lovejoy when a patient suffers—that woman
is one of theirs.

One more thought crosses Carye's mind as she heads back into
the building. No denying it, not that she'd want to: Donovan saved
Suchak's butt today.

At that moment, Suchak isn't the one Donovan is interested
in saving. At Emmanuel Hospital he is surrounded by the latest in
emergency medical equipment, all of which is faint comfort. Sitting
in the second-floor hospital lounge sipping coffee, he prepares himself for the mind-numbing ordeal he knows is about to begin. Ten
minutes pass before the ambulance arrives.

Donovan is ready to work when the decision is made to take
Chuan to the pediatric emergency room. Donovan had forgotten that
Chuan is herself just a child, sixteen years old.

In a flurry of motion Chuan is brought into the ER. The gurney
wheels are locked in place, Chuan is transferred to an examination
table and the team rushes in—trauma surgeon, respiratory therapist, nurses. And Donovan. The small room is soon packed with
ten people, maybe twelve, all seemingly in motion, focused on
one activity or another. Nobody has established who is in charge,
there doesn't seem to be time. A nurse is drawing blood. Everybody

appears to be talking at once. The lights above are as bright as artificial light can get; nothing can hide beneath their penetrating glare. Monitors all about are making their peculiar sounds, three IV poles stand at the ready.

The exam table is tilted so that Chuan's head is below her feet; the idea is to allow what little blood she has left to flow to her brain. The first thought Donovan registers on seeing his patient is that Chuan is in worse shock than he expected. Her blood pressure, taken immediately by a waiting nurse, is fifty over virtually nothing—a sure sign of shock. Forget finding the problem, Donovan tells himself. This girl needs stabilizing or she's going to die right here and now.

The IV needle inserted at Lovejoy is still in place, the tubing a transparent snake leading off to a bag of fluid on a pole. But it's not enough at this stage. Two anesthesiologists try to place a needle and catheter in Chuan's neck. If they succeed, the tubing will run down to her heart and allow the team to more immediately deliver fluids and blood to her failing circulatory system. They can't manage it; Chuan's veins are too collapsed. Ignoring the activity around them, they continue their efforts. After ten minutes Donovan sees they have prevailed.

Chuan needs blood. Desperately. Donovan decides that she can't wait twenty minutes for the lab to cross match her blood. Just looking at Chuan tells him she doesn't have twenty minutes left in her. He calls for four units of O negative blood, the universal donor supply.

Chuan is still bleeding and Donovan begins massaging her uterus, hoping to encourage it to clamp down. But all the massaging succeeds in doing is pushing more blood out.

Then Donovan notices Chuan has begun bleeding from around the three spots where she has been pricked with needles for IVs. That indicates a coagulation problem. Donovan orders plasma to replace the coagulating factors that are missing in Chuan's blood, and then ten units of cryoprecipitate, a clotting formula. Within minutes both have been hooked up to IV lines.

Donovan takes another moment to again run through the possible sources of all this bleeding. The laceration maybe, amniotic fluid flushed up into the lungs could do it, he thinks. He considers the possibility that he and the others around him will fail. Curiously he finds himself thinking, more like a child than a man in control of every advantage modern medicine has to offer, I hope she doesn't die.

The clotting formula appears to be working. The machines are spewing forth their numbers, she seems to be stabilizing. A nurse comes in with the first lab report: Hematocrits, the percentage of total blood made up of red blood cells, are 10 percent; 30 to 40 percent would be normal.

Stable does not mean healed. The IV continues to pump into Chuan replacement for the blood she continues to lose, but the body cannot long function this way. Chuan's own blood contains a myriad of biological factors that cannot be duplicated in the hospital's supply. After twenty minutes Donovan says they need to get Chuan to the OR. He's considering a worst-case scenario for permanently stopping the bleeding—hysterectomy. Take the artery that leads to the uterus and tie it shut, remove the uterus, and the problem, whatever it is, will probably disappear. And with it will go sixteen-year-old Chuan's ability to ever conceive a child.

Walking downstairs to the operating theater Donovan decides he will examine Chuan once more, this time by laparoscopy. He makes an incision just below Chuan's navel. Then he inserts a needle into the peritoneal cavity. Carbon dioxide gas is sent to fill the cavity. Then a spikelike instrument about a quarter-inch wide called a trocar is sent down. A tiny scope is set in the trocar, allowing Donovan to look all around the outside of Chuan's uterus. As he pulls out the scope Donovan is more puzzled than before. He could not find any perforation of the uterus. If it's there, it is remarkably well hidden. But still Chuan is hemorrhaging, and unless Donovan can find a way to stem the bleeding, nothing else will matter.

In desperation Donovan decides to try a technique he recalls reading in old textbooks, the lowest of low-tech. He grabs a roll of surgical gauze and a forceps and begins stuffing the gauze into Chuan's uterus, as tight a pack as he can manage. When he finishes he leaves just a bit of material sticking out. Simply put, he is trying to plug the dike. And he's used his entire roll of gauze—twenty feet.

Only two options left if this doesn't work, Donovan thinks. Call in a radiologist to place a catheter down Chuan's artery and embolize it, essentially blocking her blood supply before it reaches the uterus. This might buy time enough for her coagulation factors to recover. But if that doesn't work, if the blood supply to the uterus cannot be completely blocked off, it's time for the hysterectomy, or first maybe manually tying off the uterine artery. Okay, a third possiblity. Either way it's major surgery.

As if Chuan herself has read Donovan's mind and rejected the options, her bleeding begins to slow, halted by the tightly packed gauze. For the first time since Chuan became his patient in the recovery room at Lovejoy, Donovan begins to relax. He will leave the gauze in for twenty-four hours and hope that when he removes it tomorrow the bleeding does not start up again.

Chuan's hemorrhaging does not resume the next day. Within three days she has recovered enough to be discharged from the hospital, a testament to the sixteen-year-old body's resilience, Donovan thinks. Nobody knows what caused her bleeding. There are two best guesses: During the abortion amniotic fluid found its way into the bloodstream, causing the bleeding that led to the DIC as Chuan's clotting factors became depleted; or a sharp piece of the fetus's calvarium, or skull bone, cut through an artery.

Chapter Ten

An outside observer would think nothing changed at Lovejoy in the week after Chuan's abortion. Surgeries went ahead on schedule, internal divisions among the staff were no more noticeable or less. There was the inevitable discussion of Chuan's case among the nurses and assistants, and a few came to Carye wanting more information about Chuan's recovery and DICs in general, but the inquiries and discussion were brief.

Yet to Carye and Allene, the fallout was as evident and inevitable as if somebody had hung a banner outside the upstairs double doors reading TRAGEDY AVERTED HERE. Doctors and assisting nurses seemed to pause for a beat before stepping into the OR. Carye took a few extra calls from women who were bleeding normally after their abortions but who were abnormally cautious; all had been patients when Chuan began hemorrhaging. When Donovan finished the surgeries Friday, Allene treated the second-floor staff to margaritas at a local tacqueria.

Both Carye and Allene are almost presciently aware whenever an abortion patient from one of the city's other clinics ends up in a hospital emergency room, and they know the administrators at those other clinics will now be aware of Lovejoy's case. It is all part of the

unspoken bond between the different clinics, and the unspoken
rivalry. Even if nothing done at Lovejoy contributed to Chuan's situation, the case is counted as a black mark by those who will not
mention it to Lovejoy personnel.

Today Carye has to deal with the bad vibes she has felt around
Lovejoy since Chuan's case. This morning she counseled a twenty-
four-year-old whose ultrasound showed a biparietal of 5.6, which
translates into a pregnancy between 24 and 25 weeks. Certainly it is
beyond the 5.3 limit that Lovejoy observes and claims is set in stone,
until a case comes along and a doctor agrees to bend the barrier a bit.

Normally Carye would talk to one of Lovejoy's doctors about
this patient. The girl has never been pregnant before and is due to
start college in a few weeks. But this 5.6 biparietal will have to find
another solution. The doctors, in Carye's estimation, are just a little
bit skittish this week. Nobody wants to risk a second case from
Lovejoy ending up at the hospital within a month. Word would get
out, Lovejoy's reputation would suffer, the anti-abortion leaders
would take to the news like wolves to an injured lamb. Carye har-
bors no doubt that patients making inquiries at the city's other clinics would receive hints from counselors that Lovejoy, stuck with its
volume-business mentality, isn't quite as safe.

So Carye will not approach a doctor about bending the rules
and taking on this case. She refers the woman to a clinic in Washington that usually is willing to perform late abortions, not knowing
if the woman has the means or resolve to get there. And Carye knows
that if this woman had arrived a month or two later, or a few weeks
earlier, the atmosphere at Lovejoy would have been different and she
might have had her abortion. But not now.

Carye is also thinking about the rest of last Friday's events. The
woman who sat in the lobby preaching. Carye still cannot figure out
how everybody on the staff could fail to notice her until a patient
alerted Ginger. Allene likes to tell people who think Lovejoy too
vulnerable that her staff is aware of everything going on there. The
evidence from last Friday does not justify Allene's optimism.

"What we're going to say today is we need friendly people and we're just not getting that," Allene says. She and Carye are sitting in Allene's office plotting strategy for a luncheon meeting with Dave Austin, the new lieutenant overseeing Lovejoy's police protection. Together they discuss recent conflicts with the police. The pattern of growing indifference has continued.

When Carye called 911 Friday morning to report the sabotaged locks, she was told that technically Lovejoy had been vandalized, and all cases of vandalism are considered nonemergencies, meaning an officer could not be dispatched until late afternoon. By the time police arrived to investigate, a locksmith had changed the locks and disposed of any evidence.

With lunch still an hour away Allene confesses to a little lark she indulged in last week: She visited a psychic, something she had never done before. Lately she's been feeling a little unsure of herself, frustrated, with no single focus for her unease. So on a whim she made an appointment with a woman who recently had been written up in a local newspaper.

The psychic, Allene says, greeted her as if she had long known Allene eventually would come to the suburban office. And the woman offered two predictions. First, Allene will soon become a national spokesperson for abortion rights. The psychic's second prediction was even more specific: Some time late in the year a spy for the anti-abortion forces will come to work at Lovejoy. She invited Allene to give her the names of new employees, and offered to identify the infiltrator.

Allene and Carye walk to Besaw's, a neighborhood restaurant that serves as the setting for many of Lovejoy's most crucial meetings. The day is cool but sunny, and the restaurant's owner and waitresses smile and joke with Allene as the two women are escorted to a courtyard table. Five minutes later Austin arrives in uniform. Portland prides itself on a community policing program that encourages cooperation between the police and citizens, and Austin—bearded with metal-framed glasses, neatly styled black hair showing a hint of gray—presents a picture of an eminently accessible, modern-day policeman.

Austin takes a seat facing Carye and Allene, and the look of a thoroughly contemporary business meeting is achieved as all three place cellular telephones on the table. Austin is even more fully armed, however, with two-way police radio and mike attached to one shoulder and beeper on the other shoulder.

Allene begins by stating her concern that the police are not taking events at Lovejoy as seriously as they once did. "I have never called unless we really needed it," she says. In fact, police occasionally show up at Lovejoy in response to neighbors complaining about the commotion caused by protestors, and Allene habitually apologizes to officers in those situations, saying she knows they have more serious business to which they must attend.

Carye then explains Friday's events and the response to her report of the glued locks and the protestor in the front lobby. Throughout Carye's recitation Austin sits with arms folded across his chest. When Carye finishes he does not try to placate the two women but explains that his resources are low.

"What can we do to help you historically?" Allene asks. Then, turning to Carye, "I also question why we did a 911 on someone in our lobby." It appears they are playing good cop, bad cop—to a real cop.

Carye explains that the lobby protestor refused to leave the building after repeated requests.

"Really, Dave, I wouldn't have called for that," Allene says.

As the three continue their conversation it becomes obvious they do not share the same perspective. To Allene and Carye, accustomed to protestors violating Lovejoy's space, a trespasser sitting in their lobby for ten minutes is not that great a concern. But getting locked out of their own building, being kept from their work, constitutes a major violation and is worthy of police investigation. The police, however, have their own priorities, and in their world trespass is a greater sin than vandalism, one worthy of immediate response.

Austin maintains a conciliatory attitude. He is not here to alleviate Allene's concerns but he does not want to appear uncaring. He cannot provide an officer for every protest, he says, but when the number of protestors reaches double digits he will make sure a car is sent.

"But we would never call you for that," Allene says with a hint of frustration. Having made clear she is not an alarmist and is not attempting to exploit the Portland police as her private security force, she raises her real concern—discerning whether there has been a fundamental shift in attitude toward Lovejoy among the police. "We're also finding that the people that are coming are not very cooperative, and I've never dealt with that in all my years," she says.

Carye takes over, her tone expressing growing incredulity as she reviews the incident in which a protestor grabbed the arm of a patient and a female officer intervened. "She says to the patient right in front of me, in front of the other officer, in front of the staff, 'Is she making you do this before they'll give you an abortion?' I couldn't believe she would say this to a patient."

Austin remains expressionless and says he will look into the matter. His inscrutability has Allene and Carye off balance, still unsure of his basic attitude.

"We've had the police ask us to call them more often," Allene says. And then to have somebody come out and say something against everything we've ever been doing . . ." She leaves her statement unfinished, and silence overtakes the conversation until she begins again.

"I've never seen officers with issues," Allene says. "Some of them will say, 'Allene, I don't believe in abortion, but it doesn't matter, my job is to protect you.' Lately we've been seeing a lot of officers who seem very negative."

"Abortion politics has nothing to do with how we do our job," Austin says, his face still a mask hiding any sentiment.

"I want you to know we really support what the police have been doing," Allene says. She suggests they provide Austin, who has been on this beat eight months, a chronological review of Lovejoy's criminal and judicial history so that he will have a fuller perspective of the breadth of criminal activity that has taken place. Austin says he'd welcome that.

There is one more item on Lovejoy's agenda, the primary reason this meeting is taking place now rather than two months from now. Shelley Shannon's plea agreement is going to be heard in court next week. "This is a big deal nationwide," Carye says. "People are coming from all over the country to see this. People want to see if she's going to sing."

Carye has read a letter Shannon wrote in a newsletter distributed by the radical anti-abortion movement, a newsletter for those who consider *Life Advocate* too tame. Shannon asked her supporters to come to Portland for the hearing. Carye and Allene know that among those supporters are the people who are most likely to bring a gun or a bomb to Lovejoy.

It is unclear whether Austin is aware of the significance of the coming trial. His thinking is off on a slightly different tack—overall security at Lovejoy. He asks if they have considered requiring all patients to enter through the parking lot door to avoid protestors.

"Have you ever thought about resiting this facility to somewhere with a bigger parking lot?" he asks.

Carye and Allene politely laugh at the suggestion. Austin obviously is unaware of the many times she has had such requests made by police officials. Or that she had a national private security firm that specializes in combating corporate terrorism conduct a review of security at Lovejoy and make recommendations.

"Obviously you've never tried to buy real estate in Portland," Carye says.

"The glass in the front," Austin continues. "Is that glass dark enough so that you really don't know how many people are in there?"

Carye explains the Mylar coating that supposedly deflects and slows bullets, and the partial one-way effect it is reputed to yield. In truth, protestors outside can see inside fairly clearly.

The meeting breaks up with no one sure what progress has been made. Allene is convinced Austin is trying to help. This allays her greatest concern, that he has come to view Lovejoy a nuisance, or worse, that he is influenced by a secret, anti-abortion agenda. Austin is smart, she thinks, and she especially likes the fact that he didn't patronize her by automatically saying what he thought she'd like to hear.

Back at the office Carye adds together the totals for August and finds 440 surgeries were performed, Lovejoy's best month in years. And we probably have Rose Festival and Fourth of July weekend to thank, she thinks ruefully.

Two days later twenty-one people gather in the extra waiting room toward the back of Lovejoy's first floor. Representatives of each of the city's abortion facilities are nearly outnumbered by various police and legal notables. Cheryl Glenn from Alcohol, Tobacco and Firearms sits on one of the room's three couches, Lieutenant Austin stands toward the back of the room. With Shelley Shannon's day in court just over a week away, the city's abortion providers are sharing a heightened concern for security, but it is a diffuse anxiety because those who feel it have no idea if it is rooted in baseless fear or reality. They have managed to avoid a drawn-out trial for Shelley Shannon; instead Shannon will have one day in court, next Friday.

An assistant attorney general, standing next to a suited attorney from the district attorney's office, begins by outlining the sequence of legal events that will take place Friday. The primary issue to be decided that day is whether the new sentence for Shannon's firebombings will run concurrently with the previous sentence for the shooting of Dr. Tiller, or whether it will be added to the original sentence. The state's attorney says he anticipates consecutive sentences totaling twenty-seven years in prison.

Glenn is next. Of all the people in this room she is the one who best knows Shelley Shannon. Glenn has spent the last three years getting to know how the woman's mind works. In the process Glenn has immersed herself in the world of the radical anti-abortion movement. But even Glenn is at a loss in telling these people what to expect next Friday.

Glenn says she has heard rumors of car caravans coming in support of Shannon from Pensacola and also Wichita. She encourages everybody to assume they will arrive, though the only evidence to suggest it is Shannon's newsletter appeal. The national media that will be focused on the Portland courthouse certainly will be a draw, Glenn adds. But a one-day media event for a case already plea-bargained might not be enough to lure Shannon's supporters, most of whom are strapped for cash.

A woman administrator from one of the clinics asks what a twenty-seven-year sentence means in real time behind bars. Glenn says that Shannon has a habit of smuggling contraband into prison and getting into scrapes with other prisoners, so it is unlikely she will get much time off for good behavior.

Another administrator asks about security at the downtown courthouse.

"Why are you so worried about the courthouse?" Allene asks in peeved tone. "I think the major problem at the courthouse will be somebody being trampled by the media. It will be a circus."

Carye mentions a new protestor spotted outside Lovejoy recently holding aloft a sign that read THANK YOU SHELLEY.

Glenn reports a fire Monday at an abortion clinic in Grants Pass, Shelley Shannon's hometown. Police don't know if the fire was started by an arsonist. But in the last two weeks, Glenn adds, two arson attacks have hit Florida abortion clinics. In one case the facility was destroyed.

After the meeting has broken up with that unsettling sense that accompanies earnest preparation for an event that may not occur, Lieutenant Austin tells Allene a patrol car will be alerted and on call to Lovejoy for the week.

WEDNESDAY, SEPTEMBER 6

Allene is reading through a sheaf of papers on her desk with uncommon intensity. But this is very much an uncommon situation for Allene. Imagine discovering a history of your own life and finding it contains incidents of which you were completely unaware. The papers comprise Shelley Shannon's sentencing memorandum, seventy-two pages of evidence filed by the U.S. Attorney in an attempt to convince the presiding judge to decide that Shannon's sentence should run consecutively with her sentence for the shooting of Dr. Tiller. They contain a history of Lovejoy Allene has never known. As she hurredly turns page after page Allene occasionally makes comments without looking up. Seated across from her is Carye.

"She's so stupid," Allene says. "She had trouble finding Lovejoy." According to the report Shannon drove around Lovejoy's neighborhood, gasoline can and firecrackers in the trunk of her husband's car, unable to locate the clinic.

The report is unsettling. Shannon's philosophical conversion is nearly as unbelievable as her actions, "adventures" she called them in a computer file eventually recovered by police along with Shannon's diary. In January 1992 Shannon unsuccessfully tried to burglarize an abortion clinic in a small southern Oregon town. In April she returned and burned it to the ground. Next came Lovejoy. Shannon prepared for her attack there by practicing with fireworks on July 4. For six weeks in 1992 Shannon's husband was traveling on business, leaving her with the family car and the homemade napalm she had cooked up using a recipe from the "Army of God" manual that served as her guide into the world of terrorism.

With her husband away and unsuspecting, Shannon napalmed a clinic in Eugene, Oregon. She then drove 230 miles south to Reno, Nevada, and injected butyric acid into the wall of an abortion clinic rest room, the noxious smell causing closure of the building. A night in her car, and the next day another acid attack at a Chico, California, clinic.

A few weeks later the Pregnancy Consultation Center in Sacramento was the scene of Shannon's next arson attack, which provided what Shannon described in her diary as a "glorious state of worship." Seven months, eight clinic attacks.

But it is the report's section on Lovejoy that most draws Allene's attention. In her "adventures" Shannon describes planning the attack on the Surgicenter.

"Was reading my Bible, and God clearly said, 'I'm going to require a little more of you, Shelley.' And the Scripture I read just then was 'The way of the righteous is made plain' in Proverbs 15:19, and an idea came to me of tossing jugs of gas on the roof of Lovejoy and lighting it with a firework."

Eventually Shannon's plan would involve heaving milk jugs full of gasoline onto the roof of the Surgicenter and then tossing fireworks called ground bloom flowers to set off sparks and light the gasoline. Practicing at home with water instead of gasoline, she found it difficult to throw the gallon jugs high enough, even after experimenting with a variety of tosses.

Shannon viewed old videos of Lovejoy, taken during her protests there, to find the lowest section of roof. Her planning was haphazard, depending greatly on luck, or God. Allene reads from Shannon's diary, "I also told God I needed a five-gallon can. One day I got back from court in another city, and found in my garage a five-gallon gas can! My husband said they were throwing it out at work, so he brought it home. God worked out every other detail as well."

On the night of the Lovejoy bombing Shannon parked a block away and walked up the street carrying a suitcase with five half-gallon jugs of gasoline, newspapers to place in the jug openings as wicks, lighters, and fireworks. Shannon disguised herself with a charcoal beard, men's clothes, and a stocking cap. The fireworks would not light, and only when she threw the last one did smoke start appearing from the roof. Her efforts resulted in less than ten thousand dollars' worth of damage to Lovejoy, which opened for business as usual the next day.

The bumbling described in Shannon's account does not buoy Allene. What strikes her, and confirms suspicions she has long harbored, is the amount of help and support Shannon enjoyed during her spree. "Got really great maps and directions from A.C.," she writes. And, "Alibi was to be at W.P.'s." Much of the help was casual, but those casual helpers could become the next firebombers and shooters, Allene thinks. Nobody among the many Shannon told of her plans tried to stop her. This morning Allene is thinking about the number of potential terrorists still at large.

Carye has ordered extra clinic escorts for the weekend and upgraded Lovejoy's security alarm. But she's having trouble sleeping at night, wondering if she has missed some detail in her preparations. Tuesday evening she was alerted by a false alarm: A clinic door did not fully shut when Carye locked up for the night and later was opened by mistake. When Carye, at home, took the call from the police, her first thought was that Lovejoy had been bombed or torched. Later she recognized the danger posed by the unlocked door, practically an invitation to any protestor who might have been hanging around after hours.

As Allene finishes with sections of the report she hands them across the desk to Carye. Looking up from her own reading Carye says with a little bit of wonder in her voice, "You put Shelley on trial, and six months later she's trying to burn the building." Carye is thinking of the Lovejoy Eight trial—Shannon was one of thirty-four secondary defendants and as a result of her conviction owes Allene over two hundred thousand dollars. "She's finally getting justice."

Allene's take on the unfolding events is not so optimistic. She figures Shannon might be getting a dose of the law but she's far from through battling Lovejoy. "They'll make her a martyr," she comments.

They came seeking justice. On a gray September morning with a breeze just cool enough to remind everyone of the threat in the weather, the people whose lives center around providing and eliminating abortion focus on the stately federal courthouse in downtown Portland. Even those such as Allene Klass, who choose to stay away, have their thoughts consumed by the events taking place a mile and a half from Lovejoy.

By 9 A.M. U.S. marshals have taken positions around the building, telling observers they cannot protest on courthouse property, aware that the Advocates for Life hot-line message asks people to make a show of force.

Paul deParrie, dressed in black, is the first from Advocates to arrive, commenting that police are acting "like someone will attempt a jail break." A little later Andrew Burnett appears. "Looks like enough police," he says at first glance. Then, to a nearby officer, "It looks like you're expecting a war today."

Burnett, with the help of Life Advocate's associate editor, Cathy Ramey, unfurls a banner that reads FREE HILL & SHANNON! JAIL ABORTIONISTS! Immediately a police officer approaches and tells Burnett in an aggressive tone that the protest, on courthouse property, is illegal. The officer asks Burnett if he would like to come inside and check the statute. Burnett responds by looking up to the sky with a "Forgive them, for they know not what they do" look. Smiling, he tells the officer, "I'll take your word for it," and moves back across the street with his crew.

A few minutes later another officer tells deParrie a mistake has been made; Burnett can conduct his protest on the courthouse side of the street. When deParrie relays this message Burnett asks him to double-check. "I don't want to get arrested today," he says. Soon he crosses Broadway again to return to his station closer to the court-house. A dozen police officers move back and forth near Burnett and his group of six protestors.

At 9:30 A.M. the doors open to District Court Room 62, a muffled, lifeless chamber with burnished oak benches and panel-ing all around, outsized oil portraits of esteemed jurists along one wall and Doric columns reaching to the fifty-foot ceiling behind the judge. Off to the left is the jury box, fourteen severe-looking straight-back chairs—empty. About sixty people quickly file inside, their voices hushed as if the room has forced quiet upon them.

Shelley Shannon, wavy brown hair trailing over the front and back of her dull, prison-issue blue pants and blouse, is led inside. Only her shoes, brown leather sandals with white socks peeking through the gaps between straps, lend a hint of individuality. Shannon's skin appears sallow, her cheeks and jowls doughy, in need of sun. Her hands and ankles are joined by steel shackles. When the spectators arrive she is already seated next to her attorney on the right side of the hall. Soon the room is nearly full, abortion supporters on the left and opposing forces behind Shannon on the right. The room holds three women for each man.

Shannon, somber, unexpressive, looks very much like a woman coming to grips with her future. When she turns toward her family, seated nearby, she flashes a tense, grim smile, but it does not last. Paul deParrie takes a seat almost directly behind her, just in front of her family.

This is a sentencing hearing, not a trial. Most of what needs to be explained is contained in legal documents filed days ago and read by the U.S. district judge, James Redden.

Redden, balding and bespectacled, is a grandfatherly-looking man with a habit of leaning forward on his forearms and elbows when listening to testimony. He is a well-known Oregon figure, an Irish

Catholic from the old school of politics who served as the state's attorney general before his appointment to the bench.

Redden's face remains devoid of animation throughout the hearing, yet he never displays the disinterested look of some jurists, never appears bored. He has not presided over any of the previous cases involving Shannon, Burnett, or any of the abortion facilities in town. He has never spoken with Shelley Shannon. But earlier in the week he participated in a sentencing conference with fellow judges and probation officers, discussing the case. And he is aware that if the plea agreement had not been made and Shannon had been found guilty of all counts against her, with a maximum seventy-year sentence for each count she might have been sentenced to hundreds of years in prison.

First, Andrew Bates, Shannon's attorney, calls family members to make statements on behalf of his client. Shannon's sister reads a letter describing Shelley as "the most caring, compassionate being on earth." Shannon's daughter Angie cries when she says, "I just wanted to say that every year makes a difference in the way people change." Returning to her seat the daughter puts her left hand on Shannon's shoulder. Shannon places her hand on top of Angie's. A proud, defiant look crosses Angie's face as she walks to her seat, head erect.

David, Shannon's husband, spends much of the proceeding staring at the floor between his legs. He looks like a man who has lost control of his world, a man caught somewhere between grief and shock. A bunch of thin hair hangs over his forehead. When he approaches the judge he finds it difficult to speak. Eventually the words do come, slowly and in a hushed tone. "Your Honor, Shelley's been my wife for twenty years," he says. "She is a kind and loving person. She has been a wonderful mother. She has been active in the community. She takes responsibility for her actions. I'd like to have her back."

Assistant U.S. Attorney Stephen Peifer begins speaking with the understated confidence of a man who knows he holds four aces, or in this case, Shannon's diaries, dug up in a garden behind her Grants Pass house after investigators read a note Shannon had written referring to her backyard cache. He calls three witnesses—administrators of three of the bombed clinics.

Then, in an affable voice hinting of an Alabama boyhood, the tall, gray-haired Peifer focuses on the possibility of a nationwide conspiracy involving Shannon, emphasizing that grand jury evidence exists showing Shannon has distributed the "Army of God" manual detailing methods for destroying abortion clinics. And he recounts the progression of Shannon's anti-abortion activities from nonviolent protests to blockading to bombing and then shooting, making clear where the curve is heading.

Bates rises and puts his hand on Shannon's shoulder. A lanky, forty-two-year-old career criminal attorney who describes himself as a "bleeding heart liberal" right down to his pro-abortion stance, he tells the judge that when first approached he was hesitant to take on Shannon's case. But Shannon, he says, is not the monster he expected to find. "I found a human being, an individual who cries, an individual who, like you and I, is afraid inside, an individual, like all of these people out here who are trying to cope with life and doing the best she can and struggling. A person who feels love and fear, a person, Your Honor, not a demon."

Bates quotes an English proverb, "In a thousand pounds of law there is not one ounce of love." He paints a picture of a loving family torn apart and asks the judge to consider a fifteen-year sentence, pointing out that Shannon's arson and acid attacks all took place at night, when the abortion clinics were deserted and nobody was likely to be injured.

Accepting Shannon as a client did force Bates to confront his own political beliefs, but he is, after all, a man who has defended rapists and killers of children in his eighteen-year career. When he was first approached about the case Bates decided to telephone Shannon before making a final decision. During that talk he told Shannon he supported abortion rights but he would be open-minded about the facts of her case. And he found himself surprised by the ease of their conversation.

Shannon asked Bates two questions in that initial conversation. First, she inquired if he thought the Constitution protected murderers. Bates said no. Then Shannon asked Bates if he thought abortion was murder. Again, Bates said no. Shannon said she wanted Bates as her attorney, and Bates decided he could represent the engaging, intelligent woman after all. She did not appear the crazed zealot that he feared. What Bates did not know was the rationale behind Shannon's two questions, and that she had rejected another court-appointed attorney who said he thought abortion was murder. To Shannon, anybody who accepts that abortion is murder but still believes the Constitution does not protect murderers is a hypocrite. And she would rather have a pro-abortion attorney than a hypocrite.

Shannon's case, however, is hopeless. Her propensity for writing everything down, from the smallest detail in planning a bombing to the feelings of accomplishment afterwards, has left Bates little room for legal maneuvering.

"Praised God all the way home," she wrote after burning one clinic nearly to the ground. An entry in a manual Shannon titled "Join the Army, or How to Destroy a Killing Center if You're Just an Old Grandma Who Can't Even Get the Fire Started in Her Fireplace," offered guidance for those considering their own anti-abortion violence: "Remember, I kept praying the whole time. You would think it would be scary, but for me it was a very powerful religious experience. I saw God work when I fumbled. I sensed Him so near, so powerfully in me."

Peifer's presence completes a perfect irony. While Bates, Shannon's attorney, is pro-abortion, her prosecutor, Peifer, is a practicing Catholic who would make abortion illegal.

Shannon does not speak except to answer "No, your Honor" in a soft voice bordering on contrite when Redden asks if she wishes to address the court. Occasionally she can be seen whispering to Bates.

None of the last-minute appeals help. The U.S. Attorney's volumes of evidence prevail. Judge Redden imposes the maximum twenty-year sentence to run after the seven years remaining on Shannon's attempted murder charge. In a brief statement Redden says the issue is not Shannon's life as a wife and mother, but the fact that she has engaged in acts of terrorism.

"Terrorism in the sixties in the name of peace, or what allegedly happened in Oklahoma City in the name of patriotism, or terrorism which cost lives and property in the name of the Army of God or whatever cause is not justified," Redden says. "There is no reason, there is just no justification for this kind of conduct."

Shannon had hoped for a total combined sentence of fifteen years; now she will likely be in prison closer to thirty.

The hearing lasts thirty minutes. The crowd files out, led by a crush of men carrying video cameras and notebook-toting reporters. Burnett is still on the sidewalk, holding his banner.

The court officers have escorted Shannon out the courtroom's side door and away from the media, who have begun to realize their lost opportunity. They rush to the side door, too late. "What a zoo," one police officer calls to another.

The morning's events hardly touch Lovejoy. In addition to the regular protestors one woman shows up to hand out flowers and pamphlets. Inside Carye begins to unwind from a week of tense anticipation.

Carye has observed a police car driving by Lovejoy at regular intervals all day. Now, in the late afternoon, she has become too busy and exhausted to even notice if it is still coming around. Last night she went down to the family room in her home's basement and fell asleep on the couch before dinner. Two hours later she awoke and went straight to bed upstairs.

Throughout the morning an intelligence officer with the police called her with updates from the downtown trial. A handful of anti-abortion protestors from other areas of the country were spotted outside the courthouse but no violent incidents occurred.

Carye's decompression is coming none too soon. She knows the last few weeks have taken a toll. Yesterday a man walked in Lovejoy's front door and approached the reception window carrying a large briefcase, which he set on the counter. Carye was sitting in Allene's office, with its view of the front lobby. She flew out of Allene's chair toward the man and said, "Can I help you?" Without giving the man a chance to reply she said, "Don't open the briefcase." The man carefully placed his hands on top of the briefcase and explained—he was a carpet salesman.

Carye's office is beneath the upstairs operating room, and her desk sits directly below the suction machine used to extract tissue. Which means she is acutely aware when an abortion is being performed upstairs because the machine above her head makes a noise not unlike a vacuum cleaner. Pausing, she hears the machine go on and off a few times, which tells her the surgeon has encountered a problem with the procedure, probably difficulty removing all the contents of the uterus.

Carye counseled eleven women today, and now she is wondering how she can become the administrator Allene wants her to be with her attention so divided. Despite heavy advertising Lovejoy still has not been successful in finding a head nurse to manage the upstairs, maybe Carye's greatest distraction.

In fact, Carye has been thinking about the numbers this afternoon. Although August was Lovejoy's busiest month in years, the totals for September are way down. Last Thursday they saw only three patients instead of the usual fifteen to twenty. Carye is finding that the patient count, the numbers, are becoming increasingly important to her. Allene indirectly has begun talking as if she will someday leave the administration of the Surgicenter to Carye. And the patient count is the single most tangible way Carye can prove her administrative prowess.

Heather called last night. At dinner she was sitting around the table with her parents when her father said there was a message on the telephone answering machine for her. While the three of them paused between bites he played back the message. It came from the Portland hospital at which Heather had secretly given birth. A mistake. A hospital bookkeeper wanted to know how she should bill insurance for the birthing costs.

"Would you like to tell us about your baby?" Heather's father asked in a frozen voice.

Heather fumbled for words. "What baby?" she asked. Then her mother broke through the tension. "Oh, it must be because of your ovaries, dear," she said looking at Heather. And at that moment, with her mother patching up the tear in the cloak of secrecy Heather has so desperately tried to preserve, Heather knew with certainty that at some level her mother had been aware of the pregnancy all along. And Heather also knew that through the weeks of silently helping her maintain an illusion of secrecy, her mother was showing confidence in her daughter, silently demonstrating that she knew Heather could take care of her own problem. Either that, Heather told Carye, or her mother's denial was even more complete than either of them had ever imagined.

Finally Carye is ready to leave Lovejoy for the day, an hour after everybody else. She begins the process of closing up the building when she notices an upstairs window left open. Somebody left that window open, she thinks. Then she reflects that an entire upstairs staff left that window open. And her thoughts turn to the people who work at Lovejoy, and the revolving door it has become for much of the staff and how little loyalty most of the employees feel toward the place. All the enemies we have, hell, we've been firebombed, and nobody upstairs cares enough to make sure the windows are shut.

Allene keeps such feelings at bay with her conviction that most of Lovejoy's jobs incorporate an indefinite but very real burnout factor. Carye is not so sure. She still thinks that better benefits might help the clinic retain a more stable staff. And a more loyal one.

Heading up the stairs to shut the window Carye experiences a nagging pull at her heart and she immediately recognizes its source. Burnout is not necessarily limited to the lower-level employees. For the first time she feels an inkling of doubt about staying at Lovejoy long-term.

Chapter Eleven

Autumn arrives suddenly and hard in Portland, as if it can read the calendar. September 21, the last day of summer, was hot and sunny, a continuation of what had come before. The next morning the temperature dropped twenty degrees and the rains began. The city's longtime residents welcome the return of the rain as they would a friend too long absent but not forgotten, knowing that the rain, like an old friend, in time will overstay its welcome. This is the beginning of Portland's second season. The first is summer. The rest is rain.

The rain has settled in, but it has not yet begun to wear on people. If anything, there is a sense of impending growth in the air, inspired by the promise of rebirth in the city's numerous gardens, fed by the incipient deluge. By February daphne and forsythia will be in bloom.

In the bottom left-hand drawer of the business office desk is the folder Allene and Carye wish did not exist, and anti-abortion leaders would love to publicize. When a patient calls up after surgery and threatens or even complains, Carye pulls her records and places them in the file. If a Lovejoy doctor reports complications during surgery, that patient's file is added to the folder. Occasionally an attorney will contact Lovejoy on behalf of a patient; another file for the folder.

Lovejoy's record offers little encouragement for the litigious. The Surgicenter is sued once every three or four years. Tina, who died while Suchak was performing a tubal ligation, is the best-known case, and the Surgicenter was not responsible for that tragedy. Today Carye is placing another set of records in the file after receiving a letter from a local attorney.

The letter involves a woman who had an abortion months ago at Lovejoy and began bleeding heavily after she returned home. After calling 911 for an ambulance she checked herself into a hospital emergency room near her home and stayed overnight. Eventually she was told the bleeding was just a normal aftereffect of the abortion. But in the interim she ran up a seven-thousand-dollar hospital bill.

The woman's health insurer claims she is responsible for the bill because she checked into the nearest hospital, not one participating in her HMO plan. Last week the woman's husband called Carye and threatened a lawsuit if Lovejoy didn't pay the seven-thousand-dollar bill. Today the letter came.

Carye scarcely gives the matter a thought as she places the attorney's letter in an envelope and forwards it to Lovejoy's insurance company. She knows Lovejoy did nothing wrong and she has called their insurance representative, who says they probably are not liable. And she knows letters such as this are to be expected.

There is a prevailing impression, Carye believes, that abortions are often botched, when actually they are among the safest of surgeries. Only 3 percent of women who have abortions before thirteen weeks have any complications, and most of those are relatively minor. Less than half of 1 percent of first-trimester abortions require additional surgery or hospitalization. The real problem, Carye knows, is the existence of a large and ever vigilant audience waiting to jump on any hint of a bungled abortion; abortion just may be the most intensely scrutinized surgery around.

*

Carye enjoys schizophrenic patients. Most, she has found, display a disarming intelligence if they can be helped to focus on the subject matter. In some cases the disease is so severe that abortion counseling takes on an Abbott and Costello sort of quality with two separate conversations proceeding at the same time. As Leslie settles into the seat at the side of Carye's desk and Leslie's caseworker moves to the third seat in the corner, Carye is wondering which it will be today.

Glancing at Leslie's chart provides an easy starting point for the conversation. Leslie is thirty, according to her file, and was married for three years, until her husband committed suicide seven years ago.

"I'm sorry to see you're a widow," Carye says. "That must be very difficult."

Leslie spits out her reply. "I don't want to talk about it! I just want to get this done."

Carye looks again at the papers on her desk and learns Leslie has a hyperthyroid condition and that she is on Zoloft, Clozapine, lithium—a medicine cabinet full of psychiatric drugs aimed at combating the severe depression and episodes of rage that have characterized her life. And now she is ten weeks pregnant.

Slowly, Carye encourages Leslie to tell her a capsule version of her life. But every question is met by a drawn-out answer that only remotely relates to the inquiry. Leslie was institutionalized six years ago and was living in a mental hospital until last year, when she moved to an assisted living center. She attends a local community college. She had not had sex for seven years after her husband died, but then went to the beach for a weekend and met a man staying at her hotel. She has not seen him since.

Carye is observing Leslie with a rare intensity. It's hard not to. About halfway through her recitation Leslie jumps out of her chair and begins pacing the room. She acts as if in a constant state of distraction—twitching, walking back and forth, suddenly shifting her head to look in a new direction. Carye feels as if she is watching someone whose skin doesn't fit properly. And yet Leslie remains defiantly focused on her desire for an abortion today; discussing anything else risks becoming a flash point.

When Carye mentions scheduling the abortion Leslie stammers, "No, it won't do. I have to feed the parakeet. It needs a vitamin tonight," as if somehow having the abortion tomorrow or next week will keep her from feeding the bird.

Carye finds herself wondering if Leslie is always this incapable of participating in a conversation. Maybe, Carye thinks, being pregnant is contributing. Maybe not.

Twice during the session Leslie paces into the tiny bathroom that adjoins Carye's office. She shuts the door and Carye hears her moving about, talking nonstop nonsense, or at least nothing that makes sense to Carye.

There is no doubt in Carye's mind that Leslie wants an abortion. But she is struggling with a growing sense that she may not be able to say with certainty that Leslie understands the risks involved. And that is the necessary basis of informed consent.

Carye tries another approach. "Leslie, what are your other options? If you don't have the abortion, what happens?"

"Well, I wouldn't be able to finish college and I don't like kids."

Heartened by the reply, Carye asks, "Okay, so what does that mean?"

"I would have a baby at the hospital."

"Have you ever heard of adoption?"

At this, Leslie scowls, "I'm studying psychology."

"Is that something you've thought about or would consider?"

Leslie grits her teeth in a look of utter frustration. "*I don't want to have a baby!*" she shouts.

That's enough for Carye. But is it enough for a judge if someone takes Lovejoy to court? Carye launches into the informed consent speech and then asks Leslie's caseworker, who has remained silent until now, if she can sign the informed consent form along with Leslie. The woman refuses. If Leslie were mentally unfit in a legal sense, she or a guardian would have to sign, but since Leslie has been released from state custody, that does not apply. Carye picks up her phone, calls Lovejoy's insurance company, and is told they need backup: Carye should have the doctor go through the informed consent process a second time immediately before surgery, right down to a second signing.

Carye takes extra precaution, having the caseworker repeat back to Leslie the same informed consent information Carye has already conveyed. Then Carye reaches an informal agreement with the caseworker that the caseworker will check in with Leslie every day after surgery, making sure Leslie has changed her absorption pad, determining that Leslie's bleeding is within the normal range, taking her temperature. Carye is concerned that Leslie, who seems incredibly disconnected from her body, will bleed in the days after her abortion but she will not understand that the abortion is the cause.

Finally Leslie and her caseworker leave. Carye has not enjoyed this session. No connection was made here, she thinks. Carye is convinced that the reason most counselors feel fulfilled in their work is the personal validation they receive in speaking to strangers and having them respond. The response is the validation, it tells the counselor she is worthy of a connection. But not here. Not today.

WEDNESDAY, OCTOBER 4

There's a grim-looking father rooted in the waiting room today. A rangy, muscular man in blue jeans, black cap, and tight T-shirt, with one arm of his sunglasses tucked into the scooped neck of the shirt. He is not out of place in the manner of a bull in a china shop, for, in truth, there is little delicacy in the hallways and lobbies of Lovejoy, too many shattered dreams and broken promises for that. But this father, his jaws set stiffly as if glued in place, chin fixed firm as a vise, is a malignant presence—a stewing dad surrounded by women who are probably displeased to be in the company of any father, and especially a disapproving one.

Fathers rarely appear in the waiting room at Lovejoy. Most patients bring friends or come alone. A few ask their mothers. Very occasionally a boyfriend or husband can be spotted. Carye has observed that at Lovejoy, about the only thing fathers can be counted on to do is to express disdain for boyfriends. Never fails.

Carolee, one of Lovejoy's counselors, spots the man first. As she walks to the lobby Carolee observes a tableau that immediately tells her this next patient should make for an interesting morning. Father and mother sit side by side near the front door, but daughter Jessica is separate from them. Instead of taking a seat beside one of the parents, or directly across from and facing them, Jessica sits with her back against the same wall a few seats down. The threesome are so clearly together yet apart that Carolee does not for a moment doubt that they are a family. It does occur to her, however, that they look like three separate people tossed together, sharing a common concern but with different mind-sets and agendas. Like shipwreck survivors all in a lifeboat.

The father bears the look of a man searching for a target, somewhere he can discharge his swelling rage. Mother is a blank slate. Her hands rest in her lap, she exhibits no perceptible movement. Daughter? Well, daughter is not so easy: a strikingly beautiful blonde who could pass for ten years older than the sixteen years Carolee knows her to be. She is short, no more than five foot three, but her almost regal bearing makes her appear taller. She is wearing shorts with black socks and shoes. A second glance by Carolee reveals braces on the girl's teeth and a sullen look on her face.

Carolee herself is a bit of an enigma at Lovejoy, where boyfriends, or car and apartment hunting, are typical subjects of conversation, and brash confidence provides the prevailing backdrop. At forty-nine Carolee even looks different from the rest of the downstairs staff. She resembles one of the middle-aged Saturday morning protestors who drives in from the suburbs more than one of Lovejoy's young counselors. She wears her dark hair in a bun on top of her head. Her dress is equally restrained.

Carolee's background also makes her an unlikely employee at an abortion facility. She was raised in a strict Mormon household and still considers herself Mormon, though she strays from some of the strict dictates of her church. She has not discussed religion with most of her colleagues at Lovejoy. In fact, Carolee's older son, now twenty-six, has retained his orthodox Mormon faith, which strictly prohibits abortion. Carolee has never told him where she works.

After graduating from the University of Utah with a sociology degree twenty-seven years ago, Carolee took on the traditional role of homemaker and mother. At forty-two, with both boys in college and a storehouse of energy, she went to nursing school and then began working at Lovejoy upstairs as a surgical assistant. Eventually Allene noticed her quiet, mature confidence and asked if Carolee would be interested in counseling. Now Carolee counsels during the week and assists in surgery Saturday mornings. She works because she chooses to; her husband's career as an upper-level executive for a sportswear company provides well for the family.

Carolee enjoys the banter of the other, younger counselors, though she is unlikely to join in the talk of sports cars and boyfriends. Behind the closed door of a counseling session, however, she often finds herself crying with a tearful patient.

Carolee takes pride in her unwillingness to influence women to have abortions. The Mormon in her is never too far beneath the surface, she knows. Allene, she thinks, often sees abortion as a solution to the problems of the women who enter her building. And Carolee acknowledges Allene may be right. Often the decision to have an abortion can be the first or most empowering decision they make in their lives. Often it saves them from a lifetime of poverty and unfulfillment. Yet Carolee steadfastly refuses to accept that view. Recently she counseled a woman who said, "I think I'm ready to do this today." Carolee responded, "'I think' isn't good enough." She suggested the woman take another day or two to think and then come back.

"Jessica Johnson?" Carolee announces to the lobby. Jessica starts toward Carolee, and her mother begins to rise to follow her daughter. Stewing dad does not move. Instinct takes over and Carolee gently says, "I'd like to talk to Jessica alone for a minute." Accompanying Jessica back Carolee notices Jessica's distinctive way of walking, very light, practically on her toes, almost but not quite like a ballet dancer.

With the door closed behind them Carolee asks if Jessica knows how long she has been pregnant. Jessica quietly answers that she isn't sure, so the two head down the hallway to the ultrasound room.

Flat on her back in the ultrasound room Jessica, like many patients, begins to talk informally. It's hard to retain steely resolve with your clothes pulled up above your navel and a probe massaging gel on your stomach. She is sixteen, a sophomore in high school with a passion for horses. As one of the state's top rodeo riders she is hoping for one of the few rodeo scholarships given out by a handful of western colleges. By the time she has finished talking about riding and horses the ultrasound is over. Jessica does not ask about the ultrasound, so Carolee does not show her the picture. The two head back to Carolee's office.

"How are you feeling about having this procedure done? Is this the best choice for you?" Carolee begins once they have taken seats.

Jessica answers "Yes," not too firmly but not equivocally either. She talks about her plans for college, that she's not old enough to raise a child. She mentions that having a child would keep her from riding in rodeos. As Jessica neatly goes down her list, Carolee sees that her initial concerns upon viewing the family in the lobby are unfounded. Though sixteen, Jessica sounds mature and sure of herself. Then Jessica finishes her explanation by saying, as if in one breath, "But I don't believe in abortion and my mother and I have talked about it in the past and my mother doesn't believe in it either." Curiously to Carolee, the last sentence lacks the expression or emotion that usually accompanies those or similar words. Jessica spoke as if that was simply the last item on her list.

Carolee tries to assess what she has just heard. Jessica sounds intelligent and sure of her declaration that she does not believe in abortion. Yet Carolee's instincts are telling her that Jessica's final statement is intended as a preamble, that she will soon explain that she has indeed chosen to have an abortion. Carolee has counseled many women who claimed they didn't believe in abortion but that their cases were different and excusable in some fundamental way. And after all, Jessica is here, it does not appear she has been coerced, and this is an abortion facility.

Carolee asks Jessica, "Do you want your mother in here with you?"

"That's okay," Jessica responds with a nod of her head. The response is open to interpretation, but Carolee leaves the room and returns with Jessica's mother. She notices Jessica's father has retreated outside, where he is sitting behind the wheel of a pickup truck. As the three women settle into their seats Carolee suggests Jessica make a list of the pros and cons of having this abortion. Jessica's mother begins a nearly silent weeping. Soon Jessica is doing the same.

Dabbing at her eyes with a tissue she has taken from Carolee's desk, Jessica's mother asks questions about the actual procedure—when can it be done, will it be covered by insurance, how long will it take. Carolee, on firmer ground now and sensing her instincts were right, explains the process as matter-of-factly as she can. And as she does so, she watches both women again begin to cry, in unison yet separately. Jessica tries blinking back her tears, steadily at first, then more furiously, as if, with enough effort, she might somehow be able to blink away her pregnancy. Mother and daughter do not touch or comfort each other.

Carolee, nonplussed, is unsure of how to proceed. She chooses to press the issue by momentarily ignoring the tears and responding to the words. She reaches into the top drawer of her desk and pulls out a single-page informed consent form and a pink sheet for her counselor's notes, then begins asking the standard questions listed on the form. Jessica breaks down and is overcome with sobs.

"Do you want to go on with this today or do you need more time to think about it?" Carolee asks.

"I don't know what I want," Jessica answers.

"Jessica doesn't have any idea what's involved in raising a child," Jessica's mother says.

"It's not that I'm one of those kind of people," Jessica says with a telltale nod toward the sidewalk where Doc and Hugh hold forth. "It's just, I don't want to have one."

"You know I can't make her sign this consent," Carolee says to Jessica's mother. "She's old enough to either sign or not sign."

Breathing in, Jessica's mother speaks again. "It's her father." And like the word in a crossword puzzle that makes all the other lines come together, the mother's statement tells Carolee what is going on here. The mother finishes the explanation but she need hardly have bothered. Jessica's father has said that if Jessica does not have an abortion, she cannot come home.

Sometimes understanding only fosters more confusion. Carolee's intuition performs a back flip. A moment ago it was telling her that Jessica wanted the abortion, even though her words said she did not. Now mother and daughter are telling her why they have come for the abortion, and Carolee is thinking maybe Jessica shouldn't have it.

Carolee has been counseling at Lovejoy for ten months. In that time she has had three cases in which she needed help. This is number four she decides while looking at Jessica, who now appears not as a confident, mature young woman, but rather as an unremittingly sad teenage girl with a mother unable to help her. Carolee feels as if she has hit a wall. She has not yet dealt with a situation in which a family conflict was integrally involved in an abortion decision, and she knows Carye has.

Breaking a moment's silence, Jessica's mother asks, "Do you want me to go out for a minute?" Carolee asks the two women to wait in her office as she goes out in search of Carye.

Allene is sitting in Carye's office when Carolee appears. "I'm frustrated with this one," Carolee says. "I need help. I don't think I can make this woman do this, but she can't give a reason why she won't do it." Pausing to collect her thoughts, Carolee then continues, "She knows it's the best thing for her. She knows it's the best for the baby. It's not a religious thing." Pausing, she looks at Carye. "Will you see her?"

"Bring her in and we'll both talk to her," Allene responds.

Carolee walks across the hallway and soon returns with Jessica, then quickly leaves. Walking away she finds herself still trying to puzzle out the girl, and her own feelings as well. As a counselor Carolee feels reasonably accomplished at keeping her own values outside the counseling room. As a mother who raised two boys she had plenty of practice at guiding without judgment before she came to Lovejoy. As a Mormon she is imbued with a cautionary sense of abortion that probably distinguishes her among Lovejoy's counselors—if not in philosophy, then in degree. But now she finds herself hoping Jessica has her abortion. Carolee cannot figure out why she should feel this way; she's at a loss as to why her feelings are so involved in the first place. The thought disturbs her.

Only once before has Carolee felt the temptation to influence a patient at Lovejoy. The girl was fifteen and a drug addict. During the counseling session Carolee kept imagining the infant going through withdrawal, and then the birth defects the child might have to live with. While eating lunch that afternoon, Carolee saw pictures flashing through her mind of the life that child would live without a stable home and with a teenage junkie for a mother.

But Jessica is not that girl. Jessica at sixteen is bright and responsible. Her family is stable, her parents can help her in any number of ways. If Jessica were to continue this pregnancy, her child would have a better start in life than many. So why am I hoping this one chooses abortion? Carolee wonders.

Walking away Carolee notices Jessica's mother alone in the back hallway. She finds herself wandering toward the front lobby, where Jessica's father now sits as if sculpted from stone.

"You know, she's not sure about this," Carolee says, still standing above Jessica's father. "She does not want to sign this consent today. And you cannot make her sign that consent."

Jessica's father slowly shifts his gaze to Carolee. His eyes are those of a diamond cutter about to strike his blow. His lips are pressed so tightly together they almost disappear. "She's under eighteen," he says in a clipped voice. "She's my child. She *will* sign that consent."

Without responding Carolee walks back to Jessica's mother. She takes a seat and begins talking, hoping to gain insight into Jessica's relationship with each of her parents. By the time Carolee heads back to her office five minutes later she has come to one solid conclusion. There are two strong wills in conflict here and they belong to Jessica and her father. Mother is just a bystander.

Behind the closed door of Carye's office Allene, in the corner seat, takes charge.

"How did you end up here today?" Allene begins.

"My dad told me I had to have this done."

Carye and Allene exchange glances. They encourage Jessica to tell them about her life, and she does, from the thrill of rodeo riding to her plans for college. Abruptly, Allene tries a series of questions. She desperately wants to help Jessica envision the rest of her life, or rather two lives, one with the abortion and one without. Jessica's answers are limited to "Yes" and "No" and "I don't know."

"How would you take care of the baby?" Allene asks. "Have you wanted a baby?" "What if you have the baby and you leave home?" "Are you willing to go out on your own?" To this, Jessica has an answer. "I wouldn't have a choice because he says if I have the baby, he'll kick me out. And he's told me if I stay, I can't see my boyfriend again."

"Do you have friends who have had abortions?" Allene asks.

Jessica quickly answers. "No." In a slightly lower tone of voice she adds, "I know of a couple of people."

"How did you feel when you found out you were pregnant?" Carye asks.

"I was really happy."

Allene's turn. She looks straight at Jessica and asks, "Where do you think this is going to put your mother and father? What do you think your mother will go through with your father if you decide to carry through with this pregnancy?"

"It would be really bad." Jessica clearly is thinking now; she is quiet, but not detached.

"It doesn't seem like it's right for him to tell me what to do," she says. "He should support me no matter what I choose."

Nearly everything Jessica says involves her father, Carye has observed. Her dad introduced her to rodeo and trains her. Her dad has figured out how she can get a scholarship to college. But she doesn't talk at all about the baby's potential life.

Carye isn't sure what it is—the petulant tone of Jessica's voice, the body posture. Unlike the majority of teenagers she sees, Jessica has no slouch, conveys no diffidence or air of dismissal. She is leaning forward, her heels off the ground, intent on their conversation. Still, something is telling Carye that Jessica is putting up a front, not exactly acting, but sending a calculated message. Whatever is going on here, Carye surmises, it is not fundamentally about abortion.

Allene is thinking along the same lines. And she doesn't think a solution is going to occur until the real problem is addressed.

Jessica's resolve is no mystery to her. Allene has, after all, raised two teenage girls. She walks out and finds Jessica's father alone in the front lobby. His arms are crossed, the black cap remains on his head. She asks him to her office.

Seated in the office, Allene and Jessica's father are like two titans displaying their resolve.

"You can't force her to sign that," Allene says.

"Oh yes I can," the father responds. "I'm not sure I would stick around if she decided to keep the baby."

"You're going to have to grow up," Allene says fiercely. Jessica's father has no answer; soon he returns to the lobby. Allene rejoins Jessica in Carye's office. She waits for an opening in the conversation.

"Do you want to have a baby?" Allene asks.

"Not really," Jessica responds. "But I don't think I can do this."

"If this could all vanish and you weren't pregnant right now, would you like that?" Allene counters.

"Yes."

Carye asks Jessica if she is afraid of physical pain.

Jessica says she is.

"Is there anything you can figure out in your mind and in your heart that will allow you to go ahead with an abortion, or should we be looking at other alternatives?" Allene asks.

"Yes. I just want to do it," Jessica says.

"I can sure understand that," Carye says gently. "It's so hard to have all your brainpower focus on one thing."

Jessica gives an acknowledging laugh. A decision has been made.

"What do you want to know about what's going to happen?" Carye asks.

Before Jessica can respond Allene rises and asks a question of her own. "Is it okay if I go tell your parents that we're going to go ahead?"

"Yes," Jessica says. Then, looking at Carye she adds, "I don't know." Carye and Allene exchange "Here we go again" glances, then relax when they look at Jessica and understand she is responding to Carye's question.

"How about if I just tell you everything," Carye suggests.

Once more Allene leaves the room. First she approaches Carolee. "She's ready to go ahead with this," she tells the counselor. Carolee returns to Carye's office and takes Jessica to the counseling office in which they began. Allene escorts both of Jessica's parents into Carye's office.

Once all four are seated Allene begins by speaking directly to Jessica's mother. "It's important Jessica's father not make this an issue," she says. The mother simply nods and begins crying.

Turning to the father, Allene says, "She's doing this because of you. Because she doesn't want to lose you."

"But in return," Carye adds, "you need to ease up on her. Losing her boyfriend at the same time she's experiencing pregnancy loss is too much."

"He's a hoodlum," the father replies.

"Think about how in love you were with your first love," Carye says in a sympathetic voice. "If somebody would have told you you couldn't be with them, how would you have felt?" Carye pauses. "But think back now. Would you ever have ended up with that geek for good?"

Jessica's parents look at each other and simultaneously break out in laughter. In unison they raise their right hands, smile, and say, "We did." Jessica's mother finishes—"He was my first boyfriend." Carye notices the father's left hand has reached over and taken the left hand of his wife.

"This should be done now," says Allene. "After the abortion it should be over with."

"She's going to have to prove I can trust her again," Jessica's father says.

"How are you going to do that?" Allene asks in an exasperated voice. "She's sixteen years old. She is going to pay by reliving this memory for a long time. That's enough."

"She's a tough kid," the father says. "I've put her through a lot."

"You need to put your arms around her and tell her that you love her," Allene says.

"I've said that before," the father says.

"I'm sure you have. But right now is the time she needs to hear it the most." As Allene finishes, the only sound left in the room comes from Jessica's mother, who has been weeping throughout the dialogue.

Ten minutes later Allene opens the door and looks around. "Leah, come here," she calls. As Leah approaches the doorway Allene takes her by the hand and brings her inside the room. "This is *my* wayward daughter," she says to Jessica's father. Allies.

Back in her office Carolee begins the informed consent process a second time. As she recites the risk statistics she notices Jessica starting to cry again. Carolee decides to continue. Picking up the laminaria she says, "This begins the procedure." And as if a magician has snapped his fingers, Jessica stops crying. Suddenly she looks pleasant, almost pleased. Minutes later Jessica takes a pen off Carolee's desk and signs the consent papers without hesitation.

Watching Jessica sign, Carolee is uplifted. She feels the right decision has been made. She still will be thinking of Jessica days later, puzzled that she became so personally involved, confused that this case had her violating her personal code that resists advocating for abortion. Thinking it through she wonders why she decided to ask Carye and Allene for a second opinion. She could have told Jessica and her family to go home and talk it over, that Jessica had to be certain she wanted an abortion. Instead she took Jessica to Carye and Allene, knowing they might influence Jessica as she could not.

Wednesday is lams day: Women who will have their surgeries Thursday and Friday have laminaria inserted to begin dilation of their cervixes. While Jessica was in with Allene and Carye, Carolee went upstairs and told Suchak about the girl. Moments ago, when Suchak finished with his last patient of the day, he walked downstairs, prepared to leave the building. But now he sees the closed door of Carye's office. Remembering what Carolee told him, he remains an extra thirty minutes. Suchak recognizes Jessica's mother, who was his patient for years when he maintained a private practice. He wonders if he delivered Jessica sixteen years ago.

When word comes that Jessica has changed her mind, Suchak is ready. Carye approaches Suchak with the paperwork.

"You know I'm going to ask her if she's comfortable with this, and if she says 'No,' I'm not going to do it," Suchak says.

While Suchak talks to Carye, Carolee takes Jessica into the ultrasound room. She hands Jessica a white cloth gown that opens at the back, which Jessica dons over her shirt. Then Jessica removes her boots and blue jeans. Carolee guides her to a seat at the end of the exam table and drapes a cloth over Jessica's thighs.

Suchak enters the room.

"Hi. I'm Dr. Suchak," he begins. "I'm going to be your surgeon on Thursday." He runs through his list of questions about medical history and medications. Jessica says she uses an asthma inhaler, and Suchak tells her to bring it with her on Thursday. He asks if she has a ride home on Thursday.

"Are you comfortable having this done?"

"Yes."

"Are you sure?"

"Yes."

"We're not going to force you to do this."

"Fine."

Carolee helps Jessica lean back with her feet in two stirrups covered with lamb's wool booties, and then tells her to scoot up toward the end of the table.

Suchak begins by performing what is essentially a routine pelvic exam, inserting two fingers in Jessica's vagina to lift up the cervix. He then presses down on Jessica's abdomen to feel the size, shape, and direction of the enlarged uterus.

Next Suchak inserts a stainless steel speculum, a tool that resembles a thin duck's bill, into the vagina, sliding it up to bring the cervix into view. He wipes the cervix with a brownish antiseptic wash. With curved Bozeman forceps he picks up one laminaria—which resembles a green wooden match but actually is made of compressed sterilized seaweed—and places it in the cervical canal. Still using the forceps Suchak places a folded piece of gauze inside the vagina up against the cervix. The gauze acts as a barrier between the laminaria and the vagina, helping protect against potential infection as the cervix dilates. After he puts the gauze in place Suchak loosens the speculum and removes it as well as the forceps. The entire process has taken five minutes, and Carolee has described each step to a silent Jessica.

Jessica slowly sits up and Carolee escorts her to the adjoining changing room to put her clothes back on. Carolee reminds Jessica of tomorrow's appointment and together they return to the front lobby. Jessica greets her parents with a smile and they walk out the door together, for all appearances a happy family headed for home.

Minutes later Carye and Allene share a few thoughts in the hallway between their offices. Allene thinks the father probably has spent the day regretting his initial statement that Jessica could not come home if she does not have the abortion. "It's hard for him to back down."

Carye recalls the fear she detected in the father's voice when he asked if the surgery would be painful. "He loves her a lot," she says.

"We did one hell of a job of family therapy today," Allene finishes, as the two women head back to their offices.

Late that afternoon, alone in her office, Carye struggles to put Jessica's predicament into perspective. She finds her thinking again constrained by words, by the phrases pro-choice and pro-life.

"It kind of makes that whole pro-choice thing a joke," she thinks. From Carye's perspective, Jessica didn't have a lot of choice today. At dinner that evening Carye and Thom will try to come up with a phrase more appropriate than pro-choice. They will not succeed.

The next day Jessica comes in the front door smiling. She seeks out Allene and Carye and passes around pictures of her horse before heading upstairs for surgery. Jessica's mother comes over and gives Carolee a hug.

Three weeks later a card arrives in the mail. On the front is a picture of a dog and cat muzzle to nose. Inside is a picture of Jessica, smiling and wearing a cowgirl hat.

I give great thanks to you because, before I went into Lovejoy I felt very scared at being only 16, and with your kindness I made it through. And I think that you are a great person and that you do your job very good and that you help lots of young teen girls feel a lot better about what they're doing.

I know sometimes your job can drag you down and those people outside that place don't make it any better. But just remember you are making a difference.

Love always,
Jessica

Chapter Twelve

The noon hour has come and gone but nobody is leaving for lunch today. No words have been spoken to the staff, no directives issued by Allene, yet everybody on the first floor remains—counselors Leah, Carolee and Anneke, Carye and Allene in their offices with doors wide open, Lisa at the reception window. Tim came in a little while ago with flowers, and Allene asked him to hurry out and bring back sandwiches for the staff. Anything would do, she said, he should trust his judgment.

On the surface nothing appears out of the ordinary. Patients continue to arrive and depart, counselors shuttle from lobby to offices, occasionally leading patients back toward the exam room for ultrasounds or sending them upstairs for surgery. If there is any movement out of the ordinary, it is a subtle extra presence of staff in the front lobby and hallway, a lingering, as if some invisible bait is drawing everybody toward the center of the building.

Allene has become a hawk. A mother hawk. Standing in the doorway to her office she notices a woman follow Anneke into a counseling room. A man walks right behind the patient, a blue jacket draped over his arm. Anneke closes the door behind them. With the sure first step of a basketball player spotting an opening between defenders, Allene moves across the hallway, knocks on the door, opens it just wide enough to stick in her head and ask, "Everything okay?" Anneke nods that it is and Allene steps out, closing the door. The jacket looked suspicious.

Allene is usually in place or going to a place, a woman of straight lines. This afternoon she hovers. Her focus is on the lobby and reception area, which never leave her field of vision. When Lisa steps out to the rest room Allene takes over answering the telephone, which has been ringing incessantly the last two days. Allene thinks she knows the reason for the additional interest.

On Monday an administrator at one of the city's other abortion clinics met with Carye and told her they were raising their rates for a first-trimester abortion from $230 to $250, leaving Lovejoy alone as the low-cost provider. The administrator asked Carye to raise Lovejoy's rates, but she and Allene decided to hold the line. Allene is convinced that many women shop around for their abortions, and now Lovejoy will become their sole first option.

Lisa returns and Allene steps back to her doorway post. Her mind drifts back further—ten years. The patient was a twenty-two-year-old mouse of a young woman who knew only that she wanted an abortion. She was accompanied by her mother, a gravelly-voiced woman of about fifty who was doing her best to prevent the abortion, insisting she could take care of the baby. Both were seated in Allene's office.

"You made your bed and you should lie in it," mother said to daughter.

Temper rising, Allene countered, "If you want to have a baby, *you* should have one."

The next thing Allene remembers is looking up from the carpet, realizing she had just been floored by a powerful backhand slap. Allene knows why this memory has returned to her just now: Today could bring the second time she faces physical assault inside her building.

The threat of violence is never far from Lovejoy's doors. It does not hang in the air; the routine of daily tasks would become unbearable. Instead it remains suspended just beyond the consciousness of the people who work there. It is like Doc and Hugh outside, not objects of fear themselves, but symbols of greater menace.

There are plenty of reminders. A posting in the second-floor lounge provides guidelines for dealing with protestors and police. Carye and a few other staff members have their guns. The morning papers sporadically offer headlines about abortion clinic shootings and firebombings around the country. The patients, too, contribute with their not infrequent stories of abuse and hardship.

But today the threat has gone a step further, has taken a tangible, if not identifiable form. Over the course of the morning the downstairs staff—the people taking turns answering those incessantly ringing phones—have been threatened with violence by the boyfriend of a patient, a boyfriend who objects to his girlfriend's planned abortion and says he will do whatever he must to stop it. Carye has spoken to the man, and Lisa and Anneke.

None of the lobby watchers knows what the man looks like, whether he is fifteen or fifty. They know his name—Vincent. They have heard the anger in his voice and they are convinced Vincent's threats are real. "All you care about is killing babies," he shouted just a few minutes ago over the phone to Lisa.

Allene out loud wonders about Vincent's age. His girlfriend, Tiffany, is sixteen. Tiffany came in yesterday for counseling and lams. She is a second-trimester D & E, so she is to return today at 1:30 P.M. for a second set of lams. Surgery is set for tomorrow, Thursday. The calls from Vincent started yesterday afternoon.

Lisa, between calls, says he sounds young. She has taken three or four of Vincent's calls this morning, and each time, she says, Vincent sounded more aggressive. "Like he's working himself up to something," she says. Considering Allene's question she adds, "Sixteen sounds about right."

In his last call Vincent also said, "If you don't stop this, I'm going to come in and stop it." That's when Allene called the police. A squad car is parked outside Lovejoy's front door.

*

Tiffany was the first patient of the day Tuesday, a willowy, pretty teenager with soft brown hair and the quiet smile of a young women whose only sure thought is that boys find her attractive. She met with Anneke, said she had no idea how far along she might be, only knew that she had missed her last period. Anneke immediately took her back for an ultrasound, which revealed a seventeen-week pregnancy.

"Okay, so you're seventeen weeks along," Anneke began back at her office. "Have you made a definite decision about what you want to do?"

"If it's over four months my boyfriend said we're not going to have an abortion," Tiffany answered.

"I'm not here to try and change your mind," Anneke said in a relaxed tone of voice. This is a different Anneke from the one who counseled Shannon seven months ago. No longer does she rely on scripted, pat questions and answers. She trusts her judgment, is sure of her ability to follow a counseling session wherever it leads. Her natural curiosity is much more involved in the sessions now, and the process has become more enjoyable as it has become more spontaneous. One thing that hasn't changed is her smile, still as regular as the winter rain that has begun to hunch shoulders and sour moods around town.

"Actually we're engaged," Tiffany added.

So much for the script. Any script. Anneke paused, knowing she must now consider her responses very carefully.

"Well, congratulations. But do you think you're ready to have a child right now?"

Tiffany presented her story in bits and pieces. Her boyfriend, Vincent, is from a traditional Catholic family and doesn't believe in abortion. Vincent has dropped out of high school and lives with his mother. Tiffany still attends school, where she earns a B average and is president of the Spanish Club. She told Anneke she wants to be a doctor someday.

Vincent has other plans. He views the pregnancy as an opportunity. "Now we can get on welfare and get food stamps," he told
Tiffany last night. "Think of all the fun stuff we can buy." But to get
welfare and their own apartment they must have a child, he added.
Tiffany did not tell Vincent about her appointment at Lovejoy.

Anneke stifled an urge to voice her opinion. She has learned
that vague pronouncements about a difficult future don't influence
most sixteen-year-olds. Only specific, tangible examples that a teenager can relate to will work. So Anneke went over the list, point by
point, confronting Tiffany with the reality of caring for a baby; the
cost of a college education; the difficulty of going to school, working
for tuition money, and mothering at the same time.

"Our parents will help us," Tiffany responded.

"You should be out buying CDs, not laminaria," Anneke said.
Reining in her own feelings she said, after a pause, "I'm not here to
change your mind. I'm not here to force your opinion. But I'm sitting here seeing this beautiful young woman with her whole life ahead
of her, and you have so many other things you can do right now. Why
don't you go ahead with your dreams and have kids later?"

Tiffany had no answer, so Anneke continued, "We're always
here for you." She handed Tiffany two pamphlets, one entitled,
"Choices and Decisions about Pregnancy," intended to guide women
through the process of making a decision, the other, "Parenthood,
Adoption, Abortion," a brochure emphasizing open adoption.

Before ending the session Anneke left Tiffany with some figures
that she recently had learned from Carye: One in ten high school girls
who become pregnant finish high school, and one in ten thousand
girls who have babies during high school finish college. And a third
statistic: Over 80 percent of the men in this country don't pay their
child support. "The statistics are stacked against you," Anneke said.

Tiffany said she had to get back to school, but that she would
think about what Anneke had told her. "I just want to talk to my
boyfriend," she finished.

Returning from lunch later in the day Anneke was surprised to learn Tiffany had called back and asked for another counseling appointment after school, at 3:30 P.M. When Tiffany appeared she headed straight back to Anneke's office and sat down. With tears starting to form in her eyes, she said she didn't talk to her boyfriend but she had decided to have the abortion.

"Are you okay with that?" Anneke asked. "I know he's important to you."

Tiffany said her mind was made up, and her attitude seemed to bear that out. Even through tears she appeared more relaxed than in the morning, more comfortable. She opened her wallet and showed Anneke pictures of her friends, pointing out one girlfriend who had a baby last year and tried to kill herself a few months ago.

"I don't want my life to be over. I don't want to be stuck," she said. "I want to have a life." She added that she would go to Vincent's house after dinner and tell him of her decision.

Anneke explained the D & E procedure, emphasizing that inserting the lams today would begin the abortion and underscoring the risk involved if Tiffany should change her mind and request the lams be removed.

"I'm okay with that," Tiffany said, signing the consent form for placement of laminaria. Anneke then reviewed the entire abortion process and the risk, and Tiffany quickly signed the procedure consent forms.

In the downstairs exam room Anneke helped Tiffany change into a hospital gown in preparation for insertion of her lams. As Anneke tied the strings in back Tiffany asked, "Do you think I'm doing the right thing?"

Anneke did not like the question, not coming at this point and after the discussions they had been through. She weighed her words carefully. "My opinion shouldn't change you," she said. "But I meant it when I said you had a lot of potential, and everything you've been telling me today is reaffirming that you want to go ahead and have the abortion." When Tiffany did not immediately respond she asked, "Are you okay?"

"Yeah," Tiffany replied as Anneke left her to Dr. Lane. Carye accompanied Lane into the room. As Lane began inserting the lams Carye noticed deep purple bruises on Tiffany's legs.

"Who pinched you?" Carye asked.

"My boyfriend," Tiffany replied.

Thirty minutes later Anneke spotted Tiffany heading toward the front door. "How did you do?" Anneke asked.

"They were fine when the doctor put them in," Tiffany said. "I just felt a pinch. No cramps." Then, flashing a carefree smile, she added, "We're going to McDonald's."

Vincent's calls began late Wednesday morning, before Tiffany arrived for her second set of lams. Anneke took the first call, not knowing who it was or which patient it concerned. It was just a man with a question about a patient, insisting on talking to a doctor. Within minutes the reason for the call became clearer to Anneke, who still didn't know which patient it involved. She didn't much care.

"You don't need to talk to a doctor," she said. "You just need to talk to your girlfriend. We're here for the patient. We're not here to referee between you and the doctor."

"She doesn't have my consent," Vincent responded.

"She doesn't need your consent." In fact, consent forms for abortion don't even leave a space for the signatures of husbands; at Lovejoy boyfriends are just an afterthought.

"I'll find out who the doctor was and I'll make sure he never does an abortion again," Vincent told Anneke. In a later call he told Carye, "Either you stop this or I'll stop you from doing anything about abortion again." Carye, ever the counselor, told Vincent to come in for a talk. "I wouldn't talk to a butcher," he responded. By lunchtime most of the downstairs staff was on alert and Allene had begun her doorway vigil.

At 1:15 P.M. Tiffany arrives for her second set of lams. Anneke has not connected Tiffany with the angry call she took, and she has been too busy with patients this morning to be aware of the escalating threats. As soon as she sees Tiffany enter the building Anneke moves to her side and ushers her back to the counseling office. Immediately Tiffany explains that she wants to continue with the procedure but she's afraid Vincent is going to break up with her.

The door opens. Carye comes in and briefly informs both women of Vincent's threats. Carye finishes by telling Anneke she needs to handle this case now. As Carye leaves with Tiffany, Anneke, who came to Lovejoy after working at a domestic violence shelter, notices Tiffany has a black eye that wasn't visible yesterday. She wonders if somebody should be helping Tiffany pursue a restraining order against Vincent, or at least find some place other than home for her to spend the night.

Within minutes Tiffany's mother has arrived. Carye escorts them both to a bench behind the double doors that lead to the downstairs exam room. Allene continues to patrol the lobby, but she still doesn't know what Vincent looks like. When he arrives she is back in her office, momentarily on the phone. Lovejoy is busy and everyone is distracted. Vincent walks in and heads back toward the double doors as if he knows where Tiffany has been taken. Tiffany and the day's other D & E patients are receiving a group lecture on their procedure in a room just beyond the doors. Tiffany's mother remains on the bench directly behind the doors.

As Vincent marches toward the doors Allene intercepts him. She sees an angry seventeen-year-old boy who looks completely out of his element. With her back to the doors Allene does not waste time with her trademark smile or a polite inquiry. She confronts Vincent, not pausing for answers.

"Can I help you? You've been causing us a lot of problems today. We've got police right outside."

Vincent does not say anything, but he makes no move to leave. He has a man's body but a child's experience, and he has no idea what he should do next. His clothes drape over him in the latest gang fashion. Straight brown hair hangs to his shoulders. His expression now is dull, more confused than threatening. But he is giving no ground.

Without touching Vincent, Allene ushers him into her office. Both stand. "Now tell me why you're threatening my staff."

Vincent insists he hasn't threatened anybody.

"I would like you out of this facility."

Vincent fumbles for words. He sits. The door remains open. Over the course of about fifteen minutes Allene and Vincent converse, though Allene is doing most of the talking. When Vincent says he loves Tiffany, Allene retorts, "Love is respecting somebody else's rights. You're not anywhere close to being able to love."

Vincent talks about abortion and it is clear to Allene that he is repeating words that have been spoken to him. "I don't want my kid thrown in the garbage can," he says. "It's got ears and eyes."

"What do you have to give a child?" Allene counters. "Do you have an education?"

"I could get a job. I could go back to school. If I'm old enough to have sex, I'm old enough to have a baby."

"What did you say?" Allene fairly shouts. "It should be the other way around."

Finally, Vincent settles on a tactic. He keeps repeating that he just wants to talk to Tiffany. "Is she behind those doors?" he interjects each time Allene gives him a chance to speak. Allene has had enough. She is beginning to feel sorry for Vincent, just a little bit. She thinks he has been programmed and she thinks she knows by whom—his aunt is walking around the front lobby asking Lisa and each counselor who wanders by about paternal rights. Vincent might even be a sweet boy, she thinks, beneath the tough exterior.

Allene stands up and returns with Vincent to the lobby, where Vincent takes a position beside his aunt. "I'd like you to leave," Allene says. She starts walking toward them, herding them toward the front door without actually touching them, a motion that requires utmost confidence. Just before they reach the front door the aunt turns and says, "You are a murderer. You kill children for money."

With a smile Allene responds, "So what do you do for money?"

Behind the gray double doors leading to the exam room Tiffany fidgets on the bench beside her mother. She does not know what is occurring on the other side of the doors, but since rejoining her mother after the lecture she has hardly been thinking of anything else, repeatedly asking her mother if Vincent has shown up.

"Tell him I still love him," she says with a look full of both sadness and hope. She is torn, sure she wants the abortion and equally sure she wants this boyfriend. Nobody is restraining her from walking two steps through the doors to where Vincent can see her, but she does not rise.

Willing her daughter to remain seated beside her, Tiffany's mother, Paula, is not so conflicted. She is thinking beyond this moment, backward in time. Family history. Paula, thirty-four, could easily pass for Tiffany's older sister. They share the same wavy brown hair and innocent good looks.

"She's like every other female in our family. She has no self-esteem," Paula says. "We pick losers."

Paula was pregnant and then married at seventeen. Four times divorced, she married again at twenty-two, twenty-four, and thirty-one. "I tend to get married on dates," she wryly observes. Amazingly, Paula's mother and grandmother were also mothers by seventeen, and both married.

So many of Lovejoy's stories are about patterns and habits, women coming in for multiple abortions, generations repeating the lives of those before. Today Paula is mustering all of her motherly strength in an attempt to break the stranglehold of her family's history, starting with her daughter. This time there will be no child at seventeen. This time there will be no child bride. With each entreaty her daughter makes, with each sad look she sees on her daughter's face, Paula sees a dream dissolving. Looking at Tiffany's finger she notices her daughter is wearing the fake diamond ring Vincent gave her a few days ago. This morning Tiffany told her that no matter what happens, she and Vincent are going to marry someday.

Paula is also keenly aware of the bruise beneath her daughter's eye. Earlier Tiffany confessed to Carye that Vincent hit her. "But sometimes I hit him," she added.

In the front lobby the afternoon's patients are beginning to pick up on the scene that is being played out around them. A man in a maroon baseball cap leans over to the shorthaired woman in the chair beside him and says, "If I want to be back there with you, they can't stop me."

Tiffany willingly goes back to the exam room when her turn comes. Ten minutes later Carye helps lead Tiffany through the building's back exit and into Paula's van, which has been pulled up near the door. Vincent and his aunt are still out front, where they will remain for thirty minutes, the aunt berating the policeman who has guided them away from the building's front entrance. "She's in there sinning," the aunt insists to the disinterested officer.

Back inside Lovejoy it feels as if all the people who work there have joined in one great, collective exhale. Allene heads back to her office. Anneke approaches her just outside the doorway and says, "That was very good, what you did." Allene flashes a confident smile.

Wednesday night Tiffany stays home with her mother. Vincent does not come over to their house—Paula has made it clear she will call the police if he does. Around 7 P.M. Vincent's father calls Tiffany's house and says Vincent left a suicide note claiming he is going to jump off a bridge. At the same time Vincent has a friend phone Tiffany and tell her to call his pager, which Tiffany does. Vincent, not sounding at all suicidal, promises he will get a job and an apartment for them to live in. He also says he will support her decision, no matter what she does. He does not kill himself. On Thursday Tiffany has her abortion.

*

On a slow Thursday morning Anneke finishes her counseling and walks upstairs to turn in a patient chart. In the staff lounge she begins talking to Kim, one of the medical assistants. The topic turns to D & Es. Anneke confesses that she has never seen one performed, even though she often counsels D & E patients. In fact, she has never seen anyone under general anesthetic.

The first D & E often is regarded as a rite of passage for new counselors. It is one thing to talk about abortion, another to view a second-trimester fetus as it is removed from a woman's body. Counselors who have been operating on a detached, political plane sometimes discover the philosophical foundation of their work crumbling beneath them. Some counselors find they cannot counsel D & Es and quit, or limit their work to first-trimester patients.

In counseling sessions Anneke typically tells D & E patients their surgery will take place under general anesthetic. She explains how they will start with an IV in pre-op, and then be taken to a surgical room where they will sleep about twenty minutes and wake up in a recovery room a little sore, a little chilled possibly, and very sleepy—all normal. Rarely will a woman during counseling ask for a more detailed description of the actual surgery. When one does, Anneke provides only the most general of answers, that the doctor uses forceps to extract the fetus.

Kim extends an invitation to Anneke: A sixteen-week D & E is taking place right now. Would she like to observe? Anneke asks Dr. Lane, who agrees. Kim helps Anneke don mask, booties, hat, and scrub suit and escorts her to the operating room.

Entering the room Anneke sees a woman whose body is completely draped by blankets and whose head is covered by a blue paper surgical cap. To Anneke it appears as if her individuality has been all but erased. It is even difficult to determine the woman's age, she thinks. Anneke silently drifts to the back of the room.

Looking up, Dr. Lane invites her to stand by the table. "I'll just stay out of the way," Anneke responds softly, remaining in place.

Anesthetic has already been administered but the patient is still moving about, flopping her arms and rolling her head. This is unusual but not a cause for concern. Gently Carolee holds the patient's arms down and uses Velcro straps to keep them in place, insurance against an unexpected spasm that could pull out her IV. A cuff is placed on the patient's finger so that Marion, the anesthetist, can monitor her heart.

Anneke is surprised by the height of the stirrups, and in fact, by the elevation of the entire bed. The woman's knees are at about the level of Lane's head as he sits down on a stool between her legs. Anneke listens as Marion, a gray-haired woman with a tranquilizing bedside manner, begins talking to the seemingly unconscious patient, saying the woman's name. "Hey, honey, it's okay. I'm right here. Just relax. I'm going to be here the whole time," Marion continues.

Lane begins the surgery by reaching into the woman's cervix and removing the swollen laminaria, counting until he reaches six and knows he has them all. Next he inserts a speculum and washes the cervix with antiseptic soap. Lane picks up a ring forceps, which resembles a small salad tongs. Using the forceps to hold on to the cervix, Lane's free hand inserts two dilating rods to ensure the cervix is fully open. Anneke is surprised by the size of the dilating rods, each about the circumference of a fifty-cent piece. The rods used in first-trimester tab locals, which Anneke has seen, are closer to the size of pencils.

Lane inserts his forceps, then grabs and tugs. A clear liquid with a slight sepia tone rushes out. Anneke wonders why Lane has emptied the patient's bladder but in fact Lane has punctured her amniotic sac, releasing its fluid.

Still holding the forceps, Lane begins pulling, tearing apart the fetus. His first three tugs yield indistinguishable tissue. The fourth brings out a more solid mass, which Anneke, from her position in the back of the small room, immediately recognizes as the trunk of a fetus. But even this is not as identifiable as Anneke had expected. Tiny hands and feet, extracted next, are the most recognizable. The head is less so. The pieces of the fetus and the placenta are placed by Lane on a surgical tray to his side.

A D & E is unusual among surgeries in that the surgeon must operate by feel. No incision has been made, and so Lane cannot see what he is doing. As a result, the operation lacks the deftness of many surgeries. There is little artistry or sureness of motion as Lane pulls at the fetus. Usually it breaks apart but sometimes it is removed nearly intact. And because the contents of the uterus are invisible to him, one of the most difficult decisions Lane must make, when the fetus is not intact, is when to stop. Having decided the entire fetus and placenta are now on the surgical tray, Lane suctions the lining of the uterus to make sure no tissue has been left behind. The suction makes a sound resembling hydraulic doors opening and closing.

The entire process has taken about five minutes. Anneke heads back to the lounge as the patient is wheeled into the recovery room. Her most vivid impression is surprise that she has not been more deeply affected. The operation to her seemed routine, even clinical— the stuff of science. She recalls the appendectomy she underwent earlier this year and wonders if the operating room setting has become associated in her mind with healing, thus keeping any emotional disturbance she might have felt at bay.

Although the operation is over, the fetus is still a matter of concern. This patient, like most, has signed an extra consent allowing the extracted material to be used for medical research. Ronda, a medical assistant who also works for a biological supply company, takes the surgical tray into another room where she uses a plastic colander to strain out the blood, leaving only the separated parts of the fetus. These she places in a glass dish, taking a moment to measure one of the feet against a transparent plastic ruler to establish exact gestational age.

Earlier in the day she received her regular fax detailing what body parts are needed by which researchers around the country. The researchers specify preferences for age and, in some cases, sex. Liver, spleen, pancreas, and brain are the organs most often requested.

Peter Korn

Ronda puts the body parts into glass jars with preserving fluid. She then packs the jars in Styrofoam boxes full of ice and calls Federal Express, which will pick up all the boxes from the day's surgeries. The arrangements are handled by Ronda's company; Lovejoy supplies only the rented work space and access to the fetal material, for which it is not paid.

Later, Carye is pleased when Anneke reports her reaction. In Carye's mind, however, the ultimate rite of passage involves counseling a first-trimester patient who is having difficulty getting through her procedure, a woman who is awake and able to express her pain or sadness. That is something Anneke still has to confront.

Chapter Thirteen

No decisions, not today. Not this week, thinks Suchak, consciously trying to calm himself, as if he can think down his own blood pressure. And not here. Here, at Lovejoy, I'm just reacting. Better to go home, think things through. Make a plan.

Now there's an irony, Suchak reflects. Still trying to make plans and have the rest of the world cooperate. Guess I'm a slow learner. How can I expect the rest of the world to fall in line when I can't even count on my own body to cooperate? Suchak eases into the chair in his office. Some office for a medical director, he thinks. A corner of the first-floor staff lounge, with a desk, filing cabinet and chair squeezed in behind a couch.

Forty-eight hours since I got the news and still I'm stunned, thinks Suchak. Allergies seemed worse than usual this summer. Usually they hit around March, and by July the stuffiness and wheezing are over. Not this year. They've been dogging me right into autumn. And more severely than ever. On the weekly walks and bike rides I could hardly make it up the half-mile hill near home before starting to struggle for breath.

A visit to the internist, then an appointment with a cardiologist. No stress test, no cause for alarm. But then the cardiologist asked for an angiogram. And now I've got an appointment for a quintuple bypass a week from Monday. Talk about denial—five blocked arteries and never a clue, or at least none that I picked up on.

But how could I have guessed? It just doesn't add up. Suchak reviews the risk factors for heart disease. No family history of heart disease. No smoking, no drinking. Cholesterol levels consistently low. Okay, maybe a Type A personality. The gut says the real risk factor is Lovejoy. Maybe the stress of dealing with Allene and Carye every day has contributed to this. And maybe my heart is trying to tell me something. But heart disease doesn't happen overnight. This must have been building up for thirty years.

Tim. I wish Tim were still here. The constant battling with Carye is just too hard. But no snap decisions. There will be plenty of time to think in the hospital recovery room.

Plenty of time to think about the new house, too. When he and Myra had begun the project they'd been planning a vacation house. They'd found a beautiful spot with a view of the lake in central Washington, made plans, and here they were $250,000 later with a house that could serve them very well as a true home. Which has Suchak considering part-time work up there. The job at Lovejoy is only about twenty hours a week, and there aren't too many doctors in the country with more experience at abortions. Heck, maybe I'll just retire, he thinks.

But Suchak's new reality isn't in place just yet. He's not in the hospital as a patient, and the old aggravations haven't disappeared. He's still medical director at Lovejoy, and Friday has been a mess, close to gridlock.

Fridays have always been busy days at Lovejoy. General surgeries in the morning and tab locals in the afternoon, some days as many as two dozen in all. For five years Suchak has begun the D & Es and the occasional tubal at 7:30 A.M. and kept at it until finished, noon on a slow day, as late as two P.M. when a lot of generals are scheduled. Then another doctor, usually Chandler, takes over for the tab locals. But Chandler is slow, methodical. Some Fridays the staff is still pushing the locals through after 6 P.M., and nobody is happy about that. So recently Carye changed the scheduling. Now locals start at 9 A.M., overlapping with the generals. Two doctors working at once.

A good idea, Suchak thinks, until the unexpected occurs. Until they get another DIC like Chuan. Or even worse, two Chuans at the same time.

There's only one recovery room upstairs and only one nurse tending to patients there. The recovery room equipment includes one blood pressure cuff, one cardiac monitor for emergencies, one bathroom. Suchak can usually get through two or three D & Es in an hour. When the upstairs staff is functioning efficiently they usually manage six locals an hour, eight at most. With the locals taking place at the same time as D & Es in the late morning, six or seven women can be sharing the recovery room at the same time. Imagine the disaster if two of those women started hemorrhaging simultaneously, with one nurse on duty and one cardiac monitor. Try to explain to a jury that the recovery room was understaffed because they'd only had one recovery case turn this serious in five years, Suchak thinks. He's envisioned the courtroom scene, the battery of questions he, as medical director, would face: "Did you know this could happen, Dr. Suchak?" "Could you have protected against this happening, Dr. Suchak?" "Why didn't you?"

Suchak is not the only staff member concerned with the Friday scheduling. A few weeks ago Suchak talked about the problem with Penny, the recovery room nurse. Penny told him she had already talked to Allene about the situation. She wasn't as worried about an emergency as about the quality of care she is able to deliver every day.

Penny's job is determined by strict protocols. When a D & E patient arrives in recovery Penny must immediately take her blood pressure. She then repeats the blood pressure test at five, fifteen, and thirty-five minutes, and again when the patient is discharged, usually about an hour after her arrival.

Recovering tab local patients have their blood pressure taken when they arrive and when they leave, usually fifteen minutes later.

But it is nearly impossible for Penny to keep to that schedule with one blood pressure cuff and no help, except on those days Carolee is sent up to assist. And having only one bathroom for patients is more than inconvenient—women recovering from abortions often are nauseous.

Allene reminded Penny that the recovery room nurse has the authority to tell the rest of the staff to hold off on any more surgeries until her room clears out. Penny has wielded that power twice in recent weeks, essentially shutting down the second floor for as long as thirty minutes.

Suchak has no fight in him today, and little inclination to argue the new scheduling policy with Carye. A week from now he goes in for his own surgery. Then he will reconsider his status at Lovejoy.

One office away, nearly back-to-back with Suchak, Carye picks up the telephone and calls Allene at her beach house. Carye, too, is feeling pressure today. After a few minutes of light conversation Carye turns to business. Allene likes to keep current on the weekly patient numbers, and Carye has good news to convey—three tubal ligations coming in this week, one cash and two covered by insurance.

After setting the phone back in its cradle Carye contemplates the monthly figure. "We need numbers desperately," she thinks. She asks one of the medical assistants to look up the running total of procedures for the month. The woman comes back a minute later with the answer—195 so far. Not enough, Carye thinks. They should be up to 230 by now.

Carye has become aware that gradually Allene is letting her assume more administrative control over Lovejoy. Which makes her want to prove herself all the more. But these numbers aren't helping.

August was one of the busiest months Lovejoy has seen in years. So why, Carye wonders, was September so far down? School had begun. Maybe mothers who had to get their kids ready for the school year were waiting until they could reestablish a measure of routine in their own lives before facing up to the fact that there was a new life growing inside them.

Carye allows herself a pleasurable moment to think about yesterday's golf game, a round of eighty-eight, her best. Throughout the next few days when stress engulfs her she will let her mind wander back to that round of golf.

And as if thoughts of her mentor cannot escape for long, Carye thinks of Allene. Allene doesn't play golf. But she has found her own escape from the pressure, Carye reflects, in her garden.

Allene began redesigning her backyard garden in the spring, in preparation for her daughter's wedding. And then she fell in love with it—the sculpted stones, the blooms on the rhodies, the ancient trees way in the back she calls her forest. Even after the wedding Allene continued the reshaping.

Certainly the wedding, with over two hundred guests, was not the only stressful life event for Allene this year. For starters there has been the growing rift at Lovejoy between her director of counseling and her medical director. A few months ago Allene came to recognize she could no longer care for her father at home. His periods of lucidity were becoming increasingly rare. So Allene, everybody's caretaker, had to face the sadness of settling her father into a nearby senior care facility. Then Myron, the man with whom Allene has lived for twenty years, suffered a heart attack. Carye thinks the garden has become Allene's symbolic focus for reestablishing her house as her refuge, imposing order out of increasing chaos.

Allene, the woman who never shows stress, Carye muses. Then again, nobody else knows that every other Monday Carye accompanies Allene upstairs to check her dangerously high blood pressure with equipment in the deserted recovery room. Doctor's orders.

Even Anneke is showing signs of stress, Carye reflects. A few days ago she reported fetuses have begun to invade her dreams. The most consistent dream involves Anneke performing an ultrasound on a patient and seeing a baby bird rather than a fetus in the woman's uterus. Anneke wondered if the dreams are a sign from her subconscious that she is failing to acknowledge something about her work that disturbs her.

Carye told Anneke that she has had similar recurring dreams for years. In the most vivid, she is walking downtown and spots a fetus on the sidewalk in front of Nordstrom's. When she casually moves over to look at the fetus she notices it is early in gestation, maybe eight weeks, so she picks it up and calmly deposits it in a nearby trash can.

Anneke is also concerned about her changing attitude toward some of Lovejoy's patients. Yesterday she told Carye that she had a patient eight weeks pregnant and on welfare who confessed she took illegal drugs. The woman insisted she needed a general anesthetic because years ago she had an abortion at sixteen weeks, under local anesthetic, which severely traumatized her.

Anneke spent an hour trying to convince the woman she could get through an eight-week tab local if they administered extra Valium, but the woman refused. What bothers Anneke most is that she doesn't believe the woman, who showed no emotion, certainly no manifestation of the great fear she spoke about.

Later yesterday Anneke took calls from two women on the Oregon Health Plan who asked how far along they had to be to get an abortion with a general anesthetic. One of the women was exceedingly rude and refused to listen to Anneke's explanation of the dangers of waiting. "Just tell me," she badgered.

When Anneke replied that the minimum for a general was twelve weeks, she could not keep herself from adding, "But that's abusing the system and we can report you to your caseworker." Anneke knows her words were mostly spoken out of frustration. She also knows she has had many cases where women waited until twelve weeks to come in. What bothers her especially is that most of those women were on the Oregon Health Plan: The state, the taxpayers, would have to assume the cost of the women's unwillingness to undergo a tab local. Which led Anneke to wonder if she was becoming cynical and developing a not so well disguised bias against welfare patients.

Anneke told Carye she has reviewed medical histories of some of these women and found they had multiple tab gen abortions paid for by the state. And some had refused Lovejoy's standard offer of free birth control pills.

Carye is one of the few counselors at Lovejoy who does not express resentment of welfare patients, even when they make special requests. In her view Lovejoy is not acquiescing to their demands at all. She figures that if a patient can get through receptionist Lisa's initial grilling and then a counseling session such as Anneke has just described and still insist on the general anesthetic, she must really want it.

Carye believes that most of Lovejoy's patients are genuinely frightened, and she has seen too many women go through an abortion awake when they would have been much better off under general anesthetic.

As for Anneke, Carye is not so concerned about her growing cynicism. One afternoon this week she watched as Anneke flew out the front door with fifteen dollars Carye had just fished out of her own purse. A schizophrenic patient Anneke had counseled, who had had her abortion hours before, had called from downtown, where she was wandering around lost and out of money. She told Anneke on the phone she had misplaced her bus ticket and did not know how she could get home to Twin Falls, Idaho.

Anneke spent two hours frantically searching the Portland bus station and the surrounding seedy neighborhood before she found the patient, took her to the bus station, and gave her the fifteen dollars for a ticket home. Anneke's doing just fine, Carye thinks.

That afternoon Anneke takes a coffee break behind the reception area and tells Lisa what she learned in her first week of counseling upstairs. The first thing, Anneke says, is not to wear rings because patients like to squeeze the counselor's hand during surgery, and when a jolt of pain hits the patient it finds its way down to the counselor's fingers. Second, upstairs she can wear her comfortable sandals instead of pumps as required by Allene's unwritten dress code, because in the OR everyone has to wear blue disposable booties over their shoes anyway.

"I'm here for a morning-after pill."

Lisa, the receptionist, asks the professionally dressed black woman in front of her if she knows the first day of her last period, then takes the twenty-five dollars and begins writing up a receipt as the woman takes a seat and starts filling out her paperwork.

Leah, watching the exchange from the window of the business office a few feet away, walks up behind Lisa. "What's that girl's name?" she asks.

"Taundra Roberts," Lisa replies.

Leah suggests they try a little search on the computer to Lisa's right. Lisa, still adjusting to her job as receptionist, is pleased to be able to help. Two days ago Allene called up, and when Lisa answered the phone Allene said she sounded too robotic. So today Lisa is trying to sound more personable.

With Leah looking over her shoulder Lisa scans Lovejoy's patient records. Leah's hunch pays off when they discover Taundra Roberts has been to Lovejoy six times in the last four months, each time requesting and receiving norgestrel/ethinyl estradiol, the morning-after pill.

Leah walks back to Carye's office for a chat and returns a few minutes later to tell Taundra she cannot have the pill. Leah suggests Taundra have a Pap smear done and then start on birth control pills. She even explains that the twenty-five dollars Taundra pays for each morning-after pill will pay for an entire month's supply of birth control pills. And the pills are much safer.

In fact, Taundra's consistent use of the morning-after pill puts her at risk for increased blood pressure and stroke. The pill basically is a megashot of the hormones estrogen and progestin, which thicken the lining of the uterus to prevent a fertilized egg from becoming implanted. One morning-after pill is the equivalent of eight days' worth of birth control pills in a twelve-hour period. It is not intended to be taken regularly.

Leah explains all this without expecting any response, and she receives none. Taundra shows no sign of being upset at having her request denied, but simply turns on her heel and walks out the door, leaving Leah to wonder if she's just going to another local clinic with the same request. Maybe Planned Parenthood. She knows somebody will provide what she is after.

Returning to the computer Leah notices Taundra received her last dose of the morning-after pill at Lovejoy just five days ago. Leah walks back to Carye's office to finish their discussion. Carye surmises that the woman probably is unwilling to admit to herself that she is sexually active. Relying on the morning-after pill as birth control allows her to pretend otherwise. If she had to take a birth control pill every day, or have a doctor prescribe a diaphragm, the illusion would not be so easy to maintain. And apparently, Carye says, Taundra does not mind the loss of her regular period, which is a likely side effect.

"I don't believe in abortion."

Carolee has heard these words with some frequency of late. Earlier this month from Jessica, in fact. They are spoken fairly frequently by patients at Lovejoy.

Allene likes to tell the story of the wife of an anti-abortion advocate who snuck in the back door for an abortion while her husband led the protestors out front. Lovejoy is a place where morality and reality learn to accommodate each other.

Crystal, who has just spoken, is a tough looking woman wearing a purple windbreaker with B.U.M. spelled out across the front. Her history indicates there's conscience behind her statement. She has a fifteen-year-old son at home, but she has also put up two children for adoption, twin girls born when she was fifteen.

Crystal is thirty-three. She returned to Portland four months ago on a Greyhound bus, fleeing an abusive boyfriend in a small Idaho town. She describes a life one step off the streets, sleeping in a new boyfriend's car until recently, when she joined the boyfriend and his two teenage girls in their apartment. She also sent for her son, whom she had left with his father, a man he hardly knew. Last week she found work as a grocery store cashier. And she's about to finish her statement to Carolee.

"I never had any circumstances that put me in a position where I have to consider it," she says.

Carolee likes this streetwise woman. A lot of savvy there. Of course, Carolee likes most of the women she counsels.

Carolee's ultrasound has just revealed Crystal to be about seven weeks pregnant, as Crystal predicted it would. And the ultrasound also showed the T-shaped intrauterine device (IUD) sitting next to Crystal's amniotic sac. Crystal has heard stories about the dangers of IUD pregnancies, the risk of birth defects in children who develop with the little metal or plastic birth control devices sharing their womb.

Crystal's hard-times cynicism doesn't hold up too long with Carolee. Within minutes the younger woman is in tears, her voice, rough as gravel, beginning to break.

The IUD is supposed to work for a lifetime, Crystal says. And it's only been in place three years. "Figure that out," she says with a toss of her head.

"It's called dumb luck, I guess," Carolee answers.

On any given day Lovejoy is full of women who lack basic common sense concerning their own welfare and also women who can amaze with how much they know about their bodies and women's health. Crystal is one of the latter—high school dropout, off the streets, and able to talk about estrogen and amniocentesis like a third-year medical student. She describes to Carolee how different IUDs work, and complications from her previous pregnancies. Then she mentions that her mother died of breast cancer when she was thirteen, leaving Crystal to raise a little sister.

As a teenager, Crystal explains, she started on birth control pills. But they made her sick, and worse, they didn't work. Crystal conceived her son while on the pill. The doctor who prescribed her current IUD said it was 97 percent effective, but when it failed two months ago she knew it almost immediately. Within days she became sick and sleepy and depressed.

After a home pregnancy test confirmed the self-diagnosis, Crystal says, a doctor told her there was a chance the IUD could cause severe birth defects. In fact, the prognosis for IUD pregnancies is not as bad as the stories that have rooted themselves in the folklore of women's medicine. Carolee, who has never dealt with an IUD pregnancy, does not know enough to offer a second opinion.

What Carolee can provide is a detailed description of the abortion procedure, which will be done under general anesthetic Saturday morning. She emphasizes that Crystal cannot eat or drink anything after midnight tonight, or she will run the risk of vomiting and then possibly choking while under anesthetic. Carolee has scheduled the operation for the one day she assists in surgery, so she explains to Crystal that she will be with her throughout. "You're going to see more of me than you can stand," she says with a smile.

"So they'll remove the IUD, and the general is in case of any hemorrhaging?" Crystal asks.

"The decision was it would be more comfortable," Carolee says. "That's the real issue."

Though she has seen no evidence of cigarettes, Carolee asks Crystal how many cigarettes she smokes a day.

"You know what? I'm not a daily smoker. I smoke when I drink. And I'm not a daily drinker," Crystal says with a laugh.

Carolee looks at Crystal's medical chart and notices the woman had her last breast exam three years ago.

"You need a Pap smear," she says in a Mother Superior voice. "When did you last have a mammogram?"

Crystal contritely confesses she has never had one.

"Then you also need a baseline mammogram. I'm going to hit you with all this at once," Carolee says.

"Another thing I'm interested in is having a tubal done," Crystal says. "And I'm not sure if that's covered by Kaiser or not." Crystal is insured through the state of Oregon Health Plan, and she has chosen Kaiser Permanente as her care provider.

Carolee explains the restrictions mandated by the Oregon Health Plan: Crystal must be in a nonpregnant state for thirty-two days before the state will pay for a tubal ligation. Carolee suggests Crystal sign the consent form for the tubal Saturday after her abortion, then wait a month to make the appointment at Lovejoy.

As she is leaving, Crystal stops in the hallway and says, "Thank you very much. You made me feel very comfortable." Carolee will spend an hour after dinner researching IUD pregnancies in the medical reference books she keeps at home and wondering why, if Crystal truly doesn't believe in abortion, she exhibits so little conflict about having one.

As Carolee walks back to her office, she passes a middle-aged man with his arm around the shoulders of a sheepishly smiling teenage girl. The man and girl kiss on the lips, and then the girl goes back to a counseling room with Leah.

"Are there any shops around here?" the man asks Carolee.

"Oh sure," Carolee answers. "Two blocks down on Twenty-third Street there are all sorts. Do you want a coffee shop?"

"No, I'm going to look for a chastity belt."

SATURDAY, OCTOBER 28

Lovejoy opens early on Saturdays. Adron, the medical technician, usually arrives upstairs first to prepare the operating rooms for the day's surgeries.

A black man of fifty-eight with a neat gray mustache and a bemused smile, he comes in at 6:30 A.M. and starts by checking the schedule downstairs. Today he sees three general surgeries on the schedule. Heading to the back of the building he turns the handles on the nitrous oxide and oxygen tanks that rest just outside the back door.

Back upstairs Adron adjusts the dials on the steam sterilizer in the hallway so that it will be ready later in the morning. He tapes the surgical schedule to the door of the room used for washing instruments.

Next he checks the supplies to be used during surgery. Since Lovejoy launders its own gowns and sterilizes its own equipment, most of the material is lined up in separate neat bundles in need of a final inspection. Adron checks the tape on the top of each bundle—the white tape shows black stripes after being steamed fifteen minutes at 270 degrees, followed by thirty minutes drying. He counts the bundles to make sure they match the number of surgeries scheduled for the day.

The tab gen bundles, all in a row, each contain a vaginal speculum, eight metal dilators of varying size, a tenaculum clamp for holding on to the cervix, a ring forceps, used for grasping and removing tissue, and a sponge stick.

D & E bundles are nearly the same but they contain three larger dilators, since laminaria have already enlarged the cervical opening of D & E patients, and two large clamps.

Tab locals don't require separate bundles.

Each surgery requires a prep set consisting of two bowls with cotton balls for sterilizing the vaginal area, six sponges, and five towels for draping around the patient and for cleanup.

Adron assembled these bundles and prep sets yesterday after surgeries were completed. He moves from room to room, making certain each has the necessary equipment for the day. He places a sterile cover on a silver tray next to the operating bed and lays out a set of surgical instruments on the tray, making sure they are arranged in proper sequence. He is a stage manager alone before cast and crew have arrived. Lovejoy is a very quiet place at six-thirty in the morning.

As Adron completes his work upstairs, Crystal, accompanied by her boyfriend, walks past a group of four men "praying the rosary" on the corner outside. Crystal and boyfriend look like they could be heading for a football game: She's wearing a print dress and sandals, he's in sweatpants and sweatshirt. The boyfriend, a home remodeler, has fashionably styled long hair and a well-trimmed mustache.

"Don't let her do it, Dad," yells one man. Another protestor, who claims she is a nurse, nods her approval.

Crystal's boyfriend stops. "Mind your own business," he says. "You people should have something better to do."

"Well, you're killing a child here."

"Well, you don't understand the situation. She could die. You didn't hear her cry, hear her bawl over this."

"You're killing the baby."

Crystal's boyfriend thrusts his middle finger to the sky and guides Crystal into Lovejoy's side door.

Inside there is plenty of time to think. Crystal and her boyfriend settle into seats in the front lobby. A born-again Baptist, she begins talking about religion. When she previously lived in Portland, every year she would join hands with thousands of others to form a long chain through the city's streets, an annual anti-abortion event.

Crystal's boyfriend is flipping through the pages of an old *National Geographic*. "It's just like these sharks," he says, pointing to a picture of a great white ripping apart a smaller animal. "They get in a pack and . . ."

Carolee interrupts. "Good morning, Crystal. How are you?"

"Tired and thirsty," comes the reply. Carolee smiles and heads upstairs.

Crystal puts her head on her boyfriend's shoulder and he immediately settles his arm around her back.

"They have some nice artwork here," Crystal says as she looks around the room. Glancing out the window at the protestors she adds, "They're just trying to make a stand for what they believe in."

Every ten minutes or so Crystal walks to the rest room near the elevator. She has been craving a drink of water all morning. Her throat is dry, raspy. She leans over her boyfriend and hugs him before sitting down again.

Upstairs the staff lounge is crowded with medical assistants picking at donuts and muffins. Suchak makes a habit of bringing treats on Saturday mornings. "Sugar high. It gets them working," he comments with a smile. But standing alone in the hallway minutes later, he appears tense.

A few of the medical assistants look tired, their eyes dull, their hair just a little out of place. The conversation centers around last night's parties and dates. Plans are made for a get-together tonight at the home of one of the assistants.

Crystal was the first scheduled surgery of the morning but an anxious D & E came in early, at six forty-five, so she has been admitted. Crystal will be next, with one more D & E to follow, and tab locals will take up the rest of the morning.

Once she's past the admitting desk upstairs and through the double doors leading to the surgical area, Crystal enters the pre-op room. Kim, one of the medical assistants, hands her a gown and helps her onto a bed after she returns from the bathroom. Marion, the anesthetist, comes in and asks Crystal when she last had something to eat or drink. Five minutes later Suchak's purposeful stride brings him to Crystal's side.

Suchak is noted among Lovejoy's surgeons for his direct and formal manner. Those who like his style appreciate the professionalism and the speed of his surgeries, knowing the longer a patient is under anesthetic or on the table the greater the risk of complications. Critics consider his approach insensitive.

This morning Suchak is finding it difficult to conceal the gruffness. His heart surgery looms and no attempt to dismiss it from his consciousness has worked. He feels that in a permanent way his life suddenly has been changed but he still does not know to what. On top of which, this morning he awoke with an excruciating toothache. He will try to make an appointment with a dentist for this afternoon.

Suchak scans Crystal's chart while standing above her. "Do you want your IUD?" he asks. "We can wash it off and save it for you. Put it in your hope chest."

"I'm mad at it," Crystal responds. "I'd like to stomp on it."

Suchak, too, asks Crystal when she last had something to eat or drink. He is the fourth person to pose that question this morning. Crystal's reply is the same, nothing since dinner last night.

With chart in hand Suchak speeds over a checklist of questions about drug and disease exposures. Satisfied with Crystal's answers he says, "This isn't brain surgery." Marion inserts an IV needle into Crystal's forearm and begins feeding Versed, a relaxant, and Reglan, which will fend off the nausea that might cause Crystal to vomit. Crystal is wheeled into the operating room next door.

Once she is in place on the metal gurney, Suchak takes her hand. "I get to hold the hands of all the pretty girls," he says. Suchak uses this line with many of his patients, but it brings a slight smile to Crystal's lips.

Carolee, Crystal's upstairs counselor, is standing opposite Suchak. Counseling at Lovejoy does not end when the patient is sent upstairs. During surgery each woman has a counselor beside her, which means there are four staff members in the room—surgeon, surgical assistant, anesthetist, and counselor.

Often the upstairs counselor is one of the medical assistants so that for one surgery Tamara might be counseling while Kim assists the doctor, and for the next surgery they might reverse roles. The upstairs counselor doesn't so much counsel as comfort the patient during the abortion, important not only for the woman's emotional well-being but also because a woman moving around during surgery increases the likelihood of an instrument puncturing her uterine wall.

But Crystal has been calm and Marion is about to put her under general anesthetic. So today Carolee mostly observes, her presence enough.

Marion hooks Crystal up to propofol, the anesthetic, and applies a breathing mask for nitrous oxide, a pain reliever, and oxygen. Within a few seconds Crystal is asleep.

Suchak begins by using a number eight suction cannula, shaped like an elbowed straw, to spread open the cervix. He does not have to ask for instruments; Adron, just behind him, knows the procedure as well as Suchak. Next Adron hands Suchak a speculum. Suchak presses a button on the instrument, which forces the speculum to widen and expose the cervix. Next is the tenaculum, the long metal tool that looks like a shiny kitchen tongs, to grasp the cervix. Then a forceps to grab hold of the IUD.

"Got it just in time," Suchak jokes. The IUD was near the opening of the cervix and might have slipped out when he began suctioning Crystal's uterus. With the IUD out of the way Suchak uses a number twenty-three dilator, a metal rod with a slight cone shape, to further dilate the cervix, forcing it wider. Finally comes the suction cannula, hollow and about the width of a pencil, attached to a vacuum. Suchak reaches to turn on the machine and uses short sweeping motions to empty Crystal's uterus.

Experience tells Suchak when he has removed all of the fetus and pregnancy-related tissue. He knows one of the primary dangers here, apart from puncturing the uterine wall, is failing to fully extract the contents of the uterus. Suchak can feel the fetus as it moves through his suction device. A hard-to-describe sensation, something akin to grittiness around the uterus, tells him it is clean.

Finished, Suchak thanks Carolee, Adron, and Marion. He helps them roll Crystal back on her gurney for the trip to the recovery room. In a small metal bowl off to the side floats an unformed mass that resembles a red jellyfish—the vacuumed contents of Crystal's uterus, once a fetus. At most, ten minutes have passed from the moment Marion administered the IV anesthetic.

Crystal wakes up in the recovery room twelve minutes later. Groggy, she rests in her bed nearly an hour. Carolee, noticing the IUD on the surgical table, remarks how small it is. Marion asks if

Carolee has seen earrings made from IUDs, apparently a fashion craze among some women. Carolee laughs and assures her she has not.

Suchak, meanwhile, has proceeded to the day's remaining surgeries, a handful of tab locals, knowing that two weeks from now Crystal will not remember anything about the operation or him. In fact, she probably won't remember anything beyond the moment she arrived at Lovejoy. Versed, the relaxant she was given in pre-op, causes amnesia.

An hour later Crystal and her boyfriend drive out of the back parking lot, avoiding the protestors out front. Crystal smiles as their car turns the corner onto Twenty-fifth Street. The autumn rain has halted this morning, the sky is streaked with high clouds and occasional sunshine. On the corner Andrew Burnett blends into a handful of protestors. One of Burnett's sons, a teenager, stands next to him carrying a sign that reads FREE PAUL HILL. JAIL ABORTION PROVIDERS. Burnett's sign says FREEDOM OF CHOICE above a picture of a forceps holding a fetal head.

Burnett appears an unworried man. His step is light, he smiles. He says he just got up this morning and felt like coming to Lovejoy.

"It hurts. It hurts."

"Honey, I know it hurts. Just squeeze my hand."

There are four people in the OR. Suchak, in gown and mask, is being assisted by Carole, one of the medical assistants. The patient is Jerri, a seventeen-year-old high school junior from the suburbs of Portland. Her upstairs counselor during the surgery is Rebecca, a short, spunky woman with a quick laugh and high energy. Rebecca, thirty-one, has been at Lovejoy only two months but she's already enlivened the second floor with her street savvy and winking irreverence, her talk of "the 'hood" and previous lives in Brooklyn and Arizona.

"When you feel pain just go ahead and squeeze my hand," Rebecca repeats, standing next to Jerri, opposite Suchak.

"It hurts," Jerri says again, a little more urgency and volume in her voice.

Jerri's surgery actually is a simple tab local, no different from the other hundred or so first-trimester abortions performed each week at Lovejoy. Suchak, impatient and pained by his tooth, abruptly interjects, "Yes, I know it hurts. But you *have* to stay in control of yourself."

Rebecca begins to rub Jerri's shoulders and stroke her hair. The surgery is almost completed. Suchak has finished the suction, now all he has to do is check the tissue that has been removed. But Jerri doesn't appear to understand this. Or to her, it doesn't matter.

Jerri's cries are becoming louder, almost loud enough to be heard down the hall where the rest of the morning's patients are waiting. Some are already in pre-op, right next door.

Suchak steps over to examine the fetal tissue he has just extracted, now in the bowl on the table beside Jerri's bed. He needs to make sure he has removed it all, and his eyes comfirm what his hands have already told him—he has.

The surgery is finished, but Jerri's appeals continue. "It hurts. It hurts. I feel a lot of pain."

"Let's try some deep breaths," Rebecca suggests, sensing the growing tension in the room. But instead Jerri raises her knees from the stirrups, pulls them toward her chest and begins hugging them while emitting a piercing moan.

Suchak returns to Jerri's side. Suchak's hands reach for Jerri's ankles. A moment later the girl's feet are back in the stirrups.

"Listen," Suchak says with a barely controlled fury. "You need to get control of yourself." The move works. His commanding voice momentarily shocks Jerri out of her trance. Immediately she quiets.

"Listen here," Suchak continues. "Lift up your right arm." Jerri complies, her arm cautiously moving up as if she intends to touch the ceiling. "Put it down," Suchak commands. Jerri does. "Lift up your left arm." Again Jerri follows her doctor's orders. "Put it down. See, you have control. Now use it." And with that Suchak swiftly leaves the room, closing the door sharply behind him.

Rebecca appears nearly as stunned as Jerri. Wheeling the girl to the post-op room Rebecca gently places a heating pad on Jerri's stomach, strokes her hair, and says, "I know it hurts."

Five minutes later, having left Jerri in the care of the post-op nurse, Rebecca walks back to the second-floor lounge, enveloped by a sense of failure. In her mind Suchak went too far. The surgery was over. Jerri needed comforting, not an angry man frightening her even more. She wonders why she didn't confront Suchak, why she was too afraid to stand up for a frightened seventeen-year-old girl. Driving home an hour later she finds herself talking out the incident with her boyfriend. "I froze," she says. "I feel like a big wimp. As a woman I totally backed down."

Carye likes her beeper. Always has. Where some would consider the constant connection to their job an intrusion, she finds it a comfort, feels that it helps her keep her finger on the pulse of Lovejoy, that even when silent it tells her something. All after-hours emergency calls are directed to Carye. On a normal night she will get called three or four times. If she's getting beeped frequently from women in pain after their surgeries, she considers it a clue that the downstairs counselors are not being thorough enough helping women understand that some post-operative cramping should be expected. And that might be a sign that the downstairs counselors are too rushed. Carye knows that new counselors usually are not thorough enough telling patients what to expect and she can expect a few more calls than usual from frightened women in the first weeks after a counselor has begun work at Lovejoy.

But this Saturday night has been a quiet one. With dinner over, Carye and Thom are settling in, each with a book and a living room chair. Sure enough, just as she gets lost in her reading, Carye hears the beeping sound of the little black rectangle she has left in her nearby purse. She calls the answering service. One of Lovejoy's patients has called in, Carye is told.

Carye calls the number relayed by the answering service and is greeted by a man who hardly tries to obscure the hostility in his voice. "Can I talk to Jerri?" she says.

Jerri takes the telephone. Carye can hear the girl trying to stifle tears as she talks. She tells Carye she had an abortion this morning and she still is cramping. As Jerri describes the pain Carye senses that there is nothing abnormal, nothing that shouldn't have been anticipated and explained by a counselor. Carye tells Jerri the pain is typical and suggests she take ibuprofen and massage her lower abdomen for the pain. What isn't typical is what Jerri says next. "And that doctor, he grabbed me."

Carye asks Jerri to explain, and Jerri says that after her surgery the doctor made her put her feet down and lift her arms up. Carye recognizes that a young woman who has just had an abortion and is feeling pain probably is not the most reliable reporter of events. In fact, Jerri can't even provide the name of the surgeon who purportedly grabbed her. The only thing that is clear to Carye is the trauma the girl is experiencing. "Why was the doctor mean to me?" she asks.

The next morning, Sunday, Carye calls Jerri again, hoping she can get a clearer picture of the girl's experience. Jerri is feeling better, physically and emotionally. She doesn't even mention the doctor or how she was treated.

Hanging up the phone Carye is convinced that Jerri's initial version probably was just part of her overall reaction to the stress of the abortion and the pain. She knows that doctors sometimes are required to restrain patients if they begin kicking during the procedure—a punctured uterus could lead to serious, possibly fatal hemorrhaging.

By Tuesday Carye has forgotten about Jerri. Late in the morning she finds herself in the hallway with medical assistant Kim. "Have you heard about what happened Saturday?" Kim asks. Carye says she hasn't. Kim explains that Rebecca became upset at the way Suchak treated a patient. Rebecca has been talking to the other medical assistants. That afternoon, once the day's patients have been counseled, Carye calls down to her office Rebecca and Carole, who assisted Suchak during Jerri's abortion.

Rebecca uncharacteristically hesitates when Carye asks about Saturday morning, as if she thinks she might get in trouble for discussing the incident with the other medical assistants. Carye calmly explains that she just wants to know what happened in the OR.

Rebecca recounts her version of the events. She's sure that Suchak grabbed Jerri's ankles and forced them back down into the stirrups and certain it happened after the surgery was completed. Rebecca says she feels guilty that she froze and didn't intervene.

Hearing this, Carye considers the gray area she knows exists in these situations. What appears to be unnecessary force in the eyes of a patient or even a counselor often is warranted from the surgeon's perspective. The surgeon's first concern is the medical well-being of the patient. His mind is focused on the surgical job that needs to be done. Carye thinks of the times Suchak has had to operate on women high on crank, women unable to stop twitching or who spastically kept putting their hands in their mouths, and the tone and even force he had to use to get those women safely through their surgeries.

But it does happen, Carye thinks to herself. When surgeries mount up during the day she has seen a surgeon follow a particularly difficult procedure by becoming slightly vacant for the next, operating as if on automatic pilot. They're human, and under constant pressure. She's seen surgeons in those situations walk into the OR and address anxious patients by the wrong names, a sure sign their thoughts were elsewhere.

She recalls the times she has seen surgeons unable to get the placenta to detach from the uterine wall and slide down through the cannula, and in frustration start moving the cannula about too vigorously, risking perforation. The fact is, surgeons, especially good ones, are allowed a great deal of leeway, and nobody has yet established a precise definition of acceptable limits.

Then again, Carye has heard one of Lovejoy's surgeons repeatedly make disparaging remarks about obese patients, and she suspects the doctor is insensitive dealing with obese women. True, none of the doctors like to operate on an obese woman; in addition to making a pelvic exam more difficult, the excess fat tissue can hinder a surgeon's attempt to reach and control the cervical opening and to look inside the uterus. Last year a patient was refused surgery because of her girth: None of the doctors felt safe in performing her abortion without the backup of a hospital emergency room. None of which excuses an obese patient being treated any less gently than other patients, Carye knows.

Carye also knows that even if events unfolded as Rebecca has described them, Suchak is not the only one who bears responsibility. Might Jerri's downstairs counselor have sensed that this patient was not emotionally ready for the surgery? Might Rebecca have deduced that Jerri was not relaxed enough to begin the procedure, or done more to calm the girl so that the situation would not escalate to the point at which Suchak felt the need to take over? Some of the medical assistants, Carole for instance, prefer a surgeon who talks hard and keeps difficult patients in line. Carye looks at Carole, who has remained quiet until now, and asks for her version. Carole insists she doesn't know if Suchak grabbed the girl's ankles because she had turned her back at that moment.

But Rebecca, now that she has begun, is sure of herself. "You don't know what this feels like," she recalls the girl saying early on. And Suchak, she insists, yelled back at her, "Now listen. Do you want to do this or not?" Rebecca says it appeared as if Suchak wanted to teach Jerri a lesson.

Carye has heard enough. Within minutes Rebecca is in Allene's office repeating her story. She finishes by saying she felt like a coward. Allene looks at Rebecca and says, "Honey, you don't have to feel bad about that because you can always stop the procedure. You have that power."

In the days immediately following Allene's talk with Rebecca, business returned to something approaching normal at Lovejoy. Suchak's behavior did not dominate Allene's thinking. She has dealt with too many abortion surgeons over the years to judge them harshly. She has watched the emotional burnouts, sadly witnessed the drug and alcohol addictions that have afflicted more than a few, and come to recognize that the best surgeons, the most technically proficient, usually are saddled with eccentric personalities and stunted social skills. And as a businesswoman she knows that keeping surgeons with good hands and sound medical judgment comes first. In fact, for two days the incident with Jerri was not discussed. Not forgotten, it receded into Allene's consciousness as a folder on her desk waiting to be filed, potentially an isolated incident with no long-term consequences besides a possible talk with Suchak.

This afternoon Carye has scheduled an in-service day for the second-floor staff, a hospital's version of continuing education. A representative of Parke-Davis arrives in the upstairs lounge to conduct a seminar on patient care. Though she does not often attend these meetings, Allene decides her presence might be helpful, especially if Saturday's events have exacerbated any conflicts among the medical assistants who harbor different opinions about Suchak's behavior.

Ideally the seminar would provide a forum for some serious give-and-take between Carye and Allene on the one hand, and the nurses and medical assistants on the other. But the very presence of Allene at this meeting clearly stifles some of the criticism the staff members tend to air amongst themselves when the administrators are not around. Allene's fierce gaze and spontaneous reproaches have intimidated more than a few in the past. Still, with this session specifically focused on finding ways to improve the care and comfort of patients, there are some concrete suggestions passed about.

One often-voiced complaint from the upstairs staff concerns patients kept waiting downstairs. Like most points of conflict, this one involves a trade-off. The surgical staff would like to get women admitted, counseled, and then sent upstairs as quickly as possible. Often they find themselves greeting disgruntled patients with stories of two-hour waits downstairs before they were sent up. Generally the reason is the counselors were backed up, and nobody gets an abortion at Lovejoy without a counseling session.

In Carye's view, if the downstairs staff were to have their way and more women were sent upstairs more quickly, the result would be a change in the location of waiting rooms. The bottleneck would simply shift upstairs. And given a choice, she prefers having patients wait downstairs. Waiting downstairs the women become bored, she believes. Waiting upstairs, especially in pre-op, they turn anxious. But Carye says she will rethink the admitting procedure.

After a few more minutes of discussion Allene, sitting on the room's only couch, steers the conversation to one of her favorite topics.

"What Lovejoy is all about is to give dignity to women, and that dignity begins with giving it to each other," she begins. Though none of the upstairs staff members has mentioned Saturday's events, all know what has inspired Allene's words. Never one for an indirect approach Allene next begins talking about Jerri's surgery. "It won't happen again," she finishes in her firmest tone of voice.

Soon the subject shifts to Allene's view of Lovejoy as a workplace without hierarchy. She explains that nobody at Lovejoy, not even a doctor, has the right to talk in a belittling way to anybody else. "Everybody has a voice here," she says. The conversation turns to how a nurse or medical assistant can deal with a surgeon who appears out of control during an operation. Allene says they should just put a hand on the surgeon's shoulder or say to him, "We're just going to stop for a second."

The best surgeons fall prey to stress, fatigue, and boredom, Allene says. Lovejoy needs a fail-safe, and the nurses and medical assistants are the people she has chosen for that role. But the process works, she knows, only if the nurses and assistants, all women, don't fall into the mind-set of intimidation or awe she has seen infect support staff at many hospitals and other health care facilities, including Lovejoy. The doctors at Lovejoy all are men, and medically speaking, the doctors are all in charge. But that doesn't mean they do not make mistakes. She tells the staff that in her experience an out-of-control surgeon is actually grateful when somebody, anybody, forces him to take a time-out.

Listening to Allene finish, Carye finds herself agreeing, but she is also aware that some of the medical assistants in the room don't think what Suchak did was wrong.

Chapter Fourteen

Last night Carye took a call at home from one of the medical assistants who reported she was sick and needed a day off. No problem, Carye replied. But the conversation did not end there. Haltingly the woman hinted that something else was going on upstairs. Carye, exasperated and wanting to return to the book she was reading, asked what this was all about.

"I think that Suchak is planning to open a clinic in Yakima," the assistant confessed. In a hallway conversation last week Suchak indicated he might soon have a new job for her to consider.

By mid-morning Carye is seated in Allene's office with two of Lovejoy's other surgeons, Donovan and Lane. The door is closed.

Allene guides the conversation. They need to know more. She is concerned that the rift between Lovejoy's two floors has become so wide that Suchak could offer jobs to second floor staff and nobody downstairs and none of the facility's administrators would know about it.

Suchak is gone. Three days ago he became a patient in a successful quintuple bypass, and his recovery time is expected to last a minimum of two to three weeks. Carye says she will talk to the upstairs staff and make calls to Yakima to investigate the situation. She has another idea: Would one of the doctors call Dr. Jessel, who recently left town after years at Lovejoy and is now managing a clinic in the Midwest? If Suchak is opening a new office on his own, he will need to outfit the place with everything from ultrasound to surgical equipment. To whom did Jessel sell the equipment from his private office? Donovan says he will speak to Jessel. Allene says she will quietly begin her own investigation by making calls to her connections in the abortion field. Nobody mentions contacting Suchak.

After Carye and the doctors have left, Allene muses about the unexpected changes that may be coming her way. It has been a year of tumult anyway, with her father moving out, her daughter's wedding, her partner's heart attack. Those events she had little control over. This feels different. This feels like opportunity. If the rumors about Suchak are true, she reminds herself.

She recalls the early days of Lovejoy when she had as many as twenty-five doctors performing abortions at her facility. When she hired Suchak as medical director—a hungry surgeon with no outside practice—part of the bargain was that he would get the overwhelming majority of surgeries. And there was little opportunity to change course as the protests and violence increased. Any ob/gyns who were less than fully committed to maintaining abortion as a woman's option focused on their own practices and terminated their association with Lovejoy.

But the environment has changed. The lawsuits and injunctions have had their effect, as has recent federal legislation protecting clinics. Protests outside Lovejoy are way down, hardly a nuisance. A new crop of ob/gyns has come out of medical schools, younger doctors without established practices, unacquainted with the intensity of the earlier protests, though aware, she has to admit, of the shootings that have been taking place. Wouldn't it be nice, Allene thinks, if she could again spread the work around just like in the old days, twenty or twenty-five doctors all operating out of Lovejoy a few hours a week? Burnett and his crowd would have too many targets to do a good job of harassing anybody. Maybe Suchak, if he is indeed leaving, need not be replaced. Lovejoy could go back to being an institution with one voice at its helm—hers.

And there's another reason to think more ob/gyns might be willing to start performing abortions at Lovejoy, Allene thinks. The HMOs are imposing restraints on doctors that are rapidly shrinking incomes. They are not allowing as many difficult and expensive surgeries. Specialized practices, long the fertile ground for high incomes, have been limited. In addition, more patients are now qualifying for the Oregon Health Plan, and publicly funded medicine always translates into lower fees. Allene knows of a number of local obstetricians accustomed to salaries in the range of two hundred thousand dollars a year who are now averaging half that. This just might be the perfect time to make some changes in the composition of the medical staff, Allene thinks.

But what about Suchak? she wonders, still not believing the rumors. It makes no sense for the man to risk losing a three-hundred-thousand-dollar-a-year, fifteen-to-twenty-hour-a-week position at Lovejoy. Allene picks up the phone to begin her round of calls.

THURSDAY, NOVEMBER 16

Despite her volatility, Allene is not a woman to make snap decisions. Her preemptory manner can mask long hours of thought, her self-assuredness can make complex reasoning appear simple. But the savvy businesswoman is never far beneath the surface of quick laughter and provocative dress.

Throughout the last week Allene has pondered the best approach to dealing with Suchak. In the process she has found it impossible to avoid thoughts about the future of Lovejoy. She senses recent events, events beyond her control for the most part, are dictating she make decisions that will determine the kind of place Lovejoy will be years from now, as well as next month. Allene had planned to wait at least three years before making such decisions, which she assumed would revolve around removing herself from the facility's day-to-day operations.

Carye's inquiries with the upstairs staff have revealed that Rebecca and Tamara were approached by Suchak about jobs, but it is unclear if firm offers were made. Donovan talked to Dr. Jessel a few days ago and learned Suchak did not buy his equipment. Allene used a bit of creative detective work to get an advance copy of next year's Yellow Pages directory for Yakima and discovered a prominent advertisement for a new abortion clinic, but it did not list a doctor or an address.

Pushing Allene even more than the growing body of evidence is her heart. Twice in the two weeks before Suchak left for bypass surgery she saw Carye crying in her office after arguments with the medical director. Allene long ago accepted that she would never fully understand the source of the conflict between Suchak and Carye, or its depth. But it is becoming increasingly clear to her that something has to be done to resolve the hostility between the two.

Driving to work this morning, Allene unexpectedly was overcome with the sense that a critical event was imminent. And then, streaking along on the highway, the thought focused in her brain, as if on a piece of paper stuck to one of those picket signs outside Lovejoy: She must get rid of Suchak for Carye's sake. Carye has needed her to choose, and this is the moment.

Arriving at Lovejoy Allene set up a late morning meeting with Carye, Donovan, and Lane at Besaw's, her second office for private conversations.

"Suchak is going," she announces at the outset. She asks the two doctors if they are willing to cover Suchak's surgeries and help in recruiting more doctors to work at Lovejoy. An informal agreement is forged: Donovan will take on most of the load, which will include calling local ob/gyns who are performing occasional abortions in their offices. If they can get just five willing to work out of

Lovejoy, each would have to come in only once a month. Together the group puts together a list of seven.

Allene is placing the primary responsibility for Lovejoy's near-term future in Donovan's hands. She knows this involves some risk.

Two years ago Tom Donovan was living the American dream as defined by most medical school students. In his early thirties he already was one of the top perinatologists in the country, an ob/gyn specializing in the difficult and delicate surgeries performed on newborns and infants. In a good year he made close to five hundred thousand dollars. To complete the picture he had married his college sweetheart, and together they had started a family with a son. Too good to be true. Too good to last.

First came the cocaine. Donovan was introduced to the drug at parties and ended up an addict. His wife left him. All that remained was his work, and soon that was taken away too.

In time Donovan entered a drug rehabilitation program run by the state medical association. He remarried, had a second son, thought he was putting his personal life back together.

Then, last December, charges were brought against Donovan for having an improper relationship with a female patient. He claims he saw the woman casually only two or three times outside his office, and they never were intimate. The Oregon Board of Medical Examiners took up the case in a politically charged environment. Earlier that year the city of Portland was in an uproar as news reports revealed that a local ob/gyn who had been in practice for decades had been sexually molesting patients and the board had not followed up on complaints. That was not going to happen again.

An investigation began and Donovan told board examiners about the rehab program he had entered; the program itself is structured so that the board is unaware of doctors who voluntarily participate in it. The board immediately imposed an emergency suspension of Donovan's license pending completion of its investigation. Fortunately, Donovan's partners said they would cover for him.

It took three months before the charges were dismissed and Donovan could apply for reinstatement to the five hospitals at which he and his partners worked. Four of the hospitals immediately restored his privileges. One, Saint Vincent, a Catholic hospital, refused. Unfortunately for Donovan, Saint Vincent is the hospital where half the patients in his private practice chose to go. Donovan's partners could not cover for him indefinitely, and so they asked him to leave their group. Amazing how quickly a five-hundred-thousand-dollar-a-year practice can turn into nearly nothing. A marriage, too. Donovan and his second wife separated.

Eventually Donovan started thinking about why four hospitals reinstated him and one did not. He speculated that Saint Vincent barred him because he performed abortions at Lovejoy. Then, without hard evidence, he became certain that was the reason. There are days he wonders if the hospital was influenced by the anti-abortion lobby, or even if the woman who accused him and filed the original complaint was a plant from one of the anti-abortion groups. Donovan readily admits events have soured him on private practice; at least for now he's not sure he wants to go back to it. But he's hired an attorney and intends to sue Saint Vincent, and he's not shy about his motivation—money.

Until Allene's offer this morning Donovan had been down to a few private patients he saw each week in space leased from another obstetrician, and the occasional hours he worked at Lovejoy. Meanwhile, however, he has found a new outlet for his energy, and a new source of income, in his vending machine business.

Candy machines, pop machines, coffee dispensers—Donovan drives around the city removing the change and replenishing the supplies. He likes the business, more than he expected. He has become paranoid about people taking things away from him, he says, and this business is tangible and his. Nobody can take it away.

Donovan began performing abortions at Lovejoy as a medical resident eleven years ago, and until his recent troubles money was not a motivating factor. In fact, he was sacrificing income on his half day a week at Lovejoy. He was motivated by the same rationale that he is using on other doctors now.

"It's a dirty job that needs to be done," he says. Whereas Suchak insists he feels gratified doing the work, Donovan views abortion as necessary but unpleasant.

Donovan is aware that at Lovejoy his patients rarely smile; few are happy either before or after their operations. He could suffer that situation easily enough when it was just a few hours a week, but is uncertain how he will react to steadier work at the Surgicenter.

Some days the implications of abortion surgery are harder for Donovan to ignore than others. Not long ago he spent a morning performing perinatal surgery and saving the life of a baby born at twenty-four weeks. That same afternoon he came to Lovejoy for his half day of work and performed a D & E on a woman who was twenty-four weeks pregnant.

Donovan lives alone half the week now; the rest of the time he has custody of his two sons. Two years ago he took up smoking, and during breaks he often can be found on the bench outside Lovejoy's back door, sharing cigarettes with the medical assistants and Carye.

At the meeting's start Allene thought she was cobbling together a stopgap arrangement with Lane and Donovan. But as the four relax and become accustomed to the idea of life without Suchak, Allene's natural optimism takes over and she begins to think she may have stumbled upon a pretty good permanent plan, a way to make Lovejoy run efficiently without the overbearing and divisive presence of an upstairs, male medical director.

Carye, a more practiced worrier, is silently uneasy. Suchak may have been her nemesis but even Carye could not deny his efficiency. He was the only surgeon on staff who was never late. Though mechanical in his approach, he consistently was in and out of surgery faster than any other doctor at Lovejoy, which has always been a major part of his appeal to the nursing staff. When Suchak was operating they could count on keeping to the posted schedule and getting home on time. And for many years Suchak was that rare obstetrician who seemed immune to the burnout that afflicts so many abortion surgeons.

Carye thinks back to her first day at Lovejoy. Previously she had been working at the local feminist health center, her apprenticeship. Many of the doctors there were women, all the doctors there were addressed by their first names. The day Carye started working at Lovejoy Allene introduced her to Harold Suchak; she remembers smiling and saying, "Hi, Harold." "Dr. Suchak," came the reply in a curt, correcting voice.

That night Carye told Thom, "I'm going to find a way to make him like me." Now, just minutes after hearing the news she has long desired, Carye is overcome with a sense of failure.

Later, sitting at her desk just before finishing her afternoon's work, Allene notices Carye's dispirited face as the counselor walks by, and Allene becomes worried herself. She thought the day she dismissed Suchak would be one of elation for Carye, a liberating event. But Carye is not elated. Allene leaves for home feeling she has missed something.

FRIDAY, NOVEMBER 17

Carye's depressed feeling does not quickly evaporate. Last night Carye found herself mulling over a disturbing thought. One of her conflicts with Suchak related to the work she thought a medical director ought to be doing—staying on top of the other doctors, contacting insurance companies to drum up more business, guiding the staff. In Carye's mind Suchak disregarded his job beyond the obvious, the surgeries for which he was paid on a per patient basis. But what if, Carye thought reluctantly, the reason Suchak ignored her repeated requests was his physical condition? Suchak has been sick, his arteries clogged, for months or longer. All she is sure of is that she has won a long-fought battle but feels nothing like a victor.

Carye is leaning forward in her chair when Lisa walks in and drops a fax on the desk. Odd. It has been sent from Warm Springs, a Native American reservation that takes up a big chunk of the middle of the state. Much of the fax is unintelligible but the essence is clear: The official-looking document says that sixteen-year-old Molly Clearwater is enjoined from continuing with her abortion.

This makes no sense to Carye. She walks to the reception area, first to check the scheduling book and then to ask Lisa if she knows anything about it. According to Lisa, no Molly Clearwater has called or visited Lovejoy, nor anybody else who identified herself as a Warm Springs resident.

Puzzled but pleasantly distracted, Carye figures that the reservation must be faxing all the state's abortion facilities and that Lovejoy is not involved. She wonders what circumstances prompted the fax. Before returning to the pile of pink slips on her desk representing calls that need to be returned, she tells Lisa that if a woman from Warm Springs shows up she should be treated like any other patient. "You can't enjoin someone's civil rights," she observes.

MONDAY, NOVEMBER 20

"Molly Clearwater?"

From her post at the copy machine Carye hears Lisa repeat the name. She signals with her finger and Lisa transfers the call to Carye's office.

Picking up her phone Carye hears a scared, uncertain voice. The voice of a girl who has been intimidated, she thinks. Molly Clearwater is sixteen years old and sixteen weeks pregnant. She wants an abortion. Her parents support her decision. Her boyfriend and her boyfriend's parents, who apparently hold influence with the tribal council, want a baby. Last week they filed a motion with the tribal court, and Molly Clearwater says she was told she could not go ahead with the abortion until after the hearing.

Last Wednesday the tribal court sided with the boyfriend. As best Molly Clearwater can understand the ruling, she is no longer in the custody of her parents; the court made the tribal child protection services agency her legal guardian and told her that she must temporarily live with her grandmother, who also opposes the abortion. To Carye it sounds as if the court intends to keep tabs on Molly Clearwater until it is too late for her to have an abortion. What is eminently clear, however, is that Molly Clearwater is poorly educated and hardly able to grasp the complexity of her predicament.

"I don't know what they can do to me," Molly says.

Carye asks again, "What did they say in court?"

"That I'm enjoined," Molly replies. "They told me I can't have an abortion. But my friend told me I could."

Earlier this morning Carye consulted Dr. Lane, explaining the situation as she imagined it. Lane said he would perform the surgery, tribal injunction or not, as long as the girl is of age and certain she wants the abortion. In fact, Lane said, he would waive his fee. Now Carye tells Molly Clearwater to come in.

The injunction is just the beginning of Molly's troubles. She has no money. Carye says if she comes to Lovejoy Molly need not worry about the money. But the reservation is two hours away from Portland, Molly explains, and even if she can find a ride, she has no place to stay overnight. At sixteen weeks she will need a D & E, which will take two or three days. "I need to get some money, I'll call you back," Molly says before hanging up.

Putting her phone back in the cradle Carye only wishes she were more shocked. The week before she read in the *New York Times* about an entire town just outside Omaha, Nebraska, that conspired successfully to keep a sixteen-year-old girl from having the abortion she and her parents sought. The girl was taken from her parents' home in the middle of the night by police, placed in a foster home against her will, and ordered by a judge not to go ahead with the abortion.

Molly Clearwater never contacts Lovejoy again. After a week Carye calls the other abortion clinics in town to see if Molly called any of them, but none have heard from her.

Allene leans back in her office chair and looks at the freshly typed letter on her desk. Beneath the letter, attached by paper clip, is a check. Suchak's last paycheck.

Allene has not talked with her medical director since he left for bypass surgery over two weeks ago. As far as she knows, Suchak is unaware of the furor caused by his treatment of Jerri or the discovery of the job offers he discussed with the two medical assistants. Yesterday she composed the letter, and this morning it sits on top of the day's paperwork, never long out of view.

Tim sits across from Allene, having brought in the week's flowers. A few minutes ago Allene showed him the Suchak memorandum. Tim is slouched in his seat, relaxed. Usually when he comes into Lovejoy he and Allene find time for an informal visit, gossiping, talking about old times at Lovejoy and acquaintances they have long held in common.

Suddenly Carye rushes into the room as if she has spotted a runaway freight train, her eyes flashing. "Harold is in the lab," she says excitedly.

Tim immediately rises from his seat. "Bye. I'm leaving, Allene."

But before Tim can get out of the room Suchak blocks the doorway, his wife beside him. Allene, who usually stands to greet visitors, remains seated.

"Hello, Harold. How are you doing?" she says.

Suchak, whose normal countenance is far from easygoing, looks hard. "I'm doing very well," he says. There's a sheet of paper in his hand and everyone in the room knows what it is—next month's schedule. And Suchak's name is not on it.

"What's going on here?" he says, controlling his tone of voice but not concealing his anger. "Aren't I going to be on the schedule?"

Allene does not answer the question, but across the desk she hands him the letter and attached check. She says she intended to send both this afternoon. Standing in the room Suchak reads the letter of dismissal. Finishing, he looks up at Allene, curiously expressionless.

"Okay, okay. I'll be out of here Friday or Saturday." He turns around and walks out with his wife. He has not asked Allene why he has been let go and she has not conveyed her reasons. Neither knows how much or what the other knows. They will not speak again.

FRIDAY, NOVEMBER 24

Suchak's departure has not made Fridays any less harried or stressful. The generals and tab locals still overlap, a situation Carye will review and modify in a few months. In fact Dr. Chandler, who is performing the day's locals, is one of the slowest staff surgeons, and the second-floor waiting room is backed up even more than usual.

Yesterday Allene met with the upstairs staff and explained that Suchak was no longer working at Lovejoy. "We're going to be kinder and gentler with our patients," she said. She read them her letter dismissing Suchak.

Dear Dr. Suchak,

I'm pleased your recovery process went well and that concern is behind you and your family.

Congratulations also on your new endeavor in Yakima. The entire staff wishes you well.

I have had a vision for Lovejoy Surgicenter that you have not shared. During your absence it has become clear that my vision is possible. I need a cohesive staff proud to work at Lovejoy.

*We have returned to that. Therefore your services are no longer
required.*

*Please notify Carye how you would like your belongings
returned.*

Sincerely,
Allene Klass

Not a woman given to self-doubts, Allene nonetheless has spent
considerable time in the last forty-eight hours reflecting on her decision. Having taken the step of dismissing Suchak, she now ana-
lyzes why she did not do so earlier. She did not fire him immediately
on finding out about his alleged grabbing of Jerri. In fact, she never
asked Suchak for his version of that incident.

When it comes to Lovejoy Allene is a pragmatic woman. In her
mind Suchak, Donovan, and Lane are the best D & E surgeons available, maybe the only three who combine technical proficiency with
an ability to resist the emotional toll exacted by a heavy load of abortions. Which is why Allene has tolerated Suchak far longer than she
might have.

In the end, however, Allene expects loyalty from her employees, and she believes Suchak, in overall attitude and by talking to
the medical assistants about coming to work for him, has tried to
undermine the Lovejoy operation.

Last night Allene's thoughts wandered to a doctor she had on
staff years ago, a man who started out kind and caring but who she
watched wear down over the years like an oceanside cliff losing its
best features to the relentless attack of wind and water. First to go
was his patience, then his gentle touch. One day a patient was unable to remain still during her abortion, and the doctor reached for
his surgical tenaculums, metal clamplike devices, and cuffed the
woman's ankles to the operating table stirrups as he completed the
surgery. Allene did not dismiss the doctor immediately but in time
she did, losing a major part of Lovejoy's business in the process. The

doctor had been bringing in a hundred of his own patients a month. At least replacing Suchak will not be so hard.

And it won't be as easy as it might be, Allene reflects. Carye still is not acting as expected. Yesterday Allene watched as she snapped at one of the counselors who asked permission to take an early lunch.

Carye is not unaware of her reaction. But she still cannot dismiss the feeling of failure. She is an optimist at heart: most counselors must be, must believe people can change. Her job is helping people make over their lives, and denial is every bit as much a part of a counselor's repertoire as it is her patients'. The sad truth is most of the women Carye counsels will not change, and in the rare quiet moment Carye recognizes this. The women who come to Lovejoy because of a defect in their birth control will have been given a reprieve. Some of the young patients will take advantage of their second chance and live responsible, fulfilled lives. But many of the others will be back under similar or different circumstances, with new compelling stories to tell. Or they won't come back, but other obstacles will keep them from fulfilling their potential.

Carye says that until just two weeks ago part of her hoped Suchak would change and the two of them would find a way to co-exist at Lovejoy. So mixed in with the failure today is a sense of guilt that she might have been at least partially responsible for Suchak's departure. She never found a way to make Suchak like her.

Meanwhile, tension is building upstairs today. Chandler's pace, though partially due to the gentle attention he provides each patient, irritates some of the second-floor staff, who want to get home before the weekend traffic begins. Only tab locals are left to be performed, but as the afternoon unfolds, the surgical team is falling further and further behind schedule.

Chandler is assisted by Carole and Rebecca, the same team that assisted Suchak for Jerri's surgery. Around 3 P.M. a new patient is wheeled in, a twenty-one-year-old woman nine weeks pregnant, according to her chart. Almost as soon as Chandler inserts the cannula into the woman's uterus a clear liquid begins gushing out. Everyone in the room knows that this is amniotic fluid, which should not be evident until about twelve weeks, the point at which surgeries at Lovejoy require general anesthesia.

Chandler is intent on his work. Too intent. He begins aspirating the woman's uterus. A hand appears on his shoulder. Rebecca's. "Dr. Chandler, I think we should stop and ultrasound."

Chandler is jolted from his absorption. He removes his instruments, leaves the room, heads for the hallway telephone, and calls Carye.

A minute later Carye arrives upstairs and takes the patient to another room for an ultrasound. The scan reveals a fourteen-week pregnancy. Carye explains to the woman the tab gen procedure. The woman agrees to having laminaria inserted for a surgery under general anesthetic Saturday.

At the end of the day Allene asks Rebecca to her office. "You did exactly what was right and I'm proud of you," she says.

Chapter Fifteen

So much for a quiet day around the house. Andrew Burnett knows when it is time to change plans. The telephone has been ringing all morning from its spot in the middle of his cluttered metal desk. Burnett is news again and everyone wants to talk to him.

But if Burnett is going to spend the morning on the telephone he would rather not do it here, in the office off the kitchen. Hardly room to move around between the desk, the computer on its little stand behind his back, the beige filing cabinet to the side and the United States flag propped up in the corner.

Normally Burnett does not mind talking on the phone, but between interviews this morning he flashes back to the time a man called claiming he was from *Time* or *Newsweek*, one of the two. Shelley Shannon had just been caught and arrested for the shooting of the Kansas doctor, Tiller, and the reporter told him a grand jury had handed down an indictment accusing him, Burnett, of aiding and abetting Shannon. The caller said court officers were coming to arrest him, and asked if Burnett had any comment.

Except there was no grand jury, just as there was no conspiring with Shelley, Burnett thinks. Never did find out if the caller was a reporter trying to trick him into a scoop or a law enforcement agent trying to maneuver him into an off-guard confession. You have to be a little careful talking to people you don't know.

But they've all been calling today, so this couldn't be a ruse or a prank. The news magazines, Peter Jennings, the *Washington Post*, *U.S. News & World Report*. Don't forget the local media. They're all seeking a reaction to a lawsuit Burnett hasn't even seen yet. So, driven by curiosity, Burnett turns the interviews around, trying to find out what the reporters know.

Planned Parenthood has filed the suit. What is it they're asking for this time? No kidding, two hundred million dollars. Add up all the claims against all the defendants, and it's over a billion. Ludicrous. Where in the world did they get that figure, he wonders. We must be really bad if we did a billion dollars' worth of harm, he thinks ruefully. Or really good.

The callers expect anger, maybe fear. He can hear it in their probing questions. And this is, after all, a nationwide class action lawsuit naming him among the primary defendants, essentially claiming he and cohorts are responsible for all the shootings and deaths of abortion doctors over the last few years. This is big time, and big money. Big conspiracy, they're charging. But it's really nothing new, Burnett tries to explain to reporters.

Terrorist—that's what they're calling you, the reporters say. The abortionists began using that word ten years ago, Burnett answers, when all I did was picketing. They've gone about as far as they can go with their name-calling. Another lawsuit is hardly worthy of anger if you're Andrew Burnett. Nuisance. That's the word he settles on in his well-practiced "Here we go again" tone of voice. He has been summoned to Virginia twice this year to testify before a grand jury that is not so secretly hearing evidence about a possible conspiracy involving clinic violence. They haven't been able to put anything together, and that's after nearly a year of sessions. This is more of the same, fishing for a conspiracy they are not going to find.

By late morning Burnett tells the callers he will hold a press conference at 1 P.M. He puts on his jacket and heads out to the gray Datsun station wagon in the driveway. At the Advocates for Life house a local reporter comes by with a copy of the actual complaint.

Burnett stands in front of the fireplace in the main room downstairs, answering questions before three or four television cameras and a dozen or so reporters. He does not sound like a man who is about to change his ways.

An hour later the reporters are gone. Burnett sits around the office for a while, talking with Paul deParrie and a few other Advocates workers. The mood is upbeat, maybe because there is movement again. For all the attention we get, there is actually very little activity on our part, Burnett thinks. We do so little. So the milling reporters, the sense of something happening, seems to have energized the crew.

On Friday morning Burnett receives the caller he has been expecting. The man is around forty, dressed in a suit, drives a nice car, Burnett observes. He might be an attorney, or maybe just a process server. Either way, the man comes to the printing office, a small building adjacent to the house, and hands over two thick packets, the complaints. One for Burnett, one for Advocates. The visitor probably has been told to say nothing and reveal nothing, but simply to hand over the papers. Which he does. He also asks how he can locate the other defendants—this man has a lot of packets to deliver today.

Burnett puts the papers aside and does not look at them until after lunch. Taking them out of the envelope he scans through, looking for what it is Planned Parenthood seeks. That's what matters. Allegations are usually bogus, he's found. But in this case even the point of the lawsuit is vague. They would like him to stop putting out "wanted" posters for abortion doctors, that much is clear. Apparently the exposés of abortion doctors are their main focus. But what does "no contact with the plaintiffs" mean? And what is their real bottom line? Do they want to wipe out Advocates, or at least so severely limit its functions as to make it useless? He really doesn't know.

But this Burnett does know. The lawsuit is not about law or even politics. It's about speaking the truth. I'm just trying to speak prophetically, to follow the model of the biblical prophets, he thinks. What they really want to do is censor me. Well, they had to cut off John the Baptist's head to silence him. God called me to this; take it away and I truly don't know what else I'd do.

And then Burnett thinks he sees an unfolding pattern. In April a Planned Parenthood chapter in Texas decided it was time to collect on an outstanding judgment against Operation Rescue, and before anyone knew what was happening court officers had descended on Rescue's headquarters and removed computers, office chairs— everything of value. Just over a month ago a jury in Texas came up with an $8.6 million award for an abortion doctor against local protestors there, breaking Lovejoy's record for a single judgment. A district judge recently labeled Paul deParrie a stalker under the state's new antistalking statute, and he is barred from picketing at the home of the woman who runs the Feminist abortion clinic. And now they were after him.

They just don't stop. Their law is so precious, more precious than human life or the American Constitution. Already there are injunctions involving each of the city's major abortion facilities. How much does he owe? It used to be close to a million dollars. A little less with the setting-aside of some of the attorneys' fees. Still, at least half a million to Lovejoy, and that's without the interest. There's nothing left to take, nothing that hasn't been transferred away, but that doesn't stop them. They are after every penny. Try to put on a fundraiser, and a sheriff's deputy is likely to show up at the front door to collect the proceeds. They call it a till tab. Deputies have even come to the Advocates office and left with the petty cash.

Time to plan strategy. The first defendant listed in the suit is the ACLA, American Coalition of Life Activists, the loosely organized umbrella organization of which Advocates for Life is a member and Burnett a founder. Burnett picks up the phone and begins calling other individual defendants scattered around the country, starting with Dave Crane in Virginia, then Michael Bray in Maryland.

There are four options, as Burnett sees it. One, get some other group to pay for their defense. Over the years a number of conservative religious organizations have talked about helping them out. Burnett makes copies of the complaint and dispatches them to leaders of a couple of the organizations.

Option two, Burnett thinks, would be to raise the money himself in order to somehow hire an attorney. Not much chance of that. Or he could defend himself, option three. And alternative four, well, that would be to ignore the lawsuit, essentially to default. If the Planned Parenthood lawyers want to come out in search of more money, let them.

Lawyers. There's always Henry Kane. Kane has defended Burnett and Advocates through most of their legal battles over the years, and he's been willing to donate his time. But even if an attorney can be found to take the case for free, Burnett figures he will have to come up with about twenty thousand dollars for expenses. We spent over a hundred thousand dollars for legal expenses fighting Lovejoy's lawsuits.

And Kane retired a few years ago. Might be convinced to come out of retirement. Might not, considering how long this suit could drag on. Advocates is still fighting a lawsuit filed by Feminist in 1986.

All sorts of unusual things have been going on lately. Just a few weeks ago a visitor arrived from the Vatican of all places. The man claimed he was editor of the Vatican newspapers. He was curious about these staunch pro-lifers who weren't even Catholics, asked a lot of questions in broken English.

Well, maybe something positive will come out of this. God uses bad events to his advantage. The initial round of lawsuits was intended to get us all to quit and instead forced us out of our jobs and into full-time activism. Every time the abortionists have tried to push us further against the wall the true faithful have become more resolute.

One thing is certain. Business as usual, starting with a protest that has been planned for Saturday outside a local hospital, where one of the city's abortion doctors works. No change there. And after that a drive over to Lovejoy, where Ron Norquist says he will be leading a protest, just to say hello. Burnett has been told that Lovejoy is not involved in this lawsuit, but he suspects they must have known something about it anyway.

If there's one person more surprised by Planned Parenthood's lawsuit than Andrew Burnett, it's Allene Klass. Yesterday morning Allene was dressed for winter, a study in contrast—black and gold pin-striped pants, shimmering black silk shirt, gold belt buckle, earrings, bracelet, and watch. The effect was striking and very appropriate. The flash of her jewelry matched her flashes of anger.

The foremost object of that anger was Planned Parenthood, supposedly her ally. Some ally, she thought. On Thursday, about the time that reporters were beginning to badger Burnett at home, a fax arrived at Lovejoy informing Allene and Carye about the lawsuit. Allene, usually on top of even the smallest detail of news in the abortion world, was caught unaware. More critical was the fact that Lovejoy was completely unprepared. Late in the afternoon, watching Andrew Burnett and others tell a local television broadcaster they might step up their anti-abortion activities as a response to the lawsuit, Klass was certain she was more upset at Planned Parenthood than at the protestors.

By Friday, Allene cannot fathom Planned Parenthood's strategy. If they wanted to get Burnett, why not just buy her judgment? What's the point in amassing more awards against him when nobody can collect what they already have? Allene recalls a discussion earlier in the year with Planned Parenthood's attorney about just this subject.

This must be part of a larger plan, Allene decides. Maybe Planned Parenthood is preparing to open an abortion clinic in Portland after all and is looking to increase name recognition. Shaking her head she says to Carye, "I just don't understand this." Then she

makes a prediction: Planned Parenthood will soon begin a fund-
raising campaign, and their first mailing will feature the message that
they are on the front lines trying to keep abortion available. And as
evidence they will advertise this lawsuit.

But we're the ones likely to suffer for this, Allene thinks. If
Burnett brings out his forces on Saturday, they won't be parading in
front of the city's other abortion facilities. The Downtown clinic is
five floors up in an office high-rise, and Feminist is on the second
floor of another building. Planned Parenthood doesn't even perform
abortions in Portland, so they have little to worry about. Which leaves
Lovejoy—the biggest and best-known facility in addition to being
the one most accessible to protestors.

Allene's anger is hardly a match for Carye's on Saturday. Carye
watches from the front lobby as protestors gather outside. She considers how calm it has been for the last two months, since Shelley
Shannon's sentencing. And now Planned Parenthood has provided
more ammunition for Burnett, she thinks. Witness the scene outside, the biggest protest at Lovejoy in years. This could be just the
impetus he needs to reenergize his organization.

When she arrived this morning Carye pulled her new Volvo into
Allene's parking spot, knowing Allene would not be coming in.
Rather than walk directly into Lovejoy through the back entrance
she headed around the building toward the front. There she talked
to the volunteer escort coordinator for the day and learned three
escorts would be on duty, all sent by the Portland office of the National Organization for Women. She made sure the coordinator knew
to take pictures of all protestors with the Polaroid camera kept behind the reception desk inside.

Then Carye headed inside and upstairs to tell the staff they must
accompany all patients out to the back parking lot after their surgeries, making sure the patients get away safely. She also had the staff
move their cars out of the back parking lot to free up spaces for patients. Finally, she took a minute to talk to Donovan, who is per-

forming the morning's surgeries, reminding him to exit quickly when he is done for the day. "Be smart," she finished.

While going through these security steps an image was flashing in and out of her mind, of the protests and rescues that took place a few years ago, before the $8.2 million judgment. Today, for the first time in years, the crowd outside reminds her of those crowds, too many protestors to keep track of, protestors in the parking lot and around the side of the building. How many? She can't even count them. Maybe twenty-five. Burnett is there. Carye has seen him, along with other stalwarts from Advocates for Life.

Carye hates this chaos, feels certain this is the most endangered that Lovejoy and its staff have been in years. She hates the buzz of excitement generated by the crowd outside, the sense of camaraderie she knows is building among the protestors.

And we have Planned Parenthood to thank, Carye thinks. Sure, many of the protestors outside are in violation of Lovejoy's injunction, and Lovejoy could go after them for contempt of court. But what's the point? They'd just be back, maybe owing Lovejoy a few thousand more dollars, which they would never pay. And Allene would be out attorneys' fees. Carye does not believe the courts hold the final solution for the clinics.

Carye maintains an unorthodox view of the protests. She focuses on the fact that before Lovejoy and other clinics won large monetary awards no one was shooting at abortion doctors and staff. She considers that of great significance.

Carye thinks Shelley Shannon would not have picked up a handgun if she did not owe two hundred thousand dollars to Lovejoy. Yes, Shannon was radicalized and possibly despairing over her inability to effect change, but the judgment, Carye feels certain, pushed her over the edge. Being in debt for a sum of money she could hardly conceptualize, much less hope to earn in ten lifetimes, alienated Shannon, made her life seem particularly unreal. And it may have been that sense of unreality that prompted a mild-mannered housewife to begin shooting.

Carye has said she would love to ask Andrew Burnett a simple question: "When you think about all the money you owe, does it feel like it doesn't matter anymore, like nothing's real?"

From his twenty-third-floor office in one of Portland's downtown towers, Steve Walters, the Planned Parenthood attorney in Portland, thinks Allene and Carye are missing the point. Shelley Shannon would not have shot Tiller if Burnett hadn't been encouraging her for years, Walters says. Shelley Shannon would not have shot Tiller without *Life Advocate* supplying detailed information about the doctor and his habits.

The point of this lawsuit is to stop the killings and the bombings, plain and simple. And the way to do that is by targeting the people who are motivating and assisting the terrorists. The weapon? Monetary awards that will deter others from offering the type of assistance Andrew Burnett and Advocates for Life provide.

Prior judgments didn't push Shelley Shannon over the edge, Walters is sure. He thinks that without the lawsuits and federal legislation protecting abortion clinics, most of Portland's abortion clinics, Lovejoy included, would not be open today—the rescues would have shut them down. The correct policy, he is convinced, is to take protestors to court every time they disregard the injunctions in place, every time they cross the court-dictated boundaries on the sidewalks outside.

Walters believes Planned Parenthood has a good First Amendment basis for its case. He recognizes the danger of a show trial but is certain no shootings will take place while the trial is going on. Such violent acts would prove Planned Parenthood's case, he says. And Burnett won't let that happen, he adds, certain that Burnett exerts such control.

What Planned Parenthood is going to try to prove is that when Burnett publishes a story in *Life Advocate* providing details about an abortion doctor, he knows there are people out there who might take that information and shoot the doctor. Which makes Burnett responsible, or at least, with colleagues, a billion dollars' worth accountable.

A week later Carye takes a call from a woman obstetrician in Alaska whose patient is twenty weeks pregnant. Tests show the fetus to be severely hydrocephalic, a victim of water on the brain. The fetus likely will never make it to a live birth if left alone. If born, it might never live free of life support. The mother wants an abortion but there is nobody in Alaska who performs abortions so late. The obstetrician has called to ask how the abortion would be done at Lovejoy. Carye explains the D & E procedure and is stunned by the doctor's response.

"I don't see how anybody can talk about such a barbaric procedure so professionally," the doctor says. The rest of her diatribe makes it clear the obstetrician is not a supporter of abortion rights.

"This is the exact situation that makes it important this procedure is available," Carye counters, anger rising. "And we're the people who prevent this from being barbaric. Quite honestly I'm stunned that you would talk to me that way when you're the one who called me."

The conversation deteriorates. The obstetrician explains that her patient is on Alaska Medicaid, and Carye has to inform her that the Alaska insurance would not cover an abortion in Oregon. Carye hangs up the phone wondering how this doctor has treated her patient. Carye has seen too many people use abortion to emotionally punish women. Did this doctor use the word "barbaric" in front of her patient? It would not surprise Carye if she did; for years Carye has been mystified by her observation that some of the most insensitive abortion doctors are women.

Before continuing work, Carye has a sobering thought: It's becoming hard to tell our friends from our enemies, she realizes.

Chapter Sixteen

Winter in Portland is full of caprice. Data kept by the weather service imply a moderate season, and statistically that's true. Oregon winters are never as bitter as those in the Northeast or Midwest; a cold afternoon finds the temperature in the low forties. The rains are notable, but only for their consistency. On average, Portland receives only slightly more rainfall per year than New York or Chicago. Snow might strike Portland once or twice each winter, an inch or two usually vanished a day later.

But this winter stretches the statistics. In December the worst windstorm to hit Oregon in twenty-nine years swept in from the ocean and paralyzed much of the city with downed power lines and uprooted trees. In early February an ice storm draped crystalline coats over the trees still standing after the great blow. Streets and sidewalks became treacherous sheets of glass for two days. The next week a third calamity arrived: Unseasonable warm rain melted the ice and snow that had accumulated in the mountains. This, in turn, created massive flooding that sent citizens to the downtown waterfront to construct sandbag and plywood dikes in an attempt at protecting the city's core.

And through it all, Lovejoy remained busy. On a late spring afternoon Carye and Allene discuss a phenomenon they began to recognize years ago: Any natural disaster that drives most of the city to scurry for safety also drives patients to Lovejoy.

Carye and Allene, although sometimes awed by the hardiness of the patients, are well past being astonished. The more inclement the conditions the more determined Lovejoy's patients become. When schools close up for the rare snowstorm, Lovejoy's lobby fills. It is as if Lovejoy's patients feel they should be forced to suffer adversity to get an abortion, Carye thinks. A penance, expiation of the guilt that so often accompanies abortion, exactly what she is trying to help them avoid.

The day of the windstorm, with most businesses in Portland closed, a full slate of patients made their appointments at Lovejoy. One woman had driven 250 miles from Boise, Idaho. When the ice storm arrived, eleven women skidded their way to Lovejoy, including four D & Es. Only about a third of Lovejoy's staff came to work, and a month later Allene treated those few to a lavish dinner at an Italian restaurant in the neighborhood.

Inconvenience seems to encourage Lovejoy's patients as well. One of the busiest days at Lovejoy every year is December 31—New Year's Eve day. When everyone else is leaving work early and heading home to prepare for festivities, Lovejoy's patients are streaming in. Allene figures the women are determined to get a fresh start before a new year begins. Carye thinks health insurance is partly responsible—women using their insurance before a new deductible is imposed in January.

After a few minutes on this topic, Carye and Allene begin discussing the changes taking place at Lovejoy. Though Suchak's departure has set in motion these changes, his name is rarely mentioned now. Both women know that Suchak recently opened an office in Washington. But as a subject of conversation Suchak is not even avoided; it is as if he has been deleted from Lovejoy's institutional memory. Nobody has appropriated any of his meager furnishings from the downstairs lounge—even the desk is apparently not worthy of removing.

A slight, almost imperceptible shift in roles plays beneath the surface of talks between Allene and Carye now; over the course of the winter Allene has let Carye know that she will one day run Lovejoy.

Donovan and Lane appear to be working out well, Donovan taking the larger share of the load and happy to do it. He is nearly matching the fifteen to twenty hours a week Suchak worked.

Soon after Suchak's dismissal Donovan and Carye began meeting to review the Surgicenter's medical protocols, the rules and procedures governing patient care. There is never any doubt about who is in charge at the Surgicenter. But on issues involving medical treatment doctors always retain final authority, even at Lovejoy. Liability issues alone would demand that it be so.

Pain management was an obvious first topic for discussion. As medical director Suchak insisted on relatively low doses of pain medication to help patients after surgery. Suchak felt too many of Lovejoy's patients were either junkies or potential drug abusers, and he did not want to contribute to their descent by providing large quantities of potentially addictive narcotics.

The three drugs in question are Valium, which helps patients relax and elevates their pain threshold; Demerol, which deadens their pain; and Nubain, an antidepressant. Under Suchak most women received ten milligrams of Valium and four hundred milligrams of Advil for pain relief. Demerol was administered only in special circumstances. Suchak once told Carye he was concerned that patients receiving Demerol might be dangerously dizzy and disoriented when they left the Surgicenter.

Donovan has told Carye he thinks Lovejoy should be more liberal with medications. Demerol and/or fifteen milligrams of Valium should be available simply on request, subject to the counselor's judgment. Donovan figures that patients who don't receive enough medication to relieve pain will likely try to treat the pain on their own, with possibly harmful consequences.

Carye is pleased to find herself working with a physician whose thinking so obviously matches her own. She says she will begin the process of changing the medications protocol, starting with a meeting of all Lovejoy doctors to determine if consensus can be reached. The process is cumbersome, but a hospital or clinic cannot afford to have its policies too random and open to interpretation without leaving itself vulnerable to potential abuse down the line.

Scheduling issues are not as easy for Carye to work out with Donovan. Both he and Lane have told Carye they want to change scheduling to eliminate some of their slack time.

From the doctors' perspective, there is no reason for them to arrive at Lovejoy at the time surgeries are scheduled to begin and then wait around, often as long as thirty minutes, before the first patients reach the OR—especially when they are paid by the surgery, not for their time. The same goes for the ten-to-twenty-minute breaks they often are forced to take between tab local patients. If Donovan has his way the patients will be ready to go when the doctor arrives, and will be processed through the second floor pre-op so that one can be wheeled into the OR right after another. Then a surgeon could perform seven or eight tab locals in an hour instead of four or five.

Carye is not as concerned about how many surgeries Donovan performs in an hour. Her focus is the emotional condition of the patients. When she arrived at Lovejoy she was dismayed to see some women spending three to five hours at the Surgicenter when they came in for tab locals. Patients were usually told to arrive early in the day, which meant most arrived about the same time in the morning and had to wait for their counseling sessions and again for their surgeries. Doctors were not expected to appear until a number of patients were processed and counseled and waiting for their surgeries upstairs.

One of the first changes Carye instituted at Lovejoy was to space out the scheduling. Which means patients arrive at regular intervals, are counseled after shorter waits downstairs, and then admitted upstairs at the same pace. But it also means they arrive in the OR at intervals that cannot be precisely controlled because counselors may not be available and counseling sessions do not all last the same length of time.

Now it is rare for a woman to spend more than two hours' total time at Lovejoy, and most members of the support staff are pleased because they are dealing with fewer patients made surly by a long wait. Besides, they get paid by the hour. But it is the doctors who suffer the burden of the scheduling policy by spending extra time at Lovejoy for which they are not paid.

In fact, on a recent Friday afternoon, Carye encountered Donovan in the upstairs lounge, relaxing as he waited for a patient. She questioned him about the next day's schedule, which showed him with two D & Es and two tab gens all arriving at 6:30 A.M. Donovan confessed that after exams he told each of the women to come in at the same time. Carye rolled her eyes, knowing at least three of the women would wait most of the morning. Donovan responded that if he told four women to come in at 6:30 A.M., the odds were that maybe two would arrive on time. Carye said nothing, recognizing a battle to be fought many times.

But mostly, Carye reports to Allene, Donovan has been easy to work with. He has spearheaded a recruitment program, speaking to twelve local obstetricians so far. He has tailored his approach to the personality of each doctor, but basically appeals on two fronts. He tells surgeons that if more doctors perform abortions, it will be harder for those who want to stop abortions to target just a few with their protests and violence. Also, he explains how one afternoon at Lovejoy performing fifteen tab locals at seventy dollars each can yield eleven hundred dollars, not bad for a day off. All twelve have turned him down.

Most of the obstetricians Donovan has approached insisted they did not have the time to spare. A few in large partnerships said their contracts do not allow moonlighting. Donovan is not surprised at the response, although he had hoped to get one or two to agree to occasional surgeries at Lovejoy by now. He feels he is battling a perception around town that there already are plenty of abortion doctors, which makes appeals to conscience difficult at best.

For a moment Allene contemplates Donovan, her new de facto medical director. Allene genuinely likes the man, and her loyalty to

him is growing. She believes he is gentle with his patients and a ter-
rific surgeon, and for a doctor with those two attributes Allene is ready
to overlook any faults and baggage.

Allene remains as confident as ever and tells Carye that they
will soon have more doctors performing surgeries at Lovejoy. She
remarks that in recent weeks it has become more enjoyable for her
to come in every morning and says she has sensed more of a team
feeling developing among the Lovejoy staff. That last observation
may have been a product of Allene's natural and unabashed optimism.

The firing of Suchak did not noticeably mute the second-floor
discord. Some members of the staff upstairs were pleased to see him
go, a few remained loyal to the former medical director and resented
his dismissal. But it did not take long for everyone to recognize that
while Suchak might have provided a point of conflict, he was by no
means the source.

About a month after Suchak last set foot in Lovejoy, Carye was
forced to break up a shoving match between two medical assistants
in the upstairs lounge. The incident did not deeply worry Carye; she
attributed the fight to a personality conflict that had long existed
between the two women. Neither was severely disciplined.

Carye regards the affair understandable, if not completely excusable, within the context of the lives of the medical assistants. The
assistants remain the mystery women of Lovejoy, even to Carye. Many
are in their thirties and forties and still earn seven or eight dollars an
hour. All are consistently kind to patients, and intelligent, competent workers when they choose to be. Almost to a woman they offer
spotty work records. It is the inconsistencies that are so hard to grasp.
They fight for more work hours, yet take multiple days off. They plead
with Carye for help, more staff, but when a new assistant is hired,
invariably arguments over whose hours are being unfairly cut back
will follow.

Some of the behavior can certainly be attributed to Allene's
policies that virtually eliminate overtime pay and curtail benefits
such as paid holidays. And some might have to do with the overall

stress of working at an abortion facility. Still, the personal lives of most of the medical assistants, as Carye knows in detail, read like the plot summaries of daytime soap operas, with their litanies of divorce, wayward boyfriends, troublesome children, and recovery programs.

Carye and Allene have tried a number of strategies over the last few months aimed at squashing the insubordination that has taken root. In fact, the defiant behavior of the second-floor staff has reached a level that would not be tolerated at most businesses. Just a week ago Carye walked upstairs to find patients waiting in the lobby while all three assistants were smoking outside—and this less than a month after a staff meeting at which Carye emphasized that only two smoking breaks would be allowed each day.

A memo recently was tacked to the bulletin board in the upstairs lounge reminding the staff to limit personal telephone calls while on the job. A sign-up sheet has been placed at second-floor admitting where the medical assistants are required to record the days they work each week. But previous attempts to have staff sign in and out have failed, ignored by the assistants after a brief period of cooperation.

A number of staff meetings were called in late winter and early spring, but no fundamental changes took place. Complaints were aired. Carye came close to quitting when it became apparent that one staff meeting actually was arranged as a gripe session targeting her. Allene rallied to her support and confronted some of the upstairs staff. One was fired, another put on notice. A few days later Carye was acting as if she never would have left, but there is a sense that each managerial crisis she stares down exacts a toll.

Carye fears that Allene was right when she joked that the only thing they can count on with the upstairs staff are "pissing contests," which often involve disputed claims of who is working hard and who slacking off. Another certainty is that a year from now many of the assistants will be gone and others will have replaced them. And they, too, will be strong-willed women, the only type of woman who can work for long at an abortion facility; and they, too, will become embroiled in conflicts.

As Carye tries unsuccessfully to dampen the upstairs strife she is aware that Allene is watching her. In late winter Carye assigns Jami, a tall, serious-looking woman of twenty-five with a degree in history and experience at one of the city's other abortion facilities, to the position of second-floor supervisor. Until then Jami worked as a bookkeeper and in admitting. Carye hopes Jami can ride herd on the upstairs staff, essentially taking on the nonmedical half of the vacant head-nurse position, which Carye never was able to fill.

The strategy fails and Jami returns to her old duties. Later Allene steps in and positions Carolee upstairs in another attempt to bridge the administrative gap between the Surgicenter's two floors.

Carye is beginning to feel that Allene was right all along: The upstairs staff is not a problem that can be permanently solved, just addressed one crisis at a time. She and Allene have immersed themselves lately in helping one of the medical assistants put together a new life. The woman has decided to leave an abusive husband. Carye makes calls to help her find a place to live. Allene provides her own brand of personal and family counseling, and lends her money for first and last months' rent. Together they try to build the assistant's confidence in short sessions behind closed doors over the course of a month. This, too, is business as usual at Lovejoy.

Winter does not pass without its notable patients. For a week in February it seemed to Carye that Lovejoy was besieged by angry women making unreasonable demands. Carye believes in the power of full moons, believes they send patients with an extra measure of the bizarre her way. And so she was certain there must have been a full moon out that week.

First Carye was called upstairs to deal with a D & E patient who accused her of insensitivity because she allowed a snack machine in the lobby. Patients in for surgeries that require a general anesthetic cannot eat while they wait, and this patient thought it unfair that they should be tempted.

A few days later Carye returned upstairs after being told a visitor had verbally assaulted the entire second-floor staff. It didn't take Carye long to find the source of the tension. A compact woman who stood less than five feet tall but whose voice could peel wallpaper was pacing in the second-floor lobby. She was the sister of a patient who had been behind the double doors of the surgical area over three hours on an especially busy day—six general surgeries and twenty-six tab locals.

"Why the f—— is it taking so long," she shouted at Jami. She called one of the medical assistants "ugly." The staff upstairs could not bear this woman anymore and called down asking Carye to do something, even if it meant having the woman removed from the building.

Carye approached the woman confidently, well aware that she was twice the woman's size and weight. "My staff is feeling like you're being abusive, and that's not something that's acceptable here," she said. Calmly Carye suggested the woman wait in her car, adding that if she intended to stay in the building, she must be polite and sit down. Carye then softened, offering to find out how long it would be until her sister was out of recovery.

"Look, you fat f——, nothing should take this long!" the woman shouted back.

Not quite matching the woman in tone, Carye said, "Look, you have two choices. Either you go out and get in your car, or I call the police. This is a private facility, and you can go have a seat in the car."

The woman stormed out Lovejoy's second-floor exit. Carye turned to the rest of the women waiting in the crowded lobby and said, "That was unacceptable. Is there anyone that would like me to check on one of their friends?"

A few women responded and Carye headed back into the OR, returning in two minutes with reports. Then she looked out the second-floor window. The woman she expelled was walking around the side of the building, right toward a group of middle-aged picketers.

Carye heard the woman growl, "You don't have any right to be here."

A woman protestor gently responded, "You are a troubled . . ." She never finished the sentence. Carye watched as the diminutive woman clenched her fist, hauled back, and slugged the protestor in the arm, hard. The protestor cowered, shocked. She pulled her arms toward her body like a boxer setting himself to ward off a flurry of blows. Then, spotting Carye through the window, she shouted, "I want you to call the police."

"Look, if I'm going to call the police on this woman, you're going to have to stand in line," Carye called back. The picketer stormed off, flashing her middle finger over her shoulder.

Springtime did yield an administrative triumph of sorts for Carye. It had become increasingly and dismayingly clear to both Carye and Allene that HMOs are beginning to dominate the field of medical insurance, locking up ever greater numbers of patients. If Lovejoy is going to maintain its level of business, it will have to increase business with the HMOs.

In July Carye and Suchak discussed contacting ODS, one of Oregon's large HMOs, about contracting with Lovejoy for its abortions. Suchak thought nothing definite was decided. Carye understood Suchak would initiate the contact, and bristled for months because the surgeon never followed up. After Suchak left, Carye immediately began calling and writing letters to ODS herself, although she was aware that doctors are usually better received in that role than administrators.

After initial contacts were made, Carye put together a price schedule for various abortion procedures and sent it to ODS as part of Lovejoy's proposal. ODS responded with a counteroffer basically lowering the prices and Lovejoy's take. The money ODS offered was less than Carye had hoped because ODS, like most HMOs, is demanding discounts. Instead of billing ODS the standard insurance rate of

$530 for a tab local, Lovejoy would be allowed to bill only $235. But the fee schedule proposed by ODS narrowed the gap between Lovejoy's standard insurance rate and ODS's billable rate as gestational age increased. So Lovejoy would be allowed a greater profit on later abortions.

Carye spent about seventy-five hours on her proposal and negotiations. The tab locals would generate negligible profit, essentially serving as loss leaders for the tab gens and D & Es. But HMOs represent the future, both Carye and Allene know, and cutting costs as well as the incomes of doctors and hospitals is what HMOs are all about. This morning Allene told Carye they would accept the ODS offer. Alone in her office Carye reminds herself that the ODS contract represents good news: She has brought in twenty additional procedures a month.

But Carye remains troubled by a problem other than the bargain price demanded by ODS. The HMO also is dictating medical care. During negotiations ODS insisted that all abortions up to sixteen weeks be performed under local anesthetic, even after Carye explained that at Lovejoy abortions from twelve to fifteen weeks are routinely done under general anesthetic—tab gens in Lovejoy parlance. And sometimes a general anesthetic is prescribed for earlier cases.

The ODS administrator with whom Carye has dealt, a woman, said the HMO won't pay for the general any earlier, insisting that the "local only" policy matches the industry's standard of care. She pointed out to Carye that the other abortion clinics in town generally use local anesthetics up to sixteen weeks.

Carye's rebuttal, that the other clinics aren't surgical centers and can't offer what Lovejoy does, fell on deaf ears. In fact, some of those other facilities use Lovejoy as their backup; when a particularly difficult case comes in, they often send the patient to Lovejoy specifically because she can get a general anesthetic there.

The importance of pain relief for abortion patients is an important element of Carye's personal philosophy. She strongly feels that women should not have to suffer when they have an abortion. In our culture, she insists, pain usually is perceived as punishment, the last thing Carye wants her patients to feel, especially women in their second trimester, who usually have enough emotional trauma to deal with.

While working at the nonprofit Feminist Women's Health Center before she came to Lovejoy, Carye participated in role-playing workshops designed to teach counselors how to distract patients from their pain. The point of these lessons, Carye felt, was to minimize patients' perception of their ordeal. "It's not that bad," Carye paraphrases the guiding philosophy she was instructed to convey. Except Carye never has believed that. In time she came to think that approach, intended to empower women, was simply demeaning.

One afternoon Carye counseled a fourteen-year-old girl who had come in for an abortion at twenty weeks. The surgery would be a straightforward D & E, but it would be done, as all abortions at Feminist were, under local anesthetic. Carye stayed with the girl through the surgery, listened to her cry, "Momma, Momma, Momma," over and over again like the child she was, moaning between howls. And when the surgery was completed Carye looked at the girl's face and saw that a complete metamorphosis had taken place: She was not a little girl anymore. Something vital has been taken from this girl along with her fetus, Carye thought—the last vestige of her childhood, her adolescence. And it did not have to be this way. Within a week Carye had begun looking for a new job.

Carye did not tell all this to the ODS woman. At some point it had become obvious that the administrator was not going to be swayed by a discussion of patient comfort. Everything the woman said made it clear that her goals were all about business and profit margin.

The ODS administrator held firm. And so did Carye. Which means the final contract has Lovejoy performing ODS abortions up to twelve weeks under local and from sixteen weeks on using general anesthetic. But ODS patients between twelve and sixteen weeks will have to go elsewhere—Lovejoy will not do abortions that late under local.

Allene, while pleased at Carye's success, considers the ODS negotiations from a different perspective. Carye worked hard to get the contract, Allene knows. And she understands its significance, both for Lovejoy and for Carye, trying to prove herself as an administrator. But Allene is also aware that Carye knew for months that Suchak wasn't initiating the contacts as he should have. So why did Carye wait for Suchak to leave before recognizing she had to make the pitch herself? I wonder if she's going to get the hang of it? Allene thinks.

Two weeks later Carye confronts the human cost of the ODS contract. What most surprises her is that it took so long.

On a rainy afternoon a woman sits in Lovejoy's front lobby wrestling with a decision prompted by negotiations she had no part in. The patient is seventeen years old, ten weeks pregnant, and frightened—frightened as a child on her first visit to the dentist. This woman wants an abortion but she cannot face the pain or the idea of the pain: Carye isn't sure which it is and knows it doesn't much matter. During the woman's counseling session it was easy enough for Carye to recognize the classic profile of someone who needs to be under general anesthetic during her surgery. That's what matters. The problem: The woman is an ODS patient.

Technically the patient is on the Oregon Health Plan, meaning the state will pay for her abortion. The plan allows participants to choose a traditional insurer, with the bills paid by the state. This woman chose ODS. If she had selected another insurer for her state assistance, she would be eligible for the general anesthetic she desires.

Carye made an effort to convince the woman that extra pain medication could get her through the operation. The woman asked if she could pay the difference in cost for the general anesthetic. Even that is not possible: state health plan regulations would not allow it.

"How long would I have to wait before I can have a general?" she asked. Carye offered a convincing explanation of the dangers of waiting, though it is true that if she waits until her sixteenth week, ODS will pay for a full D & E with general anesthetic. Basically, the later an abortion the greater the risk. Later abortions mean greater dilation of the cervix, which translates into increased risk of infection and bleeding. Also, with dilation, blood vessels that feed the uterus are more open, and the softer uterus is more prone to perforation. And the general anesthetic itself presents risk. Rare as they are, most abortion deaths are linked to anesthesia.

But today's patient cannot balance her health risk against her fear. So she is out in the lobby, left alone to make her decision.

After about twenty minutes the woman leaves, but not before Carye gives her another option. In counseling the woman told Carye of a sister in Washington. If the woman were to drive across the border to Washington and immediately establish residency with her sister, Carye explained, she would qualify for a Washington state-assisted abortion within twenty-four hours, and there she could get the general anesthetic.

Weeks later Carye will learn that is exactly what the woman did. And Allene will tell Carye not to worry too much about the ODS policy. Word will get around among women, and in time ODS will learn its patients are just waiting until sixteen weeks before coming in for a D & E, costing the insurer more money. Then, Allene says, ODS will change its policy. To ODS, she reminds Carye, this is simply business.

Business. Always the first concern, Allene thinks. After family. It's been twenty-five years since she turned Lovejoy into an abortion facility, no, into a facility dedicated to women's health. And with each passing year it has seemed that her two roles, businesswoman on the one hand, promoter of women's reproductive freedom on the other, have become more confused. There are plenty of people in the feminist community willing to wave the banner of the latter, but few would shed a tear if Lovejoy failed as a business. That responsibility has been left completely in her hands.

Allene sits in her darkened office now, the spotlights above throwing shadows more than any real illumination. Slowly she feels herself relax just slightly. Allene is a woman rarely free from tension, from demands, especially here at Lovejoy. This office has never attained the status of sanctuary, only her home offers that. At Lovejoy it is nearly impossible to tell the relaxed Allene from the vigilant.

Carye is coming along, slowly. She is learning to think about the business first, to shut out the distractions, knowing that if the business doesn't succeed there won't be any prostitutes to rehabilitate or troubled teenagers to take home. Carye rarely comes to me asking to give away procedures anymore, Allene notes. Not nearly as often as before. But she still is seeing Heather and Becky regularly, still trying to fill her empty place by giving more of herself away, still allowing herself to become diverted. That's what Carye needs to learn, Allene concludes. She actually possesses a fine head for business, she just doesn't know when to say no to the Heathers of the world. And she hasn't yet learned not to worry about what she cannot change; it just doesn't come naturally for her. Too much heart, too much of her own vulnerability.

Tim was the same. Worse. Tim never would have been able to take over; he would have given away too many procedures, given in to too many demands. Maybe that's been the secret, Allene thinks. Tim, then Carye—always a softhearted administrator to provide . . . well, to balance her. A year and a half, maybe two years, and Carye will be ready. And I will be ready, too, Allene thinks, to say good-bye. Time to start taking care of myself.

A weight has been tugging at Allene's heart the last few weeks, unacknowledged only because it is one of those thoughts that does not need to be voiced; for too long it has been as a shadow, there and then not there, but never gone.

It began with a word from Carye, who was as reluctant to convey the news as Allene was to receive it. Tim is not tracking well; sometimes he is not able to remember what was said five minutes ago. And then, at other times, he can recall patients from ten years ago clear as the air on a chilly winter day. But he cannot keep counseling, Carye explained.

Carye waited weeks before telling this to Allene. And Allene will spend weeks steeling herself to talk to Tim, then telling Carye it is her task. Not everything comes so easily for this woman in black.

It's not as if Tim won't still be coming into Lovejoy, Allene reminds herself. There's plenty of work he can do here. We could designate him the unofficial lobby counselor. Hang around out front, informally comfort women waiting for surgery, explain what to expect, check on friends, sisters, and daughters who have already gone into the OR.

Before either woman brings the issue up with Tim, he will voluntarily begin cutting back on his visits, arriving around lunchtime on Fridays and leaving within the hour, as if he has reached the same conclusion on his own and does not wish to trouble his friends with the task of telling him the bad news.

But that is a few weeks off. Today Allene is reminding herself that a year ago she didn't think Tim would be alive now. He's still here, still smiling. That's worth a prayer of thanks. And Allene feels her spirits start to lift. She looks at the five different stacks of papers on her desk, each sheet another problem to deal with, another decision to be made. So, she thinks with a smile, enough looking back. What's next?

Acknowledgments

Many thanks are due. This book would not have been possible without the help and trust of many people at the Lovejoy Surgicenter, both inside and out. I have done my utmost to honor that trust. Most of the people who appear in this book have allowed use of their names. In a few cases, especially with patients, I have chosen pseudonyms and altered minor personal details and time frames so as to obscure identities.

Conversations with Meryl Weiss-Pearlman provided a starting point for this book. The chutzpah and commitment of my agent, Jennifer Rudolph Walsh, and Joan Bingham's unflagging enthusiasm at Atlantic Monthly Press made it possible.

James Marcus has proven a superb editor. Cate Cahan, Rich Cahan, Bob Rini, and Bob McGranahan have also served well when fresh eyes were needed. Pamela Hasterok's research was invaluable. Erica Troseth's reporting allowed me to be in two places at once. Curt Pesmen's general encouragement cannot be forgotten.

Dr. Murray Smilkstein provided the medical knowledge I so desperately needed. Sandy Macomber, head librarian at the *Oregonian*, saved me valuable hours with her assistance.

Also, my gratitude to the people at Caffe Fresco, where the corner table in the rear provided one writer the perfect sanctuary.

There are two more women I would like to mention, knowing that without them this book would not exist. My mother, Frances Korn, instilled in me a love of books and a sense of the written word's ability to change both the world and the writer. And Betty Smith, my wife and editor deluxe, provided inspiration at all the right moments.